Going
to Pieces

The Dismantling of
the United States of America

~ o ~

ELAINE DEVARY WILLMAN

Elaine D. Willman
P.O. 1280
Toppenish WA 98948

Dedication

I honor each courageous voice that speaks with candor and concern within these pages about what is happening to their homes, communities and country. Most especially, there are sixteen American families, known as the "Salamanca Sixteen," five of whom are now deceased. These are some of the members of the Salamanca Coalition of United Taxpayers (SCOUT) who did all they could to protect themselves against the federal government and Seneca Nation of Indians.

I dedicate *Going to Pieces* to these extraordinary citizens whose United States government not only utterly failed to protect them, but also facilitated a travesty upon them. No American citizen should ever, ever have to suffer as these American families did.

It is entirely to their credit that the surviving members of Salamanca Sixteen still choose to stand and pledge allegiance to the Flag of the United States of America. They are:

Chester "Chet" A. and Virginia Banner
*John T. and *Marie A. Brahaney*
Karen L. Ewing
Joseph D. Fluent
Alice M. Fluent
Nathan Frank
James R. and Christine Freany
Carol I. Kelly
Robert L. Johnson
Nancy C. O'Brien
Sarah C. Owens
Ronald W. and *Marjorie L. "Midge" Schubert*
Marie B. Schwab
Betty J. Seitz
Susan D. Swiech
Jerry A. and ElizabethTitus

* *Deceased*

Contents

Preface

A man's house burns down. The smoking wreckage represents only a ruined home that was dear through years of use and pleasant associations. By and by, as the days and weeks go on, first he misses this, then that, then the other thing. And when he casts about for it he finds that it was in that house. Always it is an essential—there was but one of its kind. It cannot be replaced. It was in that house. It is irrevocably lost. It will be years before the tale of lost essentials is complete, and not till then can he truly know the magnitude of his disaster.

— Mark Twain

Mark Twain's metaphor beautifully expresses my view that this country as forged and governed by the U. S. Constitution is a house burning down. America is truly "a house divided" and badly burning.

I have to get some things said. The writings here are a combination of my fact-based life experiences, and a deep desire to be heard by my countrymen.

There are two events that serve as the driving force for this manuscript. One is September 11, 2001. The other was a 6,000-mile drive across the United States, through 16 states—from the States of Washington to New York—across 17 Indian reservations.

I have lived within an Indian reservation boundary for over 13 years, am midway in completion of a doctoral degree in federal Indian policy, and work daily with community groups, across the country, that struggle with federal Indian policy. I needed to see whether life is great on some reservations and not on others. An excellent videographer and traveling partner, Kamie Christensen Biehl, joined me in the journey.

For 26 days of September-October 2004, on a 24-hour basis, we two women of very different ages, personalities and backgrounds—formed a bond and commitment to complete the harrowing project. We would record everything we could, on film and within this text.

Kamie and I share a couple of strong bonds that fold into our findings. She is of Paiute Indian descent; I am a Cherokee descendent. Kamie's grandmother was sold by her tribe for a sack of flour. My mother and grandmother were both enrolled Cherokee. My father is also of Cherokee ancestry. We value and cherish our American Indian ancestry, but we have serious questions in our heads these days.

The book is organized along the pathway of our journey, but that is to simply provide a structure within which the impact of current federal Indian policy is illustrated and explored from the voices of tribal and other citizens who endure the conditions.

The trip was not without serious personal risk for two women traveling alone. As an example, in the Duluth Tribune on March 23, 2005, we were reminded that journalists, investigators, and reporters are not always welcome within Indian reservation boundaries. At the Red Lake Indian Reservation reporters attempting to tell the story of a tragic school shooting, were harassed by tribal police with guns drawn on unarmed reporters. Two reporters were arrested by tribal police and had substantial camera equipment confiscated. Kamie and I were fully aware of these potentials before embarking on our journey. We knew our equipment could be easily confiscated, or that we could be harassed or detained, so we took every precaution.

In an era of Homeland security risks and needs, there is legitimate reason to question why the United States expends billions of dollars and the blood of thousands of our military, to free countries such as Bosnia, Kosovo, Afghanistan and Iraq from the tyranny of tribalism, while Congress simultaneously foments and facilitates a spreading tribalism as a form of governance across our own continent. There is additional concern about the lack of free press access, public "sunshine" or first amendment freedoms for tribal members and others, within many of the reservations visited.

The reader should make clear distinctions about two important conditions: The first distinction is that most American Indians (80%) honor and respect their ancestry but no longer choose to live on an Indian reservation, nor to submit to a tribal government. I fall into this category. I have a childhood, now lifetime affection for American Indian culture, many traditions and art.

Only 20% of American Indians actually live within Indian reservations and submit through tribal enrollment, to a tribal government. Just barely a half-million enrolled tribal members governed by 562 tribal governments are rapidly controlling entire regions and states containing nearly 200 million Americans. If federal Senators Daniel Akaka and Daniel Inouye have their way, most, if not all, of the State of Hawaii will also succumb. Something is wrong.

The second distinction is that every citizen has a right, even a duty, to express a voice regarding government decisions, whether local, county, state, federal or tribal. So long as Congress and courts insist upon defining tribal entities as governments, then tribal government decisions are just that - government decisions. Objecting or disagreeing with a tribal government decision is no different from objecting or disagreeing with a municipal, state or federal decision.

Few who read this book are aware that the population within Indian reservations is very diverse. According to the 2000 U.S. Census there are 33 sizeable reservations where at least 80% of the residents are non-Indian or mixed race. On most Indian reservations the population mix is equal, or there is a greater population of citizens who are not enrolled tribal members. More non-tribal residents than tribal members reside on reservations in California, Florida, Idaho, Kansas, Michigan, Minnesota, Montana, Nebraska, New York, Oklahoma, Rhode Island, Utah, Washington, Wisconsin and Wyoming. Cities and towns within Indian reservations are mirror images for cities and towns across the country—multicultural communities.

The Navajo Indian Reservation and Red Lake Indian Reservation are two of the few reservations with a predominant Indian population. They are exceptions to the rule. Decisions made by federal and tribal governments affect literally millions of other American citizens. The problem: the voice of American citizens is neither heard, nor factored into federal Indian policy.

Government is not culture. Culture is not government. Even an ethnicity, blood quantum-based government such as an Indian xii — Going to Pieces

tribe, makes decisions as a *government*, one that deeply affects both tribal members and millions of other citizens of this country. To disagree with a tribal government *decision* does not make one a *racist*, any more than to disagree with a municipal or state government decision makes one anti-American.

This story is not the romantic yesterday of "Dancing With Wolves." It is sparsely told, until now.

While tribal governments and tribal histories are prolific and well reported, there is a missing voice—now contained within these pages. It is the voice long silenced by political correctness or abject fear. It is the voice that has lifelong desired to just get along with others and be treated equally. It is the voice that generally chooses to not make waves, to respect all people, and therefore just keep quiet and keep hoping for the best of outcomes. We dare not remain quiet any longer.

Two powerful forces foretell that in the next few years, significant change must occur in our country—a change that preserves the desire and ability of American Indians to continue to respect and cherish their culture, but eliminates tribalism as a governing system in the United States. One force is the expanding outfall wrought by the Indian gambling Regulatory Act of 1988, completely out of control. The other is the risk of Homeland security gaps throughout the country, and the limited authority of federal, state and local law enforcement on vast spaces of Indian lands, vulnerable and inviting to terrorists and those who hate America.

This book makes no attempt to explain federal Indian policy from a tribal government perspective. Tribal lobbyists, federal and tribal government entities, academia and mainstream media cover these perspectives tirelessly. While some voices within these pages include enrolled tribal members and other American Indians, this book describes and explains how federal Indian policy is affecting all of us.

Elaine Devary Willman

Acknowledgements

There are rare occasions when someone dedicated to quality public service and journalism, reaches out and mentors to the following generation. The writing of this book has been greatly helped by the experienced editorial critiquing and proof reading provided by friend and associate, John Fulton Lewis. An author of some accomplishment in his own right, Mr. Lewis dedicated many hours of scrutiny and comment that is deeply appreciated.

The citizens willing to step up and speak out, also contributed hours of chapter reviews and revisions for factual accuracy, and I thank them for the sacrifice of their time and energies.

And my family, most of all, who understood our need to make a very long journey, and then found me in front of my computer for months, days and hours on end, was patient and tirelessly supportive of this goal.

I hope this reading honors the contributions of hundreds of citizens of every culture, profession and American geography, that it may reflect their present conditions in a respectful manner.

A society of sheep must in time beget a government of wolves.

— *Bertrand de Jouvenel*
French Economist
(1903 - 1987)

Chapter 1
Homeland Insecurity

A terrorist attack could strike anywhere in America at any time. No one and no place is immune.

Before moving through the road trip journey chapters, it is essential to lay out the big picture issues affecting all of the United States at this time. The discussion must begin with an assertion of the principles upon which this book is written:

- The first principle is that *all* cultures, and most certainly American Indian culture, are to be respected and cherished within the United States of America. This can and must be done in a spirit of unity.

- The second principle is that there is a clear and distinct separation between ethnic culture and governing systems. Government decision-making is not culture. Culture is not government.

One other important issue is worthy of ongoing acknowledgement. Individual American Indians have, and continue to provide, sacrifice and service to the United States military, in order to keep America safe, and our military is the better and stronger for this service. This has been the factual history from the American Revolutionary War to the current conflicts in Iraq.

This book discusses governing systems *only*, not an individual citizen's culture.

Surfacing and deterring terrorist activity requires full cooperation and collaboration of federal, state, and local law enforcement agencies in one, seamless continuum.

The Homeland Security Act of 2002 (HSA) specifically includes the involvement of tribal governments, along with federal, state, county and municipal governments and other supportive law enforcement, intelligence and emergency response agencies. The HSA passed by Congress in November 2002 was a massive reorganization of the federal government that created a cabinet-level department, the Department of Homeland Security, out of all or parts of at least twenty-two federal agencies.

Interconnectivity, coordination and collaboration are prevailing themes determined to best ensure safety of America's homeland.

In February 2003, Senator Daniel Inouye (D-HI) was one of nine senators who voted against the HSA. In a summary of remarks at a February 2003 Winter Conference of the National Congress of American Indians (NCAI), published in an American Indian news service, Senator Inouye "urged tribal leaders to capitalize on the war on terrorism in order to press their claims for tribal sovereignty."

On September 11, 2001, the very *day* of the national tragedy, the NCAI was meeting in Washington D.C. to promulgate a Tribal Sovereignty Protection Initiative, that evolved into the "Tribal Governance and Economic Act of 2002." This Act was foundational to Senate Bill 578, submitted by Senator Inouye in 2003, and entitled "The Tribal Government Amendment to the Homeland Security Act of 2002." The content of this legislation, had it passed, would have significantly balkanized the United States by creating literally hundreds of separate, sovereign, "Tribal Homelands," apart from America's national homeland.

Currently, the existing HSA of 2002 funnels Homeland Security appropriations out to the fifty states, which then distribute funds to "local governments," including Indian tribes. This was not satisfactory to Senator Inouye or the NCAI. Senate Bill 578 would have required, among other demands, the following:

1. Separate tribal homelands, apart from state lands.

2. Separate Homeland Security funding distributed directly from the federal government to Indian tribes.

3. A tribal government's ability to define the term "terrorist" as it applies to an individual "tribal homeland." This would easily allow anyone who disagreed with a tribe to be identified as not just a "dissident," but also perhaps as a "terrorist" to the tribe.

4. Full "inherent sovereign authority of an Indian tribal government to enforce and adjudicate violations of applicable criminal, civil, and regulatory laws committed by any person on land under the jurisdiction of the Indian tribal government."

The language of Senate Bill 578 would have removed the Constitutional rights and traditional, republic form of American government of several hundred thousand U.S. citizens. Citizens residing within reservation boundaries would be subject to tribal law enforcement, tribal courts, and the bill would have repealed powerful Supreme Court law that protects citizens from criminal or civil powers enacted upon them by a private tribal government. The Fourteenth Amendment providing equal protection would have been rendered null and void.

Somehow, the NCAI and Senator Inouye believed this to be a good thing. Fortunately, citizens across the country raised a vigorous opposition to such a travesty, and Senate Bill 578 disappeared, but it is not gone. Attempts to insert language contained within Senate 578 into newer bills, continues. Citizens have had to be ever vigilant to preserve their right to never be governed by a private tribal government, absent their mutual consent.

Just six months after September 11, 2001, in March 2002, the Yakama Indian Nation boasted of "visiting dignitaries" who were "civic journalists" coming to tour the tribe's radio station and newspaper. The tribe has very few visitors from foreign countries before. We would learn that these visitors were from Middle Eastern countries.

The tribal radio station is a tiny, leased building with modest provisions. The Yakama Indian Newspaper, however, is an excellent tribal newspaper, guided for years under the nationally recognized journalist, Richard LaCourse, who passed away a few years ago. I knew Mr. LaCourse, had several long visits with Richard and regarded him highly. The Native American Journalist Association (NAJA) is currently seeking funding to establish a "Richard LaCourse Fellowship." Indian journalists across the country are indebted to the respect he brought to his profession. I miss the marvelous conversations I enjoyed so much with Mr. LaCourse.

On Easter Sunday afternoon of 2002, a local individual knocked on my door, handed me some papers, and said, "You need to see these. They were in a fax machine in a tribal office, and they worry me."

The papers delivered were detailed announcements about visiting dignitaries and civic journalists, including their names and countries. There were fourteen "civic journalists" from: Algeria, Morocco, Qatar, Syria, Tunisia and Yemen. This was six months after September 11th, and these were countries not on the best of terms with the United States.

Had the journalists been from the Orient, the Americas or Europe, I would not have felt such a chill as I did then. These visitors were in a very isolated area of Washington State, at the wrong time, and from politically worrisome countries.

Immediately after the visit, the Toppenish Review newspaper and Yakama Indian newspaper carried a group photograph and short articles about the visitors, *without* identifying either their names or home countries.

What concerned me most is this: The Yakama Indian Nation's large and relatively isolated Indian reservation is bounded on the East by the Hanford Nuclear site; on the South, across the Columbia River is the Umatilla Chemical Weapons Storage Facility; on the West boundary of the reservation is the Yakama Military Training Center where troops are trained for Iraq and the War on Terrorism; and on the North, the reservation is bounded by several major dams in the Northwest, including Grand Coulee Dam.

Many tribes in the Northwest are active proponents of dam breaching in an effort to restore rivers to their natural habitat. There is little acknowledgement that when a dam is breached, the end result does not restore a river to its original formation; rather, years of built up silt and debris behind a dam releases to unpredictable results that can cause injury or death to anything in its path. There are major dams throughout the Northwest and Western states that provide life-giving water and electricity to America's homes and economy. A breached dam provides neither.

On a second front, the federal government provides substantial funding appropriations for new efforts to promote tribal government entry into energy production, energy distribution systems and energy management. Current *public* energy systems are at risk of going into *private* tribal government management, with far less accountability to citizen users and ratepayers, limited federal and no state oversight. Water and energy resources are attractive targets for terrorists.

Federal Indian policy is Top Secret. It is developed privately, between Indian tribes and the federal government, and it is nobody else's business until it arrives on your porch. The majority of tribal governments are stringently secretive, even unto their own tribal members. When private governments are secretly negotiating for such basic necessities as water rights, electricity, and more recently even air quality regulatory authority, American businesses and communities get rude awakenings, by way of terse Federal Register public notices, having a limited, perhaps 30-day, opportunity to even respond or complain.

There are daily complexities that also factor in to Homeland Security when dealing with the existence of tribal governments of strong, separatist mentalities, and less than affection for other cultures:

- Many tribal governments issue separate vehicle license plates. How does this fold into national identification systems?

- Many 911 emergency systems are literally "race-based." How can it be helpful in an emergency to have to identify one's race in order to request emergency assistance? Some of the 911 systems in Idaho, Montana and Nebraska, and likely many other states, create this obstacle.

- Tribal casinos are mega-bucks locations, substantially less accountable and audited than private sector casinos. Aren't these casinos at the very least, a quite private, "attractive nuisance" that invites money laundering, when operating on tribal lands, difficult to access by traditional law enforcement?

- Tribal governments can enroll anyone they choose. Recently in Washington State, a scam was discovered wherein a tribe was offering to sell its enrollment to encourage business advantages not available to private sector. Just *who* might be interested in such an arrangement that would imply some legal status within the United States, by a purchased tribal enrollment?

- Tribal governments insist upon identifying themselves and being treated as "separate nations." In an individual state with dozens, sometimes over thirty, such separate nations. How does a single state ensure the safety of all of its citizens when having to contend with such an internal balkanization and dismantling of state sovereignty?

- There is obvious hypocrisy of the United States to spend billions of dollars (and spill the blood of our finest military) to *end tribalism* and *install democracies* in countries such as Bosnia, Kosovo, Afghanistan and Iraq, while spending additional billions to *spread tribalism* that *replaces democracy* within America's homeland. Does Congress and the

Executive Office believe that such a travesty is unnoticed by American citizens? Is it wise to foster a governing system in this country that invites and expands a dismantling of the U.S. Constitution and its required democratic, republic form of government? Is the 14th Amendment just a fairytale?

- How long can American taxpayers and the national economy sustain a perpetual debtor/creditor society under a system that is reverting from a dwindling taxed democracy to an epidemic of untaxed tribalism?

In his recent controversial book, "The Enemies of Christopher Columbus," Thomas A. Bowden gives his readers something to contemplate:

Thus, the debate over Columbus is much wider than the question of whether he or his followers mistreated some Indians. The fundamental issue is whether the settlement of America by the bearers of Western civilization over the past five centuries was good or evil. Those who regard that process as evil want Columbus to bear blame for starting it all, and they use him as a symbol of everything they hate about the West, so as to strangle any sense of pride in the spread of civilization to the New World. . . .

Now, at the dawn of the twenty-first century, with Western civilization under martial attack by militant Islamic fundamentalists, it is more important than ever to choose sides. As President Bush said to the nations of the world at the start of America's war against terrorism, "You're either with us or against us." Those who would defend and uphold the values of Western civilization must be willing to make the same bold declaration to the enemies of Christopher Columbus.

These powerful national conditions of balkanization, separatism, ethnic supremacy, and substantial obstacles impacting continuity of law enforcement and emergency response services are dismantling America's democracy, its economy and public safety.

With such foundational concerns heavy on our hearts and minds, Kamie and I knew that something had to be done soon. So, with cameras, cell phones, coffee and other clutter, we hit the road across the United States, from Washington State to New York, on September 12, 2004. It was three years and one day after September 11th, 2001.

It does not take a majority to prevail ... but rather an irate, tireless minority, keen on setting brushfires of freedom in the minds of men.

— Samuel Adams
American Revolutionary Leader
(1722 - 1803)

Chapter 2
Two Curious and Furious Women

Her face. It was her face coming in my door at 9:30 a.m. on Sunday, September 12th, 2004. It's one of the faces I'll see the rest of my life. There are many others, but Kamie's face was my first clue that a risky trip was truly going to be all about something very unsettling.

Until I actually saw her face, I prepared myself to hear that she wouldn't arrive. She'd back out. She didn't.

There was attitude all over her face - anger, excitement, fear, and severe determination that was, at the same time, conflicted. Kamie's eyes were fierce and fiery green like a very angry mom. *Mom* is one of her favorite words, for good reason, and she was leaving her children for 26 days so she was an angry mom.

Her little town of La Center, Washington is under assault by a proposed massive Indian casino, 160,000 square feet of casino floor space and God knows what all else on 152 acres next to her town. The project will economically smother and forever change La Center. "It's my town, - I grew up here. I've raised my boys here." That's the anguish and fear all over her face.

"We *have* to do this. I know we have to do this," she pledged, with eyes that refused to cry. Her commitment to follow through, to join me on a journey across 16 Indian reservations, was clear. She showed up with cameras, tripod, research notes, and clothes— everything she needed. I packed light on clothing, and heavy on maps, reference books, background and writing materials for each stop along the way.

We set out to capture the reality of life on and near Indian reservations, to get the truth on film from the voices of people of every walk of life, tribal and otherwise. Boy did we ever, and did we ever underestimate the depth of some of the horrors we would learn.

Kamie lives life in the fast *brain*, a very intelligent and intense early 40sh, football mom whose joy is to videotape ball games of her two son's schools. She's a slender, rowdy, balls-against-the-wall type mom of two sons. Leaving them even briefly was the absolute last thing she wanted to do.

I live in Toppenish, Washington, about three hours west of La Center, Kamie's home, so the first leg of the journey for Kamie was solo, forcing herself to not turn back. Toppenish is in the south-central part of the state, an hour above the Columbia River that separates Oregon and Washington.

I moved to Toppenish in 1992, and have lived here now, longer than I've ever lived anywhere. Dad was a traveling insurance salesman so as a child I lived all over the Northwest. I married a career Army officer that prompted fourteen additional moves in ten years. Following a divorce, my kids and I bounced all around Ventura County, California where I ultimately settled in as assistant to the city manager in Ojai for ten years. I went to law school in Ventura for a couple of years, and transferred into the Masters in Public Administration program of California State University, completing a Master's degree in 1991.

With my step-mom's health failing in Spokane, it was time to move closer to her, so a job search resulted in my appointment as Community Development Director for the City of Toppenish in 1992. This is cowboy and Indian country, for real. It is not unusual to see Indian mothers with their infants on papoose boards in the stores and restaurants. The small, rural city is situated as a municipal island in the middle of the large Yakama Indian Reservation. Congress legislatively *removed* Toppenish from the Indian reservation, creating an island municipality inside the largest reservation in this State. There are several other cities across the country similarly situated.

I love this town and have loved it from day one. For a rolling stone such as I, it was incredible to meet two wonderful old-timers here, Roy Snyder and Ellis Johnson, who used to have lunch every single day at the Huba Huba cafe. They were both in their 80s, had never left town except for World War II, and were childhood friends from kindergarten. Imagine—the stability of lifelong friendship from kindergarten to over 80 years. That is the stability, the staying power through adversity and all, that is reflected in the base population of this town. I respect that commitment to community. This is now my home too. Toppenish is *my* town, just like La Center is Kamie's.

This book is about *your* town. What is happening across this country can easily arrive at your door soon. It's big-bucks tribalism coming to your neighborhood, your local government, your retail economy, your water resources, your air quality, your national parks and wildlife refuges, and your ability to be heard by a single local, state or federal elected official who has not been financially seduced, if not politically enslaved.

It is the epidemic spread of tribalism erasing democracy as you learned it and live it in the United States. With the billions and blood we're spilling to free Middle-Eastern countries of tribal tyrannies, it is sheer insanity and unconscionable that tribalism as a form of government is simultaneously escalating across American lands. The United States was populated and created by people escaping monarchies and tribalism, and all the misery and inequality that go with them.

I first met Kamie, her husband and a couple of their colleagues very late on a Friday night in March 2004, in St. Maries, Idaho, up in the panhandle of that state. I knew why I was up in St. Maries, but I was deeply impressed to hear that Kamie had traveled from La Center, Washington, to Boise, Idaho, for a family funeral, then back to La Center, and then up to St. Maries, Idaho - to join us very late that Friday night—over a thousand miles to join us for a Saturday. Something had to be deeply troubling her to put in those kinds of miles under painful family circumstances to be with a small regional gathering of community leaders for a brief weekend gathering.

I was in St. Maries because I chair a community group that is defending itself against continuous tribal government attempts to govern citizens who are not enrolled tribal members. Nothing frightens me more than to have a private government that is not mine, tell me they will, and can govern me, while I am allowed absolutely no voice in *their* government. That isn't how I was raised. That isn't how this country functions. And it sure isn't going to be allowed to start in *my* town, as I live and breathe.

As community development director for the City of Toppenish it was my role to interact frequently with tribal council leaders. One of the attractions to Toppenish for me in 1992 was its location within the largest Indian reservation in Washington. I could hardly wait to work with and interact with an Indian tribe. I was warned that I must earn their respect, must listen to any names that I'm called, just be quiet and polite, and must show up for any appointments, but expect to be kept waiting at length because of the classic "Indian time." It was deeply troubling for me to submit myself in some lesser status to a fellow human being who demands respect but does not return it. Deeply troubling, but politically necessary. This is another aspect of the problem, but I'll take that up later.

After about six months, I apparently earned respect from tribal leadership, for when I left the City in 1994 and opened my own community planning consulting firm; the Yakama tribe was one of my first and best clients for several years. My rapport with tribal leaders was very good then.

In the year, 2000, however, the Yakama tribe simultaneously announced that it was banning alcohol on the reservation, and was acquiring our public electricity distribution system. This sent shockwaves through our town, and two adjacent small towns also located on the reservation. Yakima Valley [the city, county and region are spelled with an "i"; the tribe is spelled with an "a"] is farm country, grows hops and grapes, has wineries and the ban on alcohol would have immediately shut down forty-seven businesses and service groups such as the Elks, Eagles and Veterans clubs, in three communities.

I recently read Malcolm Gladwell's *Blink*, and can remember a clear "blink" moment that changed my life and future. It was a mental moment when I realized that a tribal government could actually govern me; that a tribal government could supercede my rights as an American citizen. An unsettling awareness locked internally within me, and remains there, every day.

With the increasing federal empowerment and expansion of tribal governments, that allow me no voice or presence in their government, it became painfully clear that I and others must stand up and fight like hell. I could not imagine such a travesty put upon any American involuntarily.

The Yakama Tribe's alcohol ban would have made it a felony to have so much as a can of beer at a backyard barbecue. Folks in Santa Barbara, Seattle, Pensacola or Pittsburgh could not possibly fathom a felony charge for having beer on private property at an ordinary back yard gathering, but that's what Toppenish families were facing, along with area businesses threatened with closure.

Local Toppenish folks started the political ruckus to oppose any tribal governance over private businesses, persons and properties. The State of Washington immediately offered the tribe 4 million dollars for alcohol education and intervention if they would rescind the alcohol ban. The tribe was unwilling to comply with accountability reports required when receiving state funds, and declined the state's 4 million dollar buy-off. With little, if any, tribal alcohol services available to their members, declining this money indicated to our area that banning alcohol was not the noble purpose. The purpose was to start the process of exerting governance over non-tribal businesses and citizens.

The irony for me, at that time 24 years sober, (now approaching 30 years) was that I hadn't had a drink in decades and found myself fighting for the rights of *others* to choose to drink or not. The other terror was the thought of a private tribal government controlling my electricity service and monthly rates when the tribe had virtually no skilled labor force or successful business history, until the casino. Oh yes, the casino. This tribe got its casino operational in 1998, so by the year 2000, they were ready to flex their financial and governmental muscle—hence, the alcohol ban and utility acquisition efforts, simultaneously.

Do you have an Indian casino coming to town? It is the engine of an economic and governmental train that will entirely derail your community and economy. No exaggeration here. I mean it. We are living it. Ask Ledyard, Connecticut, or Vernon or Sherrill, New York. It will tear asunder longtime friendships among cultures that enjoyed harmony and mutual respect for many years.

The threat of a private, tribal government controlling our local economy and utilities prompted the formation of a local community group, calling ourselves the Citizens Standup! Committee (CSC) that formed to do all we could, but we were clueless about federal Indian policy, tribal government activities, or where to even start. I helped organize the group, and was elected their, thus far for five years, unpaid Executive Director.

My first job was to educate myself on federal Indian policy, locate others who could mentor me, and carry back everything I could learn to our group. That process led me to a group in New York, Upstate Citizens for Equality (UCE), which then led me to two national groups, Citizens Equal Rights Alliance (CERA) and United Property Owners (UPO), an organization that has recently reorganized as One Nation United (ONU).

From a feeling of isolation and ignorance in Toppenish, I felt like I found oxygen to breathe when these groups started channeling information and resources to our little town's citizen group. And, most important, we were not crazy and we were not alone. Indeed, there are local community groups that have been struggling for over thirty years, defending their rights to not be coerced, harassed or governed by an Indian tribe. We just didn't know that - much like most of America has no clue about what I'm talking about here; hence this cry for help.

The initial process caused our community group to meet every two weeks, doing the usual educational and public information tasks. We raised money, had information tables at community events, participated in parades, studied the U.S. Constitution with a 12-week series. We showed up at countless public hearings, wrote letters, made daily phone calls, sent emails and interfaced with elected officials wherever possible. We worried ourselves sick and had great fun simultaneously. Common trauma is bonding.

We defeated the Yakama tribal alcohol ban by sheer guts and noise that finally triggered help from the State Attorney General's Office. There were reports that tribal police units were parking, loitering and visually harassing local grocery and convenience stores in Toppenish. So we citizens contacted our local television stations and asked them to come down and catch it on camera. Four of us piled into our cars with cell phones and at a safe, non-obstructive distance, we followed the tribal police cars from store to store, and then town-to-town (some seven miles between Toppenish and Wapato, WA). We were followed by a local television crew and played a cat-and-mouse game with the tribal police for several hours, which prompted "News, Live at 11:00." The news startled our Mayor.

The next morning, the Mayor phoned the State Attorney General's Office with concern that "someone could be hurt" and that the situation on this reservation was escalating, which prompted the Attorney General to file a lawsuit challenging the tribal government's jurisdiction within Toppenish City limits.

The end result of the lawsuit was that the tribe promised the judge, under sworn oath, that they *never* had any intention of governing non-tribal businesses. This was not true as reported in local newspapers. The tribe further assured the Court that they would *never* enforce their alcohol ban against private property owners and/or non-tribal members. This was also not true as reported in local media. The Yakama Tribe promised under oath to *never* enforce their alcohol ban against non-members. That sworn promise sufficed for the Attorney General's office, and for the businesses and residents within the boundaries of the reservation.

Toppenish is nearly 80% Hispanic, 15% Anglo and only 5% Native American. We're farm country here with real farmers and real hardworking farmworkers, some settled, some seasonal. Our community parades and events are a cultural joy to behold. The mariachis and Hispanic dancers, the tribal princesses and hoop dancers, the Filipinos, the cowboys, the farmers and their enormous farm machinery - Americana at its best. All of the cultures and local industries jump into the community parades voluntarily. Tribal participants must be paid. We've never understood why such a beautiful culture wouldn't be happy to voluntarily display its culture among the others.

I started daily emails with colleagues across the country, and learned of an annual conference sponsored by Citizens Equal

Rights Alliance (CERA) in 2001 in Washington D.C., so a couple of us Toppenish folks ventured off to Washington, D.C. That was another life-changing event for me, and embedded a sense of urgency about what is happening across the country.

I came back from the national conference far more fully informed, and armed with networking resources to meet any local need. Our group started a public information and education process to continue our struggles to prevent the tribe from taking over two major dams that would have significantly impacted our farmers. We also stopped the State from allowing the Yakama tribe to detour a needed bridge replacement by closing the primary state highway into Toppenish and coincidentally rerouting traffic by their new casino for over one year. The businesses in our little town would not have survived a year without traffic, which many people in the community felt may have been the intent of the Yakama's refusal to allow the bridge replacement without a "casino detour."

For similar reasons, Kamie and I are both living in lovely communities being politically bullied and overwhelmed by the influence of tribal governments and mega-bucks gambling dollars. Something just has to be done.

Tyranny, like hell, is not easily conquered; yet we have this consolation with us, that the harder the conflict, the more glorious the triumph.

— *Thomas Paine*
American Revolutionary Pamphleteer (1737 - 1809)

Chapter 3
Battered Communities

I recently submitted a guest commentary to the Yakima Herald Republic newspaper, in Yakima, Washington, suggesting that feelings of citizens and communities situated within or near Indian reservations were strikingly similar to the feelings of a battered spouse. The newspaper published the article on January 5, 2003 and the reaction to the article was so remarkable, that I expanded upon the illustration, for a recent national newsletter. The subject seemed to strike a chord somewhere deep within many citizens in my region as well as across America. Here's what I am speaking of:

"A battered spouse deeply wishes that she could love and respect her spouse, and is likely to keep frequent beatings and humiliations to herself. She'll choose silence and secrecy for as long as she can. She may often think that if she just says the right words, or acts in a different manner, the beatings will stop. Next time will be different. Things will get better. For battered spouses, things don't get better. They get worse.

"There is an analogy here for three municipalities located within exterior reservations of the Yakama Nation, as well as other communities on other reservations across the country. These communities are currently experiencing a serious battering from a neighboring government. A government that is not of a municipality, county or state, is forcing itself upon these communities. A tribal government is pushing out for jurisdictional, regulatory and economic control of local communities through gambling, air quality, pesticides, water and water quality, area dams, utility taxation, and unwarranted obstruction of new non-tribal projects. That's quite a growing list of tools by which to threaten, intimidate, control or drive off anyone who is not an enrolled tribal member.

"I believe that most Americans fundamentally desire to love and respect each other, including tribal government systems, just as the battered spouse desires to love a spouse. But it's like trying to love a porcupine; one must do so very carefully, and the love is seldom—if ever— reciprocal. Notwithstanding enormous national financial and political clout, no one truly understands why tribes are so aggressive these days, but the general response of adjacent community members in the past, isn't working. Being nice at all times, hoping for better understandings, crossing fingers that dialogue and productive partnerships might one day occur - none of these socially preferred postures has helped at all. Pretending that everything is really O.K., that the tribe doesn't *really* mean to control or strangle non-Indian communities, is thinking like the battered wife. If we all just stay nice, maybe tribal leaders will be nice next time.

"Most area businesses and citizens in my local communities have behaved exactly as an embarrassed and frightened battered wife. Don't say anything. Don't tell anyone. Don't make it worse. Be quiet, be good and maybe it will get better soon. Is it getting better? Nope. Seldom does. Is it getting worse? Yes, conditions like this are more likely to worsen than improve, until someone says enough is enough. It stops now. It changes now.

"So what can citizens in battered and bullied communities do, to encourage fair play and better behavior from a tribal government? They can call upon resources, much like a battered wife, who has taken her last beating, must also do. She will call upon law enforcement, legal guidance and other resources that put an end to the destructive behavior.

"Likewise, citizens in the predominantly non-Indian communities must raise a great collective voice. We must demand the assistance of our State legal guidance and whatever other resources that will cause a tribal government to concern itself with its own productive development, and stop harassing its neighbors that have always supported the tribe, have never interfered with the tribe, and have only wished tribal government and tribal members all the best for a full, quality life.

"For example, here in Central Washington, no municipal, county, state or federal entity has imposed itself upon the Yakama tribe, or interfered with its future potentials. In fact area governmental leaders have gone the "extra mile" with every request made by the Yakama Tribes. No conduct has occurred that warrants the menacing, interfering actions and behaviors tribal leaders are increasing in intensity and frequency against their neighbors. Generations of mixed-cultures have been wonderful neighbors for over a century. There is no excuse for this millennium mayhem causing such jurisdictional and economic distress.

"If a battering spouse is unable to stop himself, he can be stopped. It just takes courage, speaking up, and a solid determination to do so. It is time for three non-Indian communities located within the exterior boundaries of the Yakama Reservation to take protective measures. If our homes, jobs, communities and quality of life mean anything at all to us, we can do no less.

"Since publication of this theory, I have received contacts from across the country, identifying with the feelings described. Most people truly do wish the best for their tribal neighbors and for all communities on and near Indian reservations. Citizens have been anxious and apprehensive to speak up and assert their rights on reservations, whether tribal members or not.

"We have, as citizens, submerged an innate courage, that is now surfacing across America. Mainstream media is now paying closer attention to the proliferation of Indian casinos, and corrupt political practices occurring on numerous reservations.

"The way out of oppression is first to call it by name, and then to stop submitting in silence. This is the pathway to recovery for battered spouses, battered citizens, communities and battered and bullied States."

Flashback to St. Maries, Idaho, where I first met Kamie this past March. The St. Maries event was a gathering of leaders from community groups in Washington, and Idaho. My local group sponsors an annual regional gathering and we rotate the location around the Northwest, so in March it was in St. Maries, Idaho where a newer group had formed, the North Idaho Citizens Alliance (NICA) - more about this group is coming up.

Kamie tells me, and I fully understand, that when she attended the St. Maries event, she felt overwhelmed and lost at the amount of information being tossed around the room, and at the depth of serious issues on the agenda. Federal Indian policy is, I believe, intentionally ambiguous, and therefore difficult for average citizens to grasp. Ambiguity in the courtroom almost always benefits Indian tribes. Our group had been fighting takeovers of dams, utilities, and efforts to govern our retail economy. Other groups were struggling with tribal trespasses on private property, takeovers of dock and beach jurisdictions, cross-deputizing of tribal officers and harassment by tribal police officers. The list is endless and growing.

Kamie's group, Standup for Clark County, (SCC) knew that a nearby Cowlitz Indian Tribe, having recently received its federal recognition, was proposing to put a small "cultural resource center" or something, on property near La Center, at the Interstate 5 La Center junction. Word on the street was that an Indian casino was the real deal. The pattern of secrecy, surprise, and minimization of project scope was made known to Kamie, and sure enough, with a little probing, it surfaced that a Class III tribal casino of major proportions was coming to La Center.

A brief note about gambling classifications should be made. Without going into extensive detail, The Indian Gaming Regulatory Act (IGRA) defines gambling classifications, in 25 U.S.C. 2703 [SEC. 4], as:

- **Class I** gaming means social games solely for prizes of minimal value or traditional forms, such church or school raffles.

- **Class II** gaming" means Pull-Tabs or Bingo, whether electronic, computer, or other technologic aids are used.

- **Class III** gaming means all forms of gaming that are not Class I or Class II. This Class requires substantial federal and state regulatory compliance.

With a lot of hands-on assistance from across the state and country, the Standup for Clark County group discovered that "done deals" were not done deals, and that the tribe and Portland BIA office were pulling one shenanigan after another. They learned that the process could be forced to follow the law, but that it would take enormous work and luck.

In 2002, CERA invited me to chair their national group, a position I currently hold. A fortunate coincidence of a deadline closing in on La Center citizens' for opportunity to comment or have any voice in what was now widely known as a casino coming, and an upcoming grassroots conference converged in May of 2004. I urged Kamie to come with us to Washington D.C.

I promised Kamie that she would be able to meet with her senators, congressmen, and entities such as the National Indian gambling Commission, the Department of Interior and other federal elected officials, agencies and administrators. Kamie got a baptism by fire with her first ever trip to Washington, D.C. We ran morning-to-night between one meeting and another, down lengthy "corridors of justice," for four days. Kamie, with the help of her Congressman and other resources, was able to get an environmental assessment deadline extended for La Center city council and citizen input. That single effort of a single citizen took the "Done" out of a "Done Deal." She learned another important thing that I have also come to believe.

Our system, for all its warts, works...when we work it. As we snooze, or remain politically silent and correct, we lose, and the losses have already been enormous. They are becoming truly life and government-threatening, as you will understand further by the end of this reading.

Since May, the small Cowlitz tribe proposing a tiny little casino has now mushroomed into a full-on, tsunami-colossal casino proposing 160,000 square feet of gambling floor space, 210,000 square feet of tax-exempt restaurants and retail space, convention and entertainment buildings of up to 150,000 square feet, a 250-room hotel, a parking garage for 8,500 vehicles and extensive retail enterprises. The little Cowlitz tribe has partnered with the behemoth of Indian gambling, the Mohegan Sun Casino of Connecticut. The Mohegan is coming to Washington State, and every tribe in Washington State should be very concerned, as should every single citizen.

La Center, has about 1,000 people, is very quiet, wooded and hilly; it's a beautifully greened, rural bedroom community to Vancouver and Tacoma. It has excellent schools and quiet, safe neighborhoods, and is primarily supported by revenue from four small and sedate, card rooms that are licensed and well regulated by Washington State. Once a giant tribal casino opens, the primary funding for government services and schools in La Center will very probably be run out of business within the first year. The quality of life, need for low-income multi-unit housing to accommodate low-wage casino workers, increased crime and social deterioration follows casinos like night follows day. It will permanently change life as La Center knows it today.

A grassroots conference in the Summer of 2004 in Washington D.C. had expanded from a surge of new community groups, and elected government officials, formed to deal with off-reservation tribal governance intrusions. These groups are growing in direct response to the spread of Indian gambling and tribal jurisdictional overreaching across the country. It was at this event that I looked around the room and realized that we were all gathered up, sharing our issues and essentially preaching to the choir, but that the rest of the world was oblivious to the events and effects of federal Indian policy. American Indians are not the problem. Congress and tribal governments are the problem.

Soon after the event I also learned that Kamie was an accomplished videographer. That is when two and two made four. It occurred to me that it would be very useful to go capture the stories on film in their exact locations, as told by the people enduring or surviving the oppression: governmental, social and economic threats of tribal efforts to govern beyond their people and properties, or hijack a community economy with a shiny new, tax-free casino. We needed to visually document the issues, the economic harm, and the spread of tribalism as a form of government over American citizens. We needed to talk to tribal members, teachers, bankers, farmers, cattlemen, elected officials —all walks of life within and near Indian reservations.

Kamie didn't want to go—and did want to go. I think she was furious that I asked her, and grateful to be part of something that could be effective, simultaneously. Kamie the Mom, was truly conflicted. Kamie the Citizen had no doubt whatsoever. She would go. Once she agreed, I approached private citizens affiliated with national groups for assistance. if we could secure funding, we could make the trip.

Because I live on a virtual, municipal island within an Indian reservation, and have heard frightening stories of murders, missing persons and harassment that is frequent in often lawless areas, I knew there was no way we could possibly go public for funding. The trip across reservations had to be made under the radar, during daylight hours and very carefully, especially for two women traveling far from home. The plan we formed, worked.

I put a few quiet, confidential emails out to one or two citizens in affiliate groups across the country. We asked if they could contribute to the documentary road trip expenses. Then we waited. We asked a point person in each of several communities to gather key voices, whether tribal or non-tribal that could talk candidly about the reality of life on Indian reservations.

The road trip concept was born in July, funding started coming in through August and September, but it wasn't until four days before September 12th, that we received a formal "green light" for the trip from private citizens who contributed needed funds. We had to act as if we were going, actually prepare to go, and hope that the trip could be made. The only window of opportunity for the trip was September 12th through October 7th, as I teach for a University, had to complete summer course work, and be back before Fall courses started up. Kamie could not, and would not, be away from her family for more than 3 or 4 weeks at the most either. We also needed to make the journey before Winter set in.

Kamie secured a rental car in Vancouver, Washington and drove over to Toppenish early in the morning of September 12th. I was pleased to notice Pennsylvania license plates on the rental car, figuring the additional confusion might lessen our chances of being observed. Before leaving my home, we were advised to pre-tape ourselves, explaining why two women would take on such a project, fraught with risk and controversy. Why would we put our lives on hold to get a clear picture of tribalism as it is impacting America?

We both believe that our country is imploding internally under constant tribal funding demands, land grabs, casino expansions, and with political influence escalating, eviscerating one community after another. The simultaneity of accelerating annual budget deficits in states with numerous Indian tribal governments is no coincidence.

The drive of national tribal leaders to create a *national Indian economy,* tax exempt, and free of all state and federal regulations, will be the parasitic demise of the taxpaying primary economy. Just think in terms of the numbers: over 562 federally recognized tribes; only 50 states; over 411 tax-exempt mega-Indian casinos; only 50 states; over 217 additional tribes awaiting *their* federal recognition; only 50 states. Tribalism is dramatically spreading as a form of governance in the United States.

These domestic federal Indian policies layered over ongoing Homeland security concerns were fueling our journey.

If you are unwilling to defend your right to your own lives,
then you are merely like mice trying to argue with owls.
You think their ways are wrong. They think you are dinner.

— *Terry Goodkind in* Naked Empire
Contemporary American Novelist

Chapter 4
Dangerous Woods of North Idaho

I drive frequently alone, and often long distances. I'm used to this. The remoteness of my first venture into Northern Idaho, three years ago, can be defined by the roads. Initially I was on six-lane Interstate for several hours, then exited onto two-lane Idaho State Highway 3 off of Interstate 90, heading south. The next leg of the trip was paved county road with many S-curves for about 40 miles through deep, tall forest lands, and then a narrowing graveled county road, and finally, a very narrow *dirt* road, with more S-curves through a dark woods that led to a very remote driveway. As dearly as I love the mountains and forests, this level of aloneness and isolation gave me the shivers. This is not an area in which a woman should drive alone.

Three years ago, on my initial trip to Roger and Toni Hardy's home, about the time I was hitting the narrow, winding county road through the woods, I was asking myself, "What in the world am I doing? I hardly *know* these people. I have no clue where I even *am*. What is so important to me that I would put myself in this situation?" The answer for me has always been buried like a tiny hot rock within the middle of me. Some of my fears are greater than others. If I lose my rights as an American citizen, where could I go, and how would I live? The knee-jerk reaction to this fear takes me wherever I feel I can be useful, no matter what. And isn't it strange that as an American citizen I even have to worry about these things today in 2005?

The word, "rural" describes a socio-geographic region, and has varied meanings, often associated with population density. Toppenish is a town of about 9,000 folks and is considered quite rural; certainly rural enough for me in the rolling hills of or-chards and vineyards in the Yakima Valley. Rural in Northern Idaho can mean one home per 600 acres of thick woods. That's where Roger and Toni Hardy live. It's an isolated, extreme ver-sion of rural.

Earlier, in 2002, I had been invited to St. Maries, Idaho to speak to the North Idaho Citizens Alliance (NICA), and was to be a houseguest of the Hardys. Several months earlier I had met a NICA founder, Jon Furbee, in Nezperce, Idaho, and had helped this group get its sea legs as a community organization so I was really eager to visit with them, face-to-face.

The amazing thing (God bless MapQuest) is that I actually didn't get lost, and found at the end of a narrow dirt road and driveway lined with woods several stories high, a lovely home of unique design occupied by two amazing people. They are ying and yang, absolutely. Roger Hardy is a studious, quiet intellec-tual guy, tall and somewhat fuzzy in features but sharp of mind. His wife, Toni—*Antonia* is her christened name—is classic Ital-ian, also brilliant, full of heart, emotion and flair. Toni has her own home-furnishing import business, and has created a magical home space in the middle of the undeveloped woods initially homesteaded by Toni's grandparents in 1910. If it is possible to be raging femininity in an overlarge, plaid, floppy woodsman shirt and jeans, Toni has mastered the art. Their home sets on a high wooded bluff that overlooks the southern end of magnifi-cent Lake Coeur 'd Alene. Roger is a Geologist, and a self-taught civil and architectural engineer. Rog designed an oriental theme to the exterior, with massive, tall windows, ceilings, and a lovely stone and Indonesian-tiled deck.

I anticipated a rustic dwelling, with perhaps a lived-in, threadbare, cabin ambience, and was dead wrong. Walking into Rog and Toni's home is to enter a spiritually quiet space of In-donesian nirvana in the middle of the deep Northern Idaho woods. An amazing space. Toni is a gourmet cook, an avid re-searcher, and an excellent businesswoman. Elk, deer, bear, rac-coons, and beavers are the nearest neighbors. While setting an elegant dinner table upon my arrival, Toni was reminiscing about a time when she was standing at her kitchen sink and heard a tapping on the full glass window of her front door. She stepped around the corner to see a large brown bear, standing upright on her porch, literally knocking on her door. This is rustic beyond my comfort level.

The Coeur 'd Alene tribe seems to be salivating to acquire this early and long-held homestead land of Toni's grandparents—property that includes 1.6 miles of scenic lakefront and over 500 acres. Rog and Toni are fighting with all of their might, defending against continuous tribal harassment of their shoreline property, their roads, their lands and their right to a simple voice in huge decisions that impact their property. The Environmental Protection Agency has not been a friend, nor has the State of Idaho, nor their County. These entities are either beholden to, enamored of, or intimidated by, or all of the above - the local Indian tribe. Rog and Toni, and other Northern Idaho citizens deal with a chronic political isolation as severe as the physical.

At the bottom of the bluff below their home is an abandoned railroad track that runs along the lakeshore, and even in the lake. The track traverses all of the Hardy ancestral homestead lands that include an easement made available to the old Union Pacific Railroad which carried silver mine resources and volumes of contamination seepage along here for nearly a century. Seepage into pristine Lake Coeur 'd Alene deeply worries Roger and Toni, and supposedly worries the State of Idaho and the Tribe. Supposedly. Upon abandonment of the track, Union Pacific was to have cleaned any contamination, and the railroad property provided by easement should have reverted back in full force and effect, to the adjacent landowner. What has happened instead is bitter controversy, unfinished business, that has kept Roger and Toni burning the midnight oil, tearing around to meetings all over the State and as far away as Washington, D.C.

A slick federal tool, known as "Rails To Trails" has provided Union Pacific with a neat way to avoid huge hazardous contamination clean-up costs, and has provided a tribal foot in the door upon Toni's grandparent's land—two birds with one stone, so to speak: no cleanup costs for the railroad, and the tribe acquires "management" of land that rightfully belongs to adjacent private property owners. The ruse used is a desired *public trail* as a needed stimulus for tourism and tribal economic development. Quickly cover the old track in the cheapest, fasted mode, let the seeping toxins lurk below, welcome hikers and bikers unaware of the health risk. The easement rail bed is never completely cleaned, nor returned to the landowner because who knows—one day the railroad may need the trackage again. More likely, the tribal managers of the trail will aggressively increase their harassment and persuasive control on and near Rog and Toni's land. Their private gates have been torn down as a result of tribal actions, trespassers are frequent in their isolated woods, and tribal employees display zero respect for private property, because of tribal aborigine beliefs: We were here first; you stole our land.

Roger and Toni Hardy have not yet succeeded in replacing their gates and continue to fight the expensive legal battles but the end result is that a private tribal government in which Rog and Toni have no voice, has created a public walking trail across private homesteaded land, because all promises to the homesteader have been broken. The federal government and State of Idaho fall all over themselves to honor a "trust" relationship with an Indian tribe, simultaneously breaking promises and trust with people like the Hardys who are left sucking wind. No federal or state elected officials or agencies have bothered to acknowledge the rights or needs of landowners, who own by reversion the land underneath the easement for this 70-mile railroad path of poison.

The end result of very secret, behind-closed-door Superfund Response negotiations with EPA, the tribe, the railroad and the state is a now 72 mile hiking, biking "Trail of the Coeur-d' Alenes," part of which was given by EPA to the tribe to manage, in order to spare the railroad and state an urgently needed contamination cleanup of 72 miles of toxins flowing into the Lake. Tribes are exempt from most federal and state regulations, so laying a little surface over the poisons and giving the tribe control was a quick solution, no matter the health effects upon the trail users. And ironically, the most at-risk for dangers from contamination are the residents, not the tourists, so the very people who should have been protected from exposure—the landowners—are still the most vulnerable.

This should be publicly noticed as the Trail of Continuous Contamination...use at your own risk. And, the tribe gets everything it wants and needs: more land, better access to harass private property owners, and a clever linkage between the northern and southern areas of Lake Coeur 'd Alene to pursue what is whispered as "The South Lake Tahoe Plan." Yes indeed, even more tribal class III casinos coming to replace pristine forests and recreational areas.

The federal government made promises to homesteaders as well as Indian tribes, but apparently the promises to Indian tribes are the only ones that matter. It is amazing how campaign contributions affect the minds of officeholders, but this will be dealt with later.

The net effect for Rog and Toni is the inability to have their family land—now owned by Toni's 90-year-old mother—decontaminated or returned, the painful knowledge of continuous toxins flowing into a lovely lake and their shoreline, and now their very isolated property is open to the general public for hiking and biking.

Who were the masterminds of these legal shenanigans, political liaisons, avoidance of environmental stewardship, and constructive theft of property? Enter the wondrous Environmental Protection Agency (EPA), in partnership with state officials, anxious to placate a land-hungry tribe who need not comply with federal environmental regulations. What a financial and legal relief, then, for the Union Pacific Railroad. EPA embraces a principle of protection of human health and environmental stewards unless of course, a railroad company, a politically corrupt state, and a tribal government have another desire. The toxins and Toni's family land be damned.

On this second trip, I thought the wonderful setting of Northern Idaho would be a great start for our journey and couldn't wait to surprise Kamie with what she would find at Roger and Toni's. After leaving Toppenish about noon, we buzzed through the Spokane airport's Hertz counter to add my name as a driver on the rental car we had, and then headed East and South to Harrison, Idaho. We got to Toni's about 4:30 pm, under a crisp, clear blue sky crowning the high trees. Kamie had met Rog and

Toni once briefly in March, and was warmed by their gracious-ness, and their deep appreciation for the journey we were start-ing.

The founder of the Idaho citizens group, North Idaho Citizens Alliance (NICA), Jon Furbee, joined us for a cozy, oriental gourmet dinner for five in the deep woods. Jon, Roger, Toni, Kamie and I, proceeded to talk about some of the experiences that folks in Northern Idaho endure. The juxtaposition of a quiet lovely dinner with the alarming conversational content was cap-tured on camera.

Toni served homemade, hand-rolled sushi, Thai green chicken curry, shrimp with curry leaves, jasmine rice, kai lan with garlic (Chinese broccoli), and a salad of spinach and pea leaves. I have no particular affection for gourmet cuisine, but I stand in awe of those who can actually prepare a meal such as Toni served us. It was wonderful, and totally out of synch with Northern Idaho. In my honor, she also served the strongest, most vibrant, best damn coffee I've ever had anywhere.

Jon Furbee is a very, very tall fellow who lives the life of an urban project manager at a major company in Seattle, Monday through Friday, and maximizes every minute with his family and home in the woods of Idaho on the weekends. He has a 5-hour drive to and from his work, a treacherous task on the winter roads in Washington. Jon believes in quality life for his wife and family. For him that requires a blending of a long commute to his urban profession with life in a small community in Northern Idaho. Lately, however, the quality of life around his home is being tested severely.

Sharing frequent events that occur around his home Jon told us about a few. Apparently, around Northern Idaho Indian reservations there are the equivalent to urban drive-by shootings. Young tribal kids, often high on booze or drugs, pile into pickup trucks to go "hunting," as is their "Treaty right." The pickups full of tribal kids rumble down old farm roads, and literally drive by shooting at any observable or imagined game. It doesn't mat-ter that the guns are aimed toward private homes and yards. It's the tribal members guaranteed treaty right to hunt, that's all.

Jon once heard a shot fired very loud and close to his house, and then he saw a tribal member coming onto his land to claim a dead deer. Jon went out and greeted the fellow, inviting him to leave, and to leave the deer where it was dropped. Remember, Jon's a very big guy, and Jon had a gun too. At some point in Jon's conversation with the trespasser, a tribal officer arrived. Seeing that Jon was quite serious about his views on trespassers and was on his private, deeded land, Jon was left alone - with the deer.

The mountains, forests and meadows of Benewah, Kootenai and Shoshone counties in Northern Idaho are classic Americana, settled by tribal people and homesteaders, linked by mining, rails and forestry industries, and lightly flecked throughout with very self-sustaining, hard-working Idaho folks. One of the early settlers before the 1900's was Anna O'Gara, a strict Irish Catholic woman who homesteaded O'Gara Bay on Coeur 'd Alene Lake. Ana ran a boarding house and was a dear friend and neighbor of Toni's grandparents who homesteaded on O'Gara Creek in 1910. The 500 acres of Toni's grandparents are the envy and an apparently prized goal of the Coeur 'd Alene tribe. The tribe's reservation was congressionally diminished and opened to homesteaders in the late 1800's.

What is happening in this millennium is a belated *Buyer Beware* for descendent property owners of homesteaders. Indian reservations diminished by the General Allotment Act of 1870 were legally and intentionally opened for settlers to support the development of the western states, and in this case the Northwest. There are current, legal boundaries, and "historical" boundaries of "former" Indian reservations. Within current boundaries a tribal government exercises its governance over it's tribal members and tribally owned properties. Within these boundaries, however, tribal governments have no authority over non-tribal members.

What the Coeur 'd Alene tribe has done quite blatantly is to politically expand its actual reservation of 70,000 acres by arbitrarily claiming it's former, "historical acreage" of some 345,000 thousand acres of predominantly private, deeded land, as its current reservation. What Idaho elected officials from the governor on down have done, is let the tribe have its way - all the time, every time. No elected officials want to be the first to decline a tribal request. The fear of being called a *racist* for disagreeing with a tribal government activity is the *real* Third Rail, - not Social Security.

As early as the mid-'80s, maps of the U.S. Fish and Wildlife, and other federal, state and tribal maps started magically expanding the Coeur 'd Alene reservation, from its current boundary to its former and larger, *historical* boundary, in which there is no legal tribal jurisdiction. With such mapping sleights-of-hand came efforts to expand tribal law enforcement, water rights, hunting and fishing rights, and harassment sufficient to drive off private property owners.

Historical evidence of early settlers has been intentionally removed. Apparently, settler history is offensive. Within this area, destruction of early settler history is acceptable, preservation of all things Native American is the priority. No other ethnic history is of significance in Northern Idaho, as far as Coeur 'd Alene tribal leaders are concerned.

Another great gal from Idaho, was unable to join us at dinner, but was with us recently in Washington D.C. Angie Morrow is a bright, small and delicate-faced beauty who is absolutely fearless. Her miniature frame and angelic face are deceptive. You just don't want to upset this little dynamo. With Angie, the "A" is for assertive, and if you truly anger her, the "A" is for aggressive. I dearly love the contrast of her petite power. Angie and her husband's family have a large ranch in Northern Idaho, raise tons of livestock and raise wondrous Anatolian Shepherds, magnificent and enormous dogs from Turkey. The dogs are as large as the family members, great land perimeter protectors and beautiful to behold.

Angie's parents were in the military when passing through North Idaho in 1960. They liked it so much, they too purchased 60 acres to retire on, and now have 200 acres. It was not within an Indian "reservation" when the land was purchased, but through the years the land status has been asserted to have, mysteriously, changed. Like thousands of other property owners, they are now under political pressure of a magically imposed and expanded reservation, from former to asserted actual. The Morrows also descend from Idaho homesteaders now under political pressure of a magically imposed and expanded reservation, from *former* to asserted actual.

Well, now someone *has* upset Angie. The same Rails-to-Trails corridor that affects the Hardy's also impacts Angie and her husband's land. 4.5 miles of the trail goes through their property. It is bottom land in which wild elk calve every spring, moose graze through the summer and the wildlife pass free from hunting harm, or rather, they used to. Hosts of uninvited trespassers now use the trail to access Angie's private land. To discourage trail-users from wandering all over private property, Angie was told by the Idaho Fish and Game to post the property in an appropriate manner, orange fluorescent, 10" x 10" squares painted on trees, rocks, or any object, 660' apart. Trespassers cannot be prosecuted without showing that land has been posted.

The Morrows have been posting their land along the railroad tracks for years, with no harassment from the Union Pacific Railway company. This year, after posting their land, Idaho Parks and Recreation Department, in harmonious concert with the Coeur 'd Alene tribe, actually cited Angie on her family's private lands. The first charge was Malicious Injury, carrying a possible sentence of 3 years in prison and monetary damages. This charge was reduced to Injury by Graffiti, carrying a lesser sentence. Nonetheless, Angie has had to obtain legal counsel and must argue her right to be guided by Idaho Fish and Game's regulations, the result of which caused her to be harassed on her own private property. Go figure. Angie's furious.

If Idaho Parks and Recreation Department can make this frivolous and illegal charge stick, the Tribe is waiting to demand the same for the Hardys, for refreshing the orange "No Trespassing" marks and signs they have maintained on their land for nearly a century. The Tribe already tried to have the Hardys cited several times, but so far, law enforcement refused to cooperate with the Tribe.

I introduce Angie and the Hardys as examples of truly brave and self-educated people confronting federal Indian policy, who live in a constantly defensive posture regarding their right to never be governed by a tribal government, and to never have their private properties encumbered by tribal regulations. There are thousands of Angies and Antonias, as well as Rogers and Jons throughout Idaho. They are not asleep at the wheel or apathetic. Idaho citizens vigorously write, phone, email, and visit with elected officials in person, on a continuous basis.

These citizens are simply dismissed or ignored regarding decisions that affect them, but involve tribal governments. They maintain that their state officials have failed to protect them, giving in instead to race-based pressure from the casino-rich corporate Tribe.

Northern Idaho has an underserved black eye brought about by a few skinheads and white supremacists whose odious actions have occasionally achieved national media status. Very little else in Northern Idaho receives national attention, so thousands of very decent, hardworking commoners are left in the shadows. Folks here do not keep up with New York and L.A. fashion. They dress for tasks, comfort or weather - period. What you see is what you get. The lack of pretense is entirely refreshing and credible. They are not the classic rednecks, nor are they uneducated or poor. They simply keep to themselves, bothering no one until trouble arrives on their porch or their property.

To strengthen the voice of citizens in Northern Idaho, the North Idaho Citizens Alliance (NICA) was formed in 2002. Its initial membership topped 100 right away. Several large problems are on their plate. One is the pervasive practice of allowing a tribal government to claim its former boundaries as actual boundaries, affecting the lives of thousands of Idaho citizens. Another is the Coeur d' Alene tribe's assertion to governance over private docks and shore lakebeds.

The U.S. Supreme Court awarded this tribe the lower third of Coeur 'd Alene Lake and part of the St. Joe River in 2001. The award did not, of course, include any right of strangers to enter or interfere with adjacent private properties. It has been unsettling for local property owners to have tribal members quietly boat up to their private docks, step onto them and post signs on the docks, claiming tribal governing authority and demands for a paid "tribal permits." Most property owners have refused to comply, and assert their right to access the navigable waters of the lake, a right attached to their private property. The tribe continues to pester, and property owners will likely have to endure costly litigation again, to assert rights they always had.

Following the great evening dinner at Hardys, the next morning Kamie and I met with about a dozen more St. Maries and Harrison, Idaho residents, a couple of elected officials and a local reporter. Many members of NICA were on hand.

A truly troublesome event was described cautiously by one woman. She told of a neighbor whose children were part of a middle-school biology field trip in 2003, deep in an isolated meadow, far into a forest, miles from anything or anyone. There were parent chaperones along. When the bus arrived at the distant destination, children tumbled out to be greeted by two Couer 'd Alene tribal officials. These officials held forth about the history of the tribe, the usual "we were here first - you stole our land" mantra, and then the tribal officials asked the students to stand in a very large, wide circle around the meadow.

Once the huge circle was formed, the officials asked each child to take one step toward the center of the circle and stop. They were then asked to take another step and stop, then another, and another.

After many steps toward the center of this isolated meadow, the students found themselves tightly clustered, shoulder-to-shoulder in the center of the circle. They had been instructed to step to the center until they could step no more, and then crowd up against each other. While in this position, the tribal officials then said, "How does it feel to be forced into such a small space? Are you uncomfortable? How does it feel to be so restricted? Well, now you know what your ancestors did to our people. Your ancestors stole our land and forced us into small spaces. They ordered us around like we ordered you around."

Such a school-sanctioned exercise would certainly accomplish shame, guilt and low self-esteem among students age 11 and 12. Nor did the parent chaperones object. They were few, they were far, far away from help, and they were worried about the children. And likely, they didn't want to object and be called a racist. There are some tribal voices who relish in demeaning all other ethnicities; radicals who are convinced of their special status on the planet, who demand respect, and return none. For such mentalities to have any input in the minds of 11 and 12 year olds is deeply disturbing.

A common thread among the people in so many community groups and so many states is an abiding sense of citizenship. I'm not talking just parades and flag-waving patriotism; I mean the kind of civic-minded temperament that separates the timid from the action-takers. People who, when worried, will take steps to become self-informed, will call elected officials, will write letters, will communicate with others of similar concerns, and will eventually get organized. These, to me, are the truest of citizens. We know the physical shape of the State of Idaho. The panhandle area of the state is the least populated which leads, in turn, to lesser political influence than more urbanized areas such as Boise or Pocatello.

Another is an effort to erase or remove any historical footprints of early "settlers." Apparently only tribal history matters in Northern Idaho. The backbreaking task of clearing and homesteading land even through harsh winters, building schools and communities, creating water and energy systems, and improving quality of life for everyone is just irrelevant, and a bad thing here.

One of the last vestiges of early American settlers in the area of St. Maries and Harrison, Idaho is the Rose Lake School, placed on the National Historic Register in 1985. The school represents an example of architecture from the exploration, settlement era of 1900-1924 in Northern Idaho. Tribal governments often perceive structures such as Rose Lake school as representative of an "annihilation" period and prefer no visible remembrance of early settler history within their former or actual historic boundaries.

It is stunning to me to try to grasp the concept that one particular culture or ethnicity is more special or superior to another. My core beliefs embrace a concept that all cultures and ethnicities are to be mutually respected and equally treated under the law in the United States. The history of the birth and growth of America as forged by many cultures deserves preservation and commemoration. But just like continuous erasure of the foot-prints of settlers in the Northwest, so too is the current political climate as endorsed by federal and state elected officials and federal administrators.

Antonia's recent email to me painfully summarizes what Idaho citizens who own property or live and work within or near any Indian reservation are experiencing:

> Why does this rich Tribe continue to get all these huge grants, while our counties are dying? Where is the justice and equal (not exceptional, just fair and equal) treatment, where is our right to inclusion and due process? We cannot afford lawyers, nor should we be forced into lawsuits when all we have tried to do is protect what our government said is ours?

> The railroad right-of-way, just like the city of Harrison, was (Congressionally) separated out, and the Tribe was paid for the land, on the former reservation. The land under the easement was/is included on our homestead patents as is acreage out into the Lake (now owned by the federal government, in trust for the Tribe). We brought all of these issues up before the Lake lawsuit, before the Trail implementation, all in good faith, but why are our rights not important? Do we mean nothing? It is as if we do not exist.

Politically, Northern Idaho citizens no longer exist. They have been the brave little mice defending their homes for years against enormous federal financing and the politically purchased power of the "owls"—Indian tribes. The mice have been wronged. The owls see the lands and resources of the mice, as *dinner.*

Those who expect to reap the blessings of freedom, must, like men,
undergo the fatigues of supporting it.

— Thomas Paine
American Revolutionary Pamphleteer
(1737 - 1809)

Chapter 5
The Bravest Elected Officials I Know

Most of the stops along our 6,000-mile trip were places I had never been, but Nezperce, Idaho held warm memories for me that I was eager to share with Kamie. Nezperce is about 80 miles southeast of Lewiston, Idaho, the nearest larger city. It's nestled in a lovely draw, a small, wooded canyon surrounded by high plains of farmlands. One gets their following the path of Lewis and Clark.

Nezperce is not huge. It has 435 people, unless someone died. I would bet good money that most everyone knows everything about everybody in that lovely little community. It has two res- taurants, a grocery store, a county courthouse and small post of- fice. It also has a sizeable John Deere distributor and a big gran- ary that area farmers rely upon. Although it is an economically depressed area, few people leave. It's a hard but worthy lifestyle with a quality that keeps people dedicated to their tiny town and valley.

Before describing this third visit to Nezperce, I need to tell you about the first two. Early in 2000 when my local community group was forming, we learned about a coalition of 23 govern- mental entities that formed in Central Idaho to defend them- selves against aggressive actions of the Nez Perce Tribe. I was interested in learning more about the North Central Idaho Juris- dictional Alliance (NCIJA) because I believed then, and still do, that a similar entity is needed where I live within the Yakama Indian Reservation. I contacted their Executive Director, Dan Johnson, and was invited to attend a meeting of this group in January 2001

Dan wears many hats in Nezperce. He has been at times simultaneously, a tribal attorney, a public defender, the city clerk, the town postmaster, certified public accountant, land title insurance agent, a hotel owner, and an awesome father and husband. I mean no offense by suggesting quite affectionately that if one can envision a brilliant "Harry Potter," you have Dan. He's a quixotic mind, dry wit and a deep well of thought, all packaged in a small frame, with jaunty glasses and generally, a spiffy hat. His wife, Annie is a rural Mary Tyler Moore, just vivacious, loving and very high energy. They were both raised in the Nezperce area.

Like Roger and Toni Hardy, the Johnson's families were homesteaders who spent their lives growing up in this region. They grew up among Indian children and called all cultures close friends. Dan and Annie grew up among Indian children and called all cultures close friends. The Johnsons are a very bicultural family with a sense of fairness and equality that permeates throughout the family and everything they say and do. From early adulthood on, they have given back to their community far more than they have received. They still do.

The NCIJA organized in December 1996 to "defend the members and citizens of the area from the ever expanding claims of the Nez Perce Tribe to jurisdictional legal authority over residents and property of the area within the 1863 (former) boundary of the Nez Perce Reservation." The multi-agency group includes three counties, 8 cities, 4 school districts, and 8 Highway Districts. What prompted this alliance was an incident involving the Kamiah School District that urgently needed to build a new middle school.

The Kamiah School District's subcontractors on the construction of a new middle school were ordered by the Nez Perce Tribe to comply with the Tribal Employment Rights Ordinance (TERO), which required payment of a TERO fee to the tribe, the employment of tribal members and compliance with other TERO regulations, all at a cost estimated to be in excess of $300,000 - $500,000. This would have been over and above the actual cost to construct the middle school, and would have made a desperately needed new school impossible for this impoverished rural school district. The school district property is not tribal property, nor located within the actual boundaries of the existing Nez Perce reservation. Lacking any authority or jurisdiction over the public school district did not stop the Nez Perce tribe from bullying in for a sizeable tithing from the school district.

This triggering event caused the formation of the NCIJA. An interesting fact is that the 23 governmental agencies are the very agencies that provide *all* public services within the region of the Nez Perce reservation, including education, law enforcement, public highway and road maintenance, hospital and health services. The Nez Perce Tribe provides no such public services for their 3,363 members, (Nov. 2004 Website pop. stats).

The combined, *cumulative* annual revenue of these 23 governmental agencies that provide 100% of public services and resources for over 20,000 citizens, including *all* tribal members, is *less* than the annual federal funding ($49 million) received by the Nez Perce tribe for their members. And did I mention the millions in annual revenue the Nez Perce Tribe also receives from its class III casino, sales of cigarettes and fireworks?

The small governmental agencies gathered as one voice and announced to the Tribe: "When you confront one of us, you confront all of us." From 1996 through 2001 the Tribe was frustrated by a strengthened local voice of government service providers and protectors of citizens in the region.

Then in January 2001, along came Harvard University to diminutive Nezperce, Idaho. Quite coincidentally, my first trip to an NCIJA meeting was the evening that two Harvard gentlemen were on the agenda, on behalf of the Nez Perce Tribe. The NCIJA had been relatively successful in defending themselves against aggressive actions of the Tribe, so Harvard was called in.

"The Nez Perce Tribe desires to dialogue and establish a productive working relationship with the NCIJA," said Keith Allred, Ph.D., Assistant Professor of Public Policy at the John F. Kennedy School of Government at Harvard University.

One can only imagine the level of intimidation and impact that Professor Allred's Ivy League title had in tiny Nezperce. I had the experience of watching it firsthand. It was crushing. Allred's presentation materials reassured the local governments that "the purpose of the (proposed Harvard project) program is *not* negotiation or mediation. Rather, it would seek only to provide all parties with information of an educational nature." Allred further informed the NCIJA that the Nez Perce Tribal Chairman and Council had already unanimously endorsed the concept of mediation with NCIJA, so wouldn't they also agree?

For years, local governments could not get a return telephone call from a Nez Perce tribal leader, or written answer to any communications. For years, these economically constrained local governments received menacing written notices and announcements from the Tribe, but the Tribe never responded to questions. Then came Harvard with the message: the Tribe wants to talk. If the NCIJA had declined Harvard's invitation the group would have been painted with an uncooperative, perhaps *racist* brush. Politically, they had to agree, and did. Allred promised the NCIJA that he would commence gathering facts over the next several months and return for presentation to NCIJA and the Tribe. And return he did.

I should mention that also attending this meeting was our colleague, Jon Furbee, from the Northern Idaho area. He too had come to learn about the NCIJA, and he too, believed that his area needed a similar organization to withstand the aggression of the Coeur 'd Alene Tribe. At the end of that meeting, my friend, Judy Chandler, and I were invited to spend the night in the lovely little Nezperce hotel, a historic little two-story hotel of odd, Spanish or Mediterranean architectural style. The town's first hotel was a tent on Oak Street, until this U-shaped, two story, 10-room hotel was completed in 1910. It comes complete with legends of ghosts so Judy and I were quite alert throughout the evening. It also has a wonderful restaurant and meeting spaces where the locals gather in the mornings and afternoons. After breakfast, Judy and I played Chinese Marbles in the restaurant.

Our visit to Nezperce was so illuminating, and made so welcome by the Johnsons that we decided to hold our second annual regional gathering of community groups at the Nezperce Hotel. This prompted the 2nd visit in April of 2002. It was at this regional gathering that I first met the Hardys mentioned in the previous chapter. Our regional groups numbered about 7 in 2002. We're at least double that now, thanks to the explosion of Indian casinos and land and water grabs in the Northwest.

Keith Allred returned to Nezperce, to invite the NCIJA to sign a mediation agreement with the Nez Perce Tribe in December 2002. The Spokesman Review newspaper noted, "On December 6, a bright chapter opened in the history of relations between Indians and non-Indians in Idaho. With Governor Dirk Kempthorne in attendance, the Nez Perce Tribe and the North-Central Idaho Jurisdictional Alliance - signed a Memorandum of Understanding (MOU) that commits them to building cooperative intergovernmental relations." The news article was written by Allred. The MOU completely muzzled the NCIJA. They were not allowed to express any negativity or opposition to Nez Perce Tribal issues or activities. The organization literally fell off the face of the earth during these mediations, in which long diatribes of "you stole our land," and "you owe us" were harangued upon the NCIJA at mediation gatherings. To their credit, the small government entities entered into the MOU with good faith, cooperated at all times, and suspended any litigation contemplated against the Tribe. Not so the Tribe. Their litigation and demands for 115% of the Snake River waters were rolling forward full force.

The Nez Perce also negotiated an agreement with Idaho's Governor Kempthorne that provides the Tribe with management of delisted (no longer Endangered Species) wolves in the region. Real wild wolves. Wolves that have startled Dan Johnson in his own back yard. The state legislature had authorized a state wolves management plan that somehow transferred control to the Nez Perce tribe. Farmers, cattlemen and even folks that live in town, now also have to keep a watchful eye for less-than-well managed wolves, with little to no assistance available from the Tribe. But they dare not shoot a wolf because of federal restraints against doing so.

Unable to keep silent while watching the Nez Perce litigate and negotiate with the State of Idaho for all of the area water, while struggling with ongoing law enforcement jurisdictional conflicts and wolves roaming the region, the NCIJA broke away from the stifling MOU in April 2004. The NCIJA submitted a pleading to intervene in the adjudication of the Snake River Basin Area with the filing of a 50-page memorandum in April 2004. They took horrible media press from local reporter, Jim Fisher, who on April 22· 2004 reported that withdrawal from the MOU could be a possible "declaration of another Indian war."

No, the elected officials of the 23-governmental agencies of the NCIJA are simply performing their oaths of office to protect and serve their citizens, in spite of ongoing harassment from the Nez Perce Tribe and utter abandonment by the State of Idaho. In this remote region, the elected officials cannot be purchased. And they proceed at personal risk. I consider these individuals as having a rarely found sense of courage, integrity and duty to keep providing at least minimal public services and resources for so long as they can.

So how do the wealthy tribes of Northern and Central Idaho spend their enormous monies from the federal government and gambling? It's a national pattern, quite prominent in this region. We call it the four "L's." The tribal governments buy:

1. Lobbyists
2. Legislators
3. Litigators
4. Land

Very little of huge funds pouring into tribal coffers actually trickle down to improve the quality of life and economic opportunities for tribal families. Tribal households continue to experience poverty and squalor on one reservation after another. Money is fixing almost nothing for tribal families. Money is the weaponry used to attack descendants of settlers throughout the country by purchasing federal and state political processes and power.

The Indian gambling Regulatory Act of 1988 has been the gasoline on this fire, but I'll talk about this later.

When Kamie and I drove into Nezperce on a bright September's Friday afternoon, we had the sense that we might be the first tourists in town all week. We found Dan in his musty little law office that probably hasn't changed in fifteen years. He jumped up and drove us on out to their home to find Annie, then back to the Nezperce Hotel. We settled into a corner room that gave us a window view of the whole town—both blocks. We couldn't use our cell phones because they wouldn't work down in the little hollow that is the town of Nezperce. Nor could we access the internet to catch up with families and news. We freshened up and went exploring to a local restaurant/bar and enjoyed watching the town folks interact with each other and us.

Later in the evening, we gathered in the old hotel's upstairs meeting room with some of the courageous people I've just mentioned. On camera, they talked about how much their area means to them, how long they've struggled to just withstand tribal government overreaching, and they reminisced about decades ago when cultures mutually respected each other, and everyone knew their boundaries and enjoyed the best features of an ongoing cultural diversity.

Their immediate concerns are water, wolves and law enforcement problems. Their long-term concerns include the ability of local governments to even continue providing services to the area citizens.

When there is a lack of honor in government, the morals of the whole people are poisoned.

— Herbert Hoover
31ˢᵗ President of the United States
(1874 - 1964)

Chapter 6
Buffalo Country

Do you have, or know of, bright middle school, high school or college students that dream of a career in environmental sciences, natural habitat management, or animal husbandry? Do you know young people of diverse cultures and zip codes who are, or may soon be, well qualified to pursue top jobs in wondrous natural settings across the country? Too bad, if you do.

Many of the "Last Great Places..." in which America's natural, scenic environment, which The Nature Conservancy likes to champion as treasures to be enjoyed by further generations of all citizens are now being systematically put on a restricted or potentially denied access to all but the Native American Indian population."

The Department of Interior and seven agencies of Interior (including Bureau of Land Management, Bureau of Reclamation, National Park Service, U.S. Fish and Wildlife) may has well have hung a sign out on a preliminary list of 41 national refuges, 34 national parks, wildlife refuges and hatcheries, and 15 regional water projects. The new political sign may soon say: *"Unless you are Native American, you need no longer apply for employment here."*

On April 5, 2002 the Department of Interior listed these treasured *public* spaces and natural resources as having "special geographic, historical, or cultural significance to self-governance tribes." Even "close proximity" was sufficient criteria to allow a *private* tribal government to take over the management of such national sites as:

Joshua Tree National Park (CA)	National Bison Rage (MT)
Redwood National Park (CA)	Kootenai National Wildlife Refuge (ID)
Cape Cod National Seashore (MA)	Humboldt Bay Natl. Wildlife Refuge (CA)
Glacier National Park (MT)	Sequoyah National Wildlife Refuge (OK)
Olympic National Park (WA)	Alaska National Wildlife Refuge (AK)
Mt. Rainier National Park (WA)	Mille Lacs National Wildlife Refuge (MN)

The above list is just a small sample of at least 90 major spaces across the country, now targeted by the Department of Interior for management transfer to private tribal governments, who have stringent *Indian preference* hiring practices.

Ordinarily, when job openings occur in these prestigious and well-maintained public resources, a national solicitation goes out that sets high standards and follows equal employment opportunity guidelines. National parks and wildlife refuges are able to hire the best-qualified applicant from a broad spectrum of skills, ethnicity and geography.

As one tribe after another, pushing for more land grabs, acquires control over these public spaces, future hiring practices will dutifully follow. Tribal Employment Rights Ordinances (TEROs) will severely limit opportunities for all other ethnicities the ability to work in America's great sites of our natural, most treasured resources. Public access will likely be limited or set at one fee for the general public and another fee, if any, for Native Americans. What's worse? Tribes won't have to pay for the refuges or national parks, nor fund their own management of it. We taxpayers will be forced to do that, while receiving reduced or prohibited access to these treasures. Amazing, isn't it—how enforced and false guilt, combined with revenue from a federally funded tribal gambling monopoly is rolling out those "special preferences" across all spectrums of American life.

The drive across the Coeur d' Alene Mountains and up onto the high prairies of Northwestern Montana was jaw-dropping gorgeous on a sunny, Fall day. Small communities of Polson, Pablo, Charlo, Ronan and Ravalli all neighbor the sizeable, 1.317 million acre, Flathead Indian Reservation. The area population is approximately 26,000 residents, of which about one-fifth are enrolled members of the Confederated Salish and

Kootenai Tribes. The tribe claims a total enrollment of 7,012, but indicates that just over 4,500 tribal members live on the reservation.

Kamie and I met with Montana people that have lived all of their lives, through rough weather and frequently severe financial times, never ever contemplating giving up or moving on. Times are different now. Like Idaho, Montana citizens are feeling that their elected officials no longer hear them over the ka-ching, ka-ching of casino campaign contributions. In a part of the country where a handshake was a confirmed agreement, where a man's word was good enough, and where a neighbor's need was a pleasurable duty to assist - well those values are still in place.

It's getting tougher to hold on to farms and homesteaded lands, however, with ever-increasing external political pressures exerted by the Confederated Salish and Kootenai Tribes (CSKT), amply supported by federal and state assistance.

One of our first visits in Polson, Montana was with Marv and Janet Kashke, on their lovely Christmas tree farm. Marv served as the National Bison Range Manager from 1968 until 1977. In fact, their two daughters and son spent their younger years, growing up on the Bison Range. When Marv retired from the U.S. Fish & Wildlife Division in 1988, he and Janet bought several acres of lovely bare ground overlooking Flathead Lake, and the two of them, initially living in an onsite camper, built a great home, and cultivated what is now a highly respected Christmas tree farm. The Kashkes are wonderful examples of dedicated Montanans focused on family and community.

Marv phoned me recently to report that the CSKT released an estimate of their 2004 annual Operational Management Budget in the amount of $373 million in a report released in March 2005. This $373 million for *one* single tribe is nearly the *same* amount as the entire annual *national* U.S. Fish and Wildlife's Refuge System Operational and Maintenance for the whole country in 2004.

Just outside of Charlo, Montana, is the Willow Creek Campground, 150 acres ringed with nearly 300 soft, enormous willow trees, all growing from the shoots of an original willow, planted by Dell Palmer in 1943.

"I invite the State Warden out to my property in October every year to arrest me for pheasant hunting on my land, but he won't come out any more," reports 84-year Dell Palmer. It is the State Warden's role to enforce Tribal Bird Permits, in association with a State-Tribal agreement for hunting regulations.

Over a period of time in recent years, the State Warden had cited Del for failure to obtain a Tribal Bird Permit. All five times Dell requested a jury of his peers in the County Court of the Justice of Peace. His peers acquitted him on each occasion, and Dell prevailed. "This is my land and I have no duty or debt to a tribal government. I have my own government." However, Dell does obtain the appropriate Montana State hunting, bird and fishing permits.

Talking with Dell on the phone is like listening to the booming voice of Perry Mason, as played by actor Raymond Burr. Dell is a strong, muscular fellow—his own man. He takes no guff from any one; but then he doesn't give any, either. I find Montana men wonderfully deceptive, made of bison-hard shells and gentle, warm hearts. And the best ones are like Dell, survivors—in their senior years.

Dell and Bernice Palmer are classic Montanans whose great-grandparents were drawn by attractive advertisements placed by the federal government in the early 1900s, inviting settlers to homestead throughout the state, including lands of *former* Indian reservations. Dell is descended from the Palmer family of London England, one of whom came to America as an indentured servant until he had worked off his passage. After receiving his freedom, the original Palmer served under Captain Miles Standish, a renowned leader of the Plymouth Colony in Massachusetts. Dell comes from strong, stock with a deep love of country flowing through his veins. Bernice's ancestors also homesteaded in Eastern Montana. Bernice recalls being born in a small log cabin in the middle of nowhere.

At 84, Dell still bucks bales, drives a tractor, handles all the irrigation on his acreage, raises horses, and tends exquisitely landscaped habitats and ponds that are home to six graceful and nearly tame swans. Before converting his land to a dreamlike campground, Dell bought the land and opened the Silver Thorn

Dairy in 1943, raising registered Holstein cows, while also raising a family of three sons and a daughter—all of whom, along with six grandchildren and six great-grandchildren, still live within a few miles or a few minutes of the folks. Farm, ranch and dairy families cherish their land and family relationships above all else.

The Salish-Kootenai Tribes' increasing expansion of the tribal rights under the Treaty of Hellgate of July 16, 1855, on and around the Flathead Reservation, is a pattern across Indian reservations in the Northwest. Somehow, the "exclusive right to take *fish* in all streams" running through a reservation, has now become, in the minds of aggressive tribal leaders, the *exclusive control of all fish and all waters, above the ground, underground and beyond the boundaries* of the reservation.

Somehow, the "*privilege* of hunting, gathering roots and berries" translates in the year 2005 to "complete and exclusive jurisdiction to license, regulate and control hunting and fishing activities of all citizens throughout the (even former) lands, including private property, within the reservation. Never mind that tribal self-government was and is intended to be *self*-governing authority over tribal members only, and tribal properties only.

Hunter-gatherer, nomadic societies have no claim to land they once only owned as long as their warriors could occupy and defend it. This is true throughout the world, and once another group of people occupy and lay claim to it, the prior occupants lose their rights to it.

The National Bison Range is near Moiese, Montana, within the *former* boundary of the Flathead Reservation.

One of Dell's son's, Skip Palmer, works for the National Bison Range, and has for many years. Skip's a naturalist, a lover of land and animals, a cowboy who looks like something's missing when he takes off the cowboy hat. Skip spent some time explaining to Kamie and me the unpredictable and dangerous nature of the bison, coupled with a vulnerability if not managed properly.

"It is not like herdin' cattle, or sheep or horses. Bison are wild animals. They're damn dangerous if you don't know what you're doing, and damn dangerous even when you *do* know what you're doing." he said.

"They may seem slow but even at 2,000 pounds, buffalo can run as fast as a horse." We sensed and saw what Skip was saying as we drove through the range late one afternoon. The male bison, even at great distances, never took their eyes off our vehicle - watched every move we made. I was pleased that they weren't too close, and in awe of this mysterious animal and the magnificent lands they roam.

The Bison Range is home to between 300 and 500 bison that roam an 18,500 acre range. Annual roundups involving many local volunteers gather the bison for vaccinations, identification and other needed care. Very dedicated and highly trained, local volunteers spend hours in continued training, take their work very seriously and prioritize the safety and well being of the bison.

Area residents are concerned that the Bison Range will be transformed into a cultural center focusing on Salish-Kootenai cultural history, and that the bison and range will become a secondary matter. The annual Bison roundup is extremely difficult, serious and quite dangerous business. Many of the local trained volunteers who are not tribal members, are uncertain about whether their experience will be welcome and utilized by the tribe. The Bison Range is held dear to all America, not just one specific tribal government.

Skip tells us that the U.S. Fish and Wildlife (USFW) service is truly fortunate to be able to draw upon America's finest and most qualified people to manage the Bison Range and other USFW refuges. Skip's not political, and not one to keep his views to himself. "I dearly love my job, but I love the First Amendment too. I worry about changing the hiring criteria for this range. I worry about inexperienced management and staff around these bison. I worry about this American Icon, this place being converted to some Indian museum or cultural center, instead of its original and sole purpose —to preserve and honor the American Bison."

Marv Kashke former manager of the National Bison Range, echoed everything we heard and learned, and he, too, believes that the range, as well as all other U.S. wildlife refuges, national parks and habitats should remain under the sole control of the federal government, and not a private tribal government.

So, upon my return from our road trip, in October 2004, I wrote a letter to Matt Hogan, then Director of U.S. Fish and Wildlife Service, opposing transfer of management of America's National Bison Range to an Indian tribe. Below are a couple of excerpts:

...The American public has been wondrously benevolent toward federal government preferential funding for Indian tribes that has accomplished, to mention but a few programs:

> Separate tribal governments
> Separate Indian health services
> Separate Indian educational programs
> Separate Indian housing programs
> Separate Indian gambling monopolies
> Separate "sacred" grave protection resources
> Separate tax benefits and tax exemptions

As enamored as Congress, the Department of Interior (DOI) and other federal agencies must be to fund duplicative programs for Indians who have been equal citizens since 1924, Congress and the DOI would be ill advised to now abdicate America's precious wildlife refuges and national parks to one small segment of our society. Converting such a beloved natural resource to a "separate" tribal wildlife refuge is completely unthinkable. Enough is enough.

Throughout America, as I write this letter, are thousands of college students of every culture and ethnicity, pursuing academic and professional goals in environmental habitat, natural resource management, animal husbandry and other natural resource endeavors. Many have dreams of the ultimate career - to work in and for a revered national park or wildlife refuge. ...

How, and more important, <u>why</u>, would the DOI or U.S. Fish and Wildlife Service remotely consider hijacking major national parks, wildlife refuges, and public resources enjoyed and revered by <u>all</u> Americans, to limit public access and employment, by way of an executed annual funding agreement (AFA) with a single, private, tribal government that strictly enforces Indian-preference hiring? And what incentive does a private tribal government have to honor the considerations of other American citizens?

We assert that ... America's natural habitats, wildlife refuges, and national parks, are indeed, sacred to <u>every</u> American citizen, and most certainly not sacred to <u>only one</u> small ethnic culture in this country.

The political and illogical myths that a piece of American ground, or a specific species is more sacred or special to only one culture in our country deeply insults the descendants of America's founders, early settlers and homesteaders whose hard work and shedding of blood forged our amazing country. Our national parks and public resources are hallowed grounds for stewardship by federal and state agencies answerable to all citizens.

For nearly one hundred years, every visitor to the National Bison Range has experienced reverence and respect for the mission and stewardship of the Bison Range. America's national parks and wildlife refuges belong to *all* of its citizens. The accountability of federal agencies must not be subverted or subcontracted to a private tribal government that has no accountability to every American citizen.

Ironically, a prominent French author and philosopher, Jean Francois Revel, who disagrees with anti-American rhetoric, does make the following illuminating comment: *'Clearly, a civilization that feels guilty for everything it is and does will lack the energy and conviction to defend it-self.'*

My letter was one of literally thousands of letters, phone calls, emails, and communications from across the country. Most prominently, Susan Rennau, a nationally recognized author of 21 books on wildlife conservation and hunting, has been the strongest, most tireless voice to call America to action in order to ensure that the National Bison Range, and at least 90 other magnificent American natural and historic resource properties, remain under the management of federal or state agencies, and at all times, available to the general public, including equal opportunity employment for America's best and brightest.

It hasn't mattered. On December 15, 2004 the Confederated Salish and Kootenai Tribes (CSKT) and the U.S. Fish and Wildlife Service (FWS) signed an annual funding agreement (AFA) that transfers approximately half of the refuge staff positions and budget at the National Bison Range in Montana to the CSKT. This AFA is the precedent-setting door that opens the door for other tribes to take over management of some 90 national public treasures.

So far, millions of American citizens weighing in with vigorous protest on this issue have simply not mattered. Susan Rennau recently updated us with news about the Bison Range transfer of management to the CSKT:

> The National Bison Range agreement has gone through as of March 15, 2005. No one from the CSKT showed up at the National Bison Range to do any of the work for the first nine days of the contract. Of the 10 jobs turned over to the CSKT, 7 of them are vacant and the CSKT has no one to fill them. The money to pay the 10 workers, though, has been transferred to the CSKT prior to any work being done. The new Civil Service position, paying $63,000 plus benefits, called 'tribal coordinator' is not filled yet the money for this position has been transferred to the CSKT. That's quite a deal for a contractor, wouldn't you say?

The volunteers at the NBR are leaving because no federal tort laws protect them under the agreement and most of the current Civil Service workers are resigning rather than join the CSKT.

Apparently, maintenance employees at the Bison Range are being now offered four options, if one could call any of these actual "choices":

1. Resign from the USFW and hire on with the CSKT.

2. Remain with the USFW and be on loan to the tribe.

3. Accept a transfer to another refuge. The problem with this option is that the same issues, of tribal management takeovers are likely to be the problem at other refuges soon.

4. Get fired.

Skip Palmer has recently opted to remain with the USFW, and be placed on "loan" to the tribe, which means that he is paid by the federal agency to perform work for a tribal government. He'd like to continue wearing his USFW uniform, but there's a possibility that he'll be asked to wear a tribal uniform.

U.S. Fish and Wildlife, federal administrators and elected officials have sealed the proverbial "Done Deal." So giving America's gem, the National Bison Range over to a private Indian tribe opens the ugly door for also giving 90 more amazing wildlife refuges and national parks over to private tribal governments. The tribal land grabs continue and the loss to the American public in incalculable.

Such is the power of casino money in the pockets of America's coin-operated elected officials.

Oppression is but another name for irresponsible power.

— Charles Cotesworth Pinckney,
Federal Convention Delegate,
Early Abolitionist, South Carolina
(1746 - 1845)

Chapter 7
Murder and Malaise in Montana

"They wouldn't let me see her. They were sure I couldn't bear it." Naomi Costa was telling us about the death of a grown daughter on the Crow Reservation. This would be the second daughter she has lost. This would also be the worst Thanksgiving Day of Naomi's life. Kamie and I had been following the case of two young Indian women who had been brutally murdered on the Crow reservation. On September 20th, 2004, we were fortunate to be able to meet with family members and others associated with the case.

Naomi, an enrolled Crow tribal member, is now the sole support of four grandchildren. Her daughter, Koren Dicbert was brutally beaten and murdered on a late Friday night in November 2003. Koren's body, and the body of another young woman, La Fonda Big Leggins, were found in a ditch by the side of remote highway on the Crow Reservation, on Thanksgiving Day 2003. Koren was a Crow tribal member, and La Fonda was an enrolled Sioux tribal member from Fort Peck, in northeastern Montana. The women had been victims of grisly beatings and left to die. A severe blizzard immediately after the girls went missing, would make search and discovery nearly impossible for days, maybe months.

Naomi had reported her daughter missing on November 18, 2003, a matter that came to the attention of Bob Pease, former Senior Special Agent of the Bureau of Indian Affairs (BIA). Bob, an enrolled Crow tribal member, took the report of the missing young women very seriously. He has spent thirty years of his life serving in law enforcement for Indian agencies, either tribal or BIA, in five different states. Pease knew what *missing* can mean on reservations where everyone generally knows everyone. Following procedure, Pease notified the Billings FBI office about the girls.

"The FBI agent said, 'Ah they're probably just out there drunk somewhere. They'll turn up.' I didn't appreciate his attitude," Pease said. The FBI ignored the initial days when Koren and La Fonda were just missing. Bob immediately started interviewing locals, asking questions all around, checking with family members and friends. None of his initial effort produced any leads. Then a day or two before the discovery of the girls' bodies, an important turn of events happened when an informant reported that one of the perpetrators had been talking about what he had done. The informant reported that the girls had been taken out to a place called The Pussy Pond, beaten to death and then taken somewhere and dumped, but the informant didn't know exactly where the bodies were located.

Koren and La Fonda were missing for about ten days when a driver on an isolated gravel road, State Highway 50-A, saw two bodies in a ditch, and called Bob Pease. Again, Pease immediately responded to the scene, and called the FBI. And called, and called again, while working the crime scene. When one FBI Agent finally arrived on scene, Bob wanted to erect a tent over the crime scene to warm and melt the snow, for an evidence search of the crime scene. The FBI Agent just wanted to wrap up the site visit, and get on with it, instructing Pease to "just call the coroner and have the bodies picked up." Since FBI has exclusive jurisdiction of murder and major crimes on Indian reservations, Pease followed the instruction, and called the coroner who came and collected the bodies. Then the coroner and FBI agent left the scene.

"The FBI agent was on the crime scene maybe an hour and a half; he wanted to get back to Billings to do his physical workout exercises," said Pease.

"I went back out to that scene the next day. Some of the snow had melted and I found the murder weapon." Pease continued. "Someone could hold that weapon and bash heads and faces, causing wounds consistent with what happened to these girls." In his entire law enforcement career, Pease had never worked such a brutal crime scene.

Pease would work the next several days, around the clock, continuing with interviews and further investigation. With the FBI as lead agent, it was Pease, as Senior Special Agent of the BIA that conducted 90-95% of the investigation on this case. He also located the bloody clothing of the murder suspects. Pease contacted the FBI again, for a warrant which should have taken a few hours, but ultimately took another two or three days. All of the forensic evidence, blood samples, murder weapon, and clothing, were sent to the FBI forensic lab back East, where it still remains, a year and a half, so far.

Area newspapers had reported that the last time Koren and La Fonda were seen, they had left a local bar with three brothers, Eugene, Randy and Moses Rising Sun, all enrolled tribal members of the Northern Cheyenne Indian reservation that borders the Crow Reservation. There is no love lost between these two tribes.

With sufficient evidence obtained, Pease went to the Crow Tribal Court and asked for tribal court charges to be brought against the Rising Sun brothers. A warrant for arrest was granted. "It was about two weeks before Christmas, that I went over to the Northern Cheyenne Reservation and picked up the Rising Sun brothers."

Currently, Bob Pease is the Under-Sheriff of Big Horn County which encompasses the Crow Indian Reservation.

When Kamie and I met with Naomi, her sister Jessica Costa, and her son, Justin, in September 2004, it had been nearly one year. There was no progress to report on any pending murder charges. The contrast of a soft voice, a gentle countenance upon the face of this attractive older Indian woman, telling of such horror and heartache was nearly too much to hear. There was no help available to Naomi for assistance with raising her grandchildren. She works fulltime and does the best she can, but her pain is such that she said, "It is all right if I die now. I want no more pain."

There are occasions in my life when I've had the experience of sitting near a person whose presence is so intense, it is actually tangible and numbing for me. The emotional pain of another human being can sometimes blanket one in a momentary paralysis. That's what happened to me when I first looked into Naomi's eyes. I struggled to keep any composure. Kamie and I had read about this atrocity and were grateful that Naomi would come and meet with us to tell her story.

We had selected a private room at a local business, had the camera's ready and chairs in place. The two Crow women and son walked in and sat down. I looked into Naomi's eyes and was struck with a depth of reflected pain, as though her eyes were a bottomless well of sorrow. This was the second death of a grown daughter of Naomi. As a grandmother, Naomi was now the sole provider for four grandchildren, two that were children of Koren. In the many months that followed Koren's death, Naomi felt entirely alone, and reported few, if any resources available to her through Crow tribal programs, leaders, or anyone, anywhere. No help or information was available to her from the FBI, the U.S. District Attorney's office or county and state law enforcement either.

It was as though her daughter was dead. What's the big deal? The oldest Rising Son brother, Eugene, was taken into federal custody on unrelated drug charges and remains in federal custody today. The younger brothers, Randy and Moses, were eventually taken into custody by the Crow tribal police, on very strong circumstantial evidence, and held in the Crow tribal jail for nearly a year. Crow tribal law imposes a maximum sentence of one year for any major offense. Even if murder charges could have been brought by the tribal court, the boys would have already served a maximum available sentence, under tribal law. When no formal charges could be brought by the Crow Tribe against the younger brothers, the boys were released by the tribal court in November 2004, and banned for one year from the reservation.

Kamie and I were very troubled as to why justice for these two young Indian women was so delayed and denied. The stumbling block in securing justice for Koren has been the FBI. It seems that from November 2003 until this publication, there just hasn't been time to process the forensic evidence and DNA evidence taken from Koren's crime scene. Odd, within 24 hours, the FBI processed DNA from a cigarette butt left at the scene of a federal judge's home recently. And likewise, when the beautiful young North Dakota woman was missing, DNA evidence was processed in less than 2 weeks. But it is going on two years that Naomi has waited for the needed factual evidence to bring charges against her daughter's killers. The U. S. District Attorneys Office and FBI have not filed any charges yet.

Bob Pease shared some thoughts about the delay in FBI evidence processing. He told us that the pattern of FBI assistance on Indian reservations is sorely inadequate, slow or unresponsive. For decades there's been a low prioritization of crime on many Indian reservations.

Quite often brand new FBI Academy graduates are assigned to Indian reservations but are not thrilled with their assignment. Within the bureaucracy, being assigned to an Indian reservation is viewed with disdain. Some FBI agents are reluctant, and often resent their assignments, or worse, hold a negative attitude about Indians.

"I'm sure that there are FBI Agents that love Native Americans and Native American history, that would volunteer for the assignment to Indian reservations, but that's not the practice," said Pease.

In recent decades on the Yakama Reservation there have been about thirteen missing Indian women whose cases have never been solved. This is likely a scenario on numerous other Indian reservations. These crimes happen throughout the country, but with greater frequency and less attention by law enforcement, on Indian reservations. It is not as though the lives of these women were not intrinsically valuable. They were. It is not as though the mourning and loss to the families wasn't severe. The loss was severe and forever. Perhaps a poor FBI work performance record contributes to so many unsolved crimes on Indian Reservations.

Another problem lies in the pervasive conflicts among overlapping systems of law enforcement and judicial systems. Tribal police and courts have authority only over misdemeanors. The FBI and U.S. District Attorney's office have jurisdiction over felonies identified in "The 18 Major Crimes Act." This act applies to the tribal members who are located within exterior boundaries of all Indian reservations. Tribal police are often, for the most part, less trained and held to different skill and academic standards than traditional law enforcement agencies of cities, counties and states.

Somehow, the energy and diligence of federal agencies investigating crime on Indian reservations have been limpid or absent. Where this gets additionally critical is now in matters of Homeland Security on Indian reservations.

Nearly a year after the murder, the Crow Tribal Chairman, Carl Venne, and about 300 other Crow tribal members, rallied to help Naomi. They organized several busloads of tribal members into Billings, to conduct a ceremonial march and to lodge a complaint against the FBI and the U.S. District Attorney's office in Montana.

A well publicized and calmly conducted march was conducted in Billings, with specific advance notice sent to both FBI and the U.S. District Attorney's office. The complaint was legitimate. When the Crow Tribal Chairman and Naomi arrived at FBI and U.S. Attorney offices, they were informed that absolutely no one was available to meet with the Crow Tribal Chairman and Naomi Costa. Even with local news reporters along, these agencies saw no need to acknowledge Naomi Costa's pain. Heading into Summer of 2005, the U. S. District Attorneys Office and FBI have not yet filed any charges.

[More recently since return from our journey, in April 2005, I received word of a similar investigation problem, this time with the homicide of a 23-year old Crow Tribal member, Steven Bearcrane. The Billings Gazette newspaper stated that on February 2nd, Yellowstone County sheriff's deputies, responding to a report of a shooting, were told by Bobby Holcomb, age 53, that he shot Bearcrane during a physical confrontation. Holcomb's claim is that that he and young Steven had argued, and that he shot Bearcrane in self-defense. Bearcrane apparently had no weapon on him.

Holcomb called 911 and Yellowstone County Sheriffs responded, although Bearcrane was an enrolled Crow tribal member, and the Leach man Ranch was on the Crow Indian Reservation and next door to the Bearcrane family allotment where the family resides. It was several hours before the Bureau of Indian Affairs Criminal investigators were called to the scene, even arriving after media was on scene.

In charge of the scene was the very same FBI agent that handled the case of the two murdered girls. There is concern that the very same indifference and attitude was present. Holcomb has not been charged with a crime and has been released. Family members report that Steven had befriended Holcomb, as a rather lonely "drifter" who moved from ranch to ranch. The two men knew each other well.

Steven leaves a 3-year old daughter and an extensive, grieving family. He graduated from Billings Senior High School six years earlier, and was so highly respected by his peers and faculty, that his family was contacted by the school principal, to arrange planting a tree on school grounds, in Steven's memory.

As in the Koren Dilbert investigation, the Bearcrane family is very upset with the FBI agent assigned to the investigation, and also that Yellowstone County Sheriff's, rather than BIA conducted the bulk of the initial investigation.

The Bearcrane family believes that the homicide was not racially motivated as the two men were friends. The family was told by the BIA Criminal Investigator that the investigation conducted by Yellowstone County appears to be taking on racial overtones, as more effort seems directed to point to Bearcrane as a perpetrator, when he was unarmed, rather than as a victim of homicide.

One of Steven's aunts is a tribal attorney, and another works in the U.S. District Attorney's office in Billings. Recently, the federal prosecutors office in South Dakota has been called in to investigate whether Holcomb was justified in the shooting death of Steven. The Bearcrane family is distressed that Holcomb has been released without charges.

Steven's little daughter turned 3 a month after her father's death. Her family says she carries her father's pictures daily, in a little backpack, and that she often says, "let's go to Bob's and get daddy." "Bob" was Holcomb, Steven's friend who shot him. The

Bearcrane family wants fair investigation and prosecution of the perpetrator, just the same as Naomi Costa does].

One could say that because law enforcement conflicts among, federal, state and tribal governments exist, law enforcement and judicial practices, normally available to U.S. citizens, provide little, if any, constitutional guarantees to enrolled tribal members. The result is a prolonged or absent justice, or, as will be seen in future chapters, large areas of absolute lawlessness in the United States. Justice and due process is often lacking in Indian Country.

Kamie and I had the pleasure of having a long lunch and conversation with Linda Solberg, a freelance journalist living in Billings, Montana, whose interest in and respect for American Indians is pronounced. Linda and her husband, Richard, run a radio station and an online Big Sky Newsletter. Linda has communicated closely with, and done everything possible, to assist Naomi Costa. The Solbergs see hope for progress among the current Crow Tribal leadership and its members, but also see serious issues that will be slow to correct, or may never be corrected.

The most serious conditions on the reservation are lack of educational attainments, domestic violence and drug and alcohol abuse. Crow tribal children are not scoring well on standardized tests given in grade schools and high schools. They are doing quite poorly. Spousal and child abuse are rampant on the reservation, as are drugs, alcohol and meth labs. These latter issues relate back to the law enforcement problems just described. Apparently, when progressive leadership is exerted, adequate programs to assist family members are offered. If leadership changes, these programs deteriorate or dwindle away.

The Crow Tribe, under the current leadership of Chairman Carl Venne, is moving through a transition from the traditional tribal council form of government, to a tri-lateral form of government inclusive of separate executive, legislative and judicial bodies. The Crow tribe adopted a new constitution in 2000 and has an elected legislature in place. It is working on refinements to create a viable government that can dispense with the Bureau of Indian Affairs, and become more autonomous, but not disassociated with the federal government.

Two lingering cultural practices associated with traditional council governments are impeding the progress of forming an effective new government for the Crow tribe. One is the influence of powerful family tribal leaders. The other is the mindset of traditional Crow members who are untrusting of entrepreneurial business such as establishing a separate corporation for oil and gas exploration, arms length from tribal government. Another is a tendency among the old guard members to focus on receipt of their *per capita*, small funds, perhaps a couple of hundred dollars, distributed to enrolled tribal members quarterly. Per capita funds do not ordinarily support tribal households, but they are sufficient to keep many remaining enrolled tribal members across the country tied to a reservation.

Changing from one form of government to another is a substantial endeavor under the best of conditions. But if ruling families continue to exert nepotistic influence, and tribal members resist change, it really doesn't matter what the new system of government is; the system will remain dysfunctional. At present, the current Crow Tribal Chairman has exclusive power over all branches of government. There is no separation of power, thus making the Crow Tribal Court system, a "kangaroo" court. The Chairman has the power to fire Crow Tribal judges.

Kamie and I had the privilege of being the guest of Christ Kortlander, who many people refer to as the unelected Mayor of Garryowen, Montana. Chris *owns* the historic town of Garryowen, and the unique and well-appointed Custer Battlefield Museum. Chris is an expert in historical rarities and has a magnificent collection within the museum and his exquisite home above the large museum. Moments that gave us goose bumps and some needed serenity, were times spent on the upper balcony of Chris' home where we could see the entire Custer Battlefield and listen to Chris tell us about exactly what happened, and where and when. Some of our most spiritual and beautiful film footage was taken at Custer's Battlefield.

For many years Chris lived the Los Angeles good life, with a home in Malibu and a historical rarities business. Then came the Malibu fire of 1993, and he was literally burned out of home and business, rescued by helicopter, barely escaping with his life.

This was a deeply discouraging time for him. Somehow, Chris remembered little Garryowen, Montana and bought the whole tiny town, and built the Custer Battlefield Museum and Gift Shop, a gas station, a Subway Sandwich shop, bed and breakfast, and a federal post office.

Here is a quick example of Chris' courage and what he experienced as a new, non-tribal business owner located on privately deeded land within the exterior boundaries of the Crow reservation. Upon purchase of the town and operation of his corporations, the Crow tribal government imposed a 4 and 1/2% resort tax against non-Indian owned tourist-related businesses. Taxation without representation as provided in the U.S. Constitution gave Chris his legal foundation to defend his constitutional guarantees, and not submit to the tax.

The tribal government then issued a letter, signed by the tribal chairman, notifying Chris that his property and real estate would be seized, which would put him out of business. Chris refused to submit to their threats, and told the tribal officials to back off, in stronger words than reported here. This matter garnered the attention of national news media with two separate CNN interview broadcasts of Chris and Montana's Senator Conrad Burns. Senator Burns said, "Congress needs to figure out the jurisdictional conflict issues." The Crow tribal government did not waiver in their demands.

Chris ultimately contacted then Governor Mark Racicot and told the Governor, "I'll burn this place to the ground before I will let the tribe run me off my property and out of my businesses. This is unconstitutional, and what is right is right. They are not my government, YOU are!" Governor Racicot contacted Senator Burns who contacted the tribal government chairwoman at the time, and told her to think hard about any move that they might make because there would be ramifications.

The Crow Tribal Chairwoman, at the time, was a federal felon, convicted of the crime of conversion of federal funds. Two preceding Tribal Chairmen, and one subsequent Tribal Chairman, were also convicted of the same offense; four Crow Tribal Chairmen in a row are felons. The current Crow Tribal government has written policy that assures no discrimination against felons.

Six years and $200,000 in legal fees and business costs later, Chris and his associates, whose legal case was folded into a similar U. S. Supreme Court case from Arizona, set a national Indian policy precedent in a unanimous (9-0) victory in Washington D.C. The nation's highest court, in *Atkinson v. Shirley* (2001) ruled that: "Indian tribes have no civil jurisdiction over non-members on private property unless there exists one of three exceptions: 1) express Congressional delegation of authority; 2) a consensual, contractual relationship; 3) jeopardy to the tribe's political integrity, economic security, and health and welfare of the tribe."

Chris is a handsome and very organized *Mayor*. He and his businesses and lessees employ more Native Americans than any other business in the State of Montana, other than government. He recently was presented the Governor's Award for Tourism in 2004 for his expertise in promoting tourism and the phenomenal historical experience he offers to Montana visitors. Chris actually took a little ghost town, Garryowen, and built the town into one of the top five tourist attractions in Montana.

A specific incident has caused Chris to become forever vigilant regarding law enforcement within the exterior boundaries of the Crow Indian Reservation. In 1997, Chris dialed 911 to report an in-progress armed robbery with shots fired in his facilities. He got into an argument with the Big Horn County Sheriff dispatcher who needed to know the race of the perpetrator and victim before she would dispatch help. Chris could not believe that. In a desperate and dangerous scenario involving "shots fired," the dispatcher had to know the race. Larson Medicine Horse, an enrolled Crow tribal member is the Sheriff of Big Horn County. This was Medicine Horse's policy. The policy caused Chris great concern. He joined the Big Horn County Sheriff's Office, where he served for two years. To change departmental policy, Chris then opposed Sheriff Medicine Horse in a very close and heated election. Sheriff Medicine Horse fired Chris for political differences.

Sheriff Medicine Horse's policies, much like the delays and confusions that Naomi Costa endures, illustrate the danger and complexity when law enforcement jurisdictions and authority are organized around race.

Chris's alter ego and right arm. Rhonda, is his delightfully warm and patient, top administrator at the Custer Battlefield compound. I say patient, because Chris is so passionate, intelligent and driven, he can actually be exhausting to those unable to keep up with him. The joy is that he knows this about himself and highly values his colleagues and workers. Rhonda is an admirable facilitator and smoother, for all of Chris's dreams and goals.

The Information Specialist at the Custer Battlefield Museum is Faron Iron, an enrolled Crow tribal member who has served as an executive committee member, and a former member of the Land Advisory Board—the 107th Committee, under three Crow tribal government administrations. Faron is also an ex-Marine. His gentle countenance and conversation reveals a well-read, highly educated individual who cares very much about what is happening within the Crow culture. Faron opposes current Crow governmental policies and practices, which could explain why he is not a part of their leadership at this time. Faron is a progressive thinker who values the history and traditions of Crow culture but also values academic and economic development. He thinks the climate fostered within the reservation mentality is stifling, uninspiring and controlling—conditions which keep tribal families in a rut, one generation to another.

"This establishment thrives because of the perverted interpretation of sovereignty. The Indian establishment—I'm talking about the tribal government and the Bureau of Indian Affairs—wield a lot of power in Washington. They purport to be Indian experts and they speak for the common Indian, but it isn't so," says Faron. "They protect the system itself, which benefits them. As far as the people, they merely serve as statistics to qualify for funds or whatever else they need. The people are basically to be used, is what it is."

Faron insists that, "the ruling class, or the Indian establishment, are the ones that stay on top of these entities. A system has been created wherein no one is accountable. Monies are not being used for their designated purpose."

What Faron was reporting was confirming of another chronic practice on Indian reservations, the redirecting of designated federal funds. For example, federal monies designated for education are often used to acquire "perks" for tribal leaders or those who please them.

I asked Faron, "Would the loss of tribal government destroy the Crow Indian culture?"

He responded, "I really don't believe that. That is one of the arguments I've heard over the years—that if you do away with the reservation and the tribal government, people are going to lose their culture; they're going to be assimilated, and so on. But, if you look at other ethnic groups, the Jews and Greeks and so on, even the Germans—they keep their culture if they so desire. They come to this new land, the United States of America, the Irish, -and if they want to keep portions, or all or none of their culture; it is basically a personal decision. And they've been able to thrive in various parts of the world, and have maintained their culture."

Faron continued, "If tribal sovereign immunity were curbed or really done away with, and if tribal governments were made to be responsible and accountable for their actions, I think that would be a step in the right direction. This tribe here, the Crow tribe - a lot of us have been brainwashed over the generations that this reservation system, or enrollment, or being enrolled in a tribe is part of your Indian identity. And again, it is kind of unique because that's the only race that has an enrollment system."

Faron called our attention to a report that was published in 1989 from a Senate Sub-Committee for Indian Affairs. "It does mention that for every dollar that is appropriated for the Indian, 75 to 90 cents is absorbed by the Bureau of Indian Affairs for administrative costs. A dime to a quarter makes it to the tribal bureaucracies and they absorb a large portion; and pennies, if any, trickle down to the people who need it" said Faron. "As I mentioned earlier, this present Crow Tribal administration has funding that has been given to its tribal bureaucracy and it just disappears. The programs are never actually implemented and utilized as intended."

The Crow Indian Reservation illustrates the frustration of a tribal government, which recently is actually trying to modernize to a more equitable system of governance, within entrenched cultural attitudes and leadership practices that resist or refuse change. Even the best of systems implemented are failing to provide adequate law enforcement, education and general public safety for tribal families. Old monarchies interacting with federal and state agencies are not creating thriving spaces for tribal families. Worse, law enforcement services that are based upon the color of one's skin or race can result in unfairness, injustice, or no law—at all.

There is one more upside-down-world story to share that has occurred since our visit on the Crow Indian reservation in September 2004. In April 2005, a multi-agency, heavily armed force—FBI, Bureau of Land Management (BLM), National Park Service Rangers, Big Horn County Sheriffs, Office of the Inspector General—armed with weapons drawn and a search warrant, descended upon the Custer Battlefield Museum in Garryowen, Montana. According to the Big Horn County News website, the agents were looking for American Indian artifacts, and the search warrant was based upon "four named artifacts—three buttons and a suspender buckle."

This event required 24 federal agents who sealed off access to the museum and lovely tourism compound, with a fleet of vehicles on site the entire day, searching for possible violations of the Native American Grave Protection Act (NAGPRA). Six computers were seized and later returned, and employees experienced a harrowing day, complying with agents armed to the teeth.

Here is my question: Why is a violation of NAGPRA immediately addressed with such an enormous and costly federal and state force, but there are no available law enforcement personnel to expedite evidence and move to prosecute the killer's of Naomi Costa's daughter, Koren Diebert?

This is a perfect, albeit upside-down, demonstration of the misguided priorities of federal Indian policy entirely oriented to serve tribal *governments*, not individual tribal *members*.

Surely the death of a tribal woman's daughter is as great a priority as four old buttons and a suspender buckle.

My heart goes out to Naomi Costa, and to Mr. Kortlander who must muddle through the insanities of federal Indian policy.

I am for doing good to the poor, but I differ in opinion of the means. I think the best way of doing good to the poor, is not making them easy in poverty, but leading or driving them out of it.

— Benjamin Franklin
American Revolutionary Philosopher, Diplomat
(1706 - 1790)

Chapter 8
"Reservation Bound" in Wyoming

Grandmothers, mothers and little girls will fondly remember their first "Mrs. Beasley" doll. Well, lo and behold, she lives in Riverton, Wyoming, complete with the little silver-haired bun, and wire-rimmed glasses perched on the end of her nose. One difference: this Mrs. Beasley, as a senior citizen activist, kicks butt. She would probably chastise me for saying, "kicks butt."

I'm speaking of Barbara Dickinson, a woman who called me a couple of years ago, worried sick about the conditions of tribal families on the Arapaho and Shoshone reservations in Wyoming. Barbara's a retired nurse who has traveled the world with a Mother Theresa vigilance and love of the downtrodden and needy. On the phone she said, "Elaine, these people are struggling under such troublesome conditions. Drugs and alcohol are tearing families apart and now the Arapaho want to bring in a third addiction, gambling. It will destroy their people."

Kamie and I traveled from where the Buffalo roam in Montana to where the deer and the antelope play in Wyoming— literally. One of the joys of this 6,000-mile journey was the splendor of American's beautiful lands, and tracing the paths of American history. We had come from the Northwestern tribes of Washington and Idaho, through the Lewis and Clark trails across and atop Lolo Pass, along to the Big Sky and buffalo in Montana, and now to the serene landscapes of Wyoming. This is a magnificent country, indeed.

Nearing Riverton, and getting hungry, we had noticed a sign that said "Hell's Half Acre—1/2 mile." I asked Kamie, "Hey Kam, do you want to have lunch in Hell?" She said, "Sure."

As we pulled into Hell's Half Acre, we spotted the little wayside restaurant with a small parking lot, pulled in, locked the car and wandered over to a parking lot fence. It was there we just froze. We were looking at one of the strangest geographic phenomena I had ever seen. Directly below us and for a range of 320 acres beyond, was a very deep canyon created by melting coal and lava, complete with enormous stalagmites on the canyon floor, standing several stories tall, like natural security guards daring anyone to entire such an ominous, cavernous mystery. The strata of colorful walls lining the canyon pock marked by dark little caves, seemed like scenes from an unearthly time and place. The little parking lot fence we were standing near was at the very lip of this gigantic canyon so looking straight down, many hundreds of feet, and then beyond, was just spine tingling. This truly *was* Hell's Half Acre, a once boiling cauldron carved into our planet. So, what we thought was a clever little name for a wayside restaurant was manifested before our eyes, and no doubt before the eyes of the first man on this continent.

After lunch in Hell, we were just forty miles from Riverton, so we met Barbara at a motel where she had arranged our lodging. Barbara had also arranged a very full schedule of events for the following day, and for the morning of the next day, that we would spend in Riverton. Our immediate need was for Kamie to have some down time, to process film, catch up with news from her boys and her community group, and just rest. While Kamie did that, I met Barbara for a long, long chat over dinner and a review of upcoming meetings about the Arapaho and Wind River Shoshone tribes, and Riverton community issues.

Both of these Wyoming tribes are fairly private and low profile in comparison to larger tribes, with bigger casinos and hired lobbyists. Neither of these tribes is fond of the other, although they share contiguous reservations, the Wind River Shoshone reservation being larger. The local impression is that the Arapaho is more politically vigorous, and is, in fact, pursuing expanded Class III tribal casino gambling. The Arapaho Tribe is larger in enrollment, approximately 7,500, but smaller in reservation size. The Shoshone has about 3,500 members on a larger reservation land base.

The Wyoming tribes are not known to be particularly wealthy, but the Arapaho is working on changing that through gambling. The Shoshone people are more placid, traditional, and content to maintain their culture without imposing upon others. Living many years within the boundaries of the Yakama Indian Reservation, I felt that there was something very authentic and legitimate about the atmosphere and ambience of the Wind River Shoshone Indian Reservation. Perhaps it was the absence of neon lights or glitzy, modern buildings.

I had a personal and serious desire to visit Sacajawea's grave on the Wind River Shoshone reservation, which is discussed in the following chapter, so early the next morning we headed to Ft. Washakie (pronounced WASH-a-key), to the famous "Bird Woman's grave nearby. Sacajawea, of course, was the Indian woman who participated in the Lewis and Clark Corps of Discovery Expedition across the Louisiana Purchase lands, as sanctioned by President Thomas Jefferson in 1803.

It was on this road that we had a startling moment of having two oncoming cars speeding toward us when the second car nearly ran us off the road, and then *did* deliberately run the car it was chasing, off the road. Kamie braked to a screeching halt and said, "Let's go back." I said, "No, Kamie, they might be armed and we're not equipped to help. Keep going. Get *out* of here." I panicked. She consented and we proceeded on, but that was quite a disturbing experience. I had seen road rage, but not ever so intentional.

From Sacajawea's burial site, we drove nearby to meet and visit Anciel and Marietta Twitchell. At the time, Marietta was running for elected office, to be a Fremont County Commissioner in Wyoming. Cecil is of Shoshone ancestry. Quite coincidentally, in this conversation, we discovered that Anciel, and the love of my life, Grant, whom you will meet in the next chapter, were related and grew up together as young boys in Lander, Wyoming. They are first cousins. Marietta provided us with some general background information on county government, and what their lives have been like living for years within the reservation. They feel close to their Indian neighbors, have close ties to their home and lands, and wouldn't consider living anywhere else, fiercely cold winters notwithstanding.

Following that visit we headed for a tour and conversation with staff at the Fort Washakie Cultural Center. Details of this stop are also in the forthcoming chapter.

At 2:00 that afternoon, Barb Dickinson had convened a gathering of local elected officials and businessmen to an informational presentation by Darrel Smith, a historian and federal Indian policy researcher from South Dakota, as well as a long-time cattleman. Barb had also asked me to address this group with my perspectives on federal Indian policy and information on current federal legislation moving through Congress.

The situation in Riverton is this: both tribes are on the move. The Arapaho is moving to expand tribal gambling. The Shoshones are rumored to be pursuing reacquisition of ceded lands North of the Wind River, lands currently held in private ownership by the descendants of legitimate homesteaders.

Barbara senses these serious winds of change, and worries about the social and economic impacts upon tribal families, as well as the entire City of Riverton's economic systems. Since Barbara has been following Indian land claims and gambling patterns in other states, she sees nothing but huge problems coming soon to Riverton, and has been doing all she can to inform and educate elected officials and community leaders. She has been very effective in this regard.

Our time in Riverton was more focused on sharing information, than on gathering information from community members. To Barbara's credit, a good number of elected officials are listening and networking, sensing that "Mrs. Beasley" might be right. Times could soon be seriously changing, and not necessarily for the better.

Because Barbara has a deep spiritual and socio-medical foundation, she loses sleep at night over the conditions occurring among tribal families of the neighboring tribes. She very much wanted us to meet a teacher in an Arapaho Indian school, to listen to the teacher's perspectives. Kamie and I discussed subtle, inconspicuous strategies for unobtrusively entering the school, to be minimally disruptive when meeting with a teacher named

Christine. To our amazement, as we arrived at the door of her room, there was a large paper sign posted on the door, that said, "Quiet - videotaping in progress." So much for inconspicuous.

The Arapaho Indian School is fairly new in appearance and well appointed. It's a lovely one-story building of red brick and bright windows. It had very wide halls, was clean and quite welcoming.

Christine proceeded to tell us about how much the students love their school, but how difficult it is to engage parents in student activities or to discuss student needs and progress.

"We send notices home. We telephone. We knock on doors. It's very hard to even find the parents." said Christine.

"I'll give you an example," Christine said. "We have a lovely 14-year old student who carried a birthday gift for her mother around the whole community for over two weeks, trying to find her mother. The girl lives here and there, with relatives that take her in for awhile, but she has no core family."

The family structures have shattered under the oppression of alcohol, drug abuse, methamphetamines, and poverty. "And now they want to increase gambling here," wailed Christine. "These children cannot survive a *third* addiction rampant through the families."

Christine reports that far too many of the students are very depressed, have a sense of hopelessness and despair. She spoke of a sullen, junior high school boy who rarely spoke, but had "Reservation Bound," broadly scrawled on a 3-ring binder. She asked him what he meant by that. He said, "It's useless. I'll never get out of here. This is nowhere."

For the 20% of American Indians that continue to exist within the federal reservation system, this student's lifestyle and outlook is fairly typical. Tribal families—American Indian people—for the most part, are not thriving, are not experiencing opportunities for improved quality of life under oppressive tribal government systems that tend the leadership well, but leave the flock quite lacking. This was becoming increasing obvious to Kamie and me as we continued our journey from one Indian reservation to another. We had to keep each other's spirits buoyed, and keep focused on our own goals, to shake off the sadness and sorrow we were spending our time with every day of this trip.

Christine smiled warmly when talking about how the students treat the teaching staff at the school. "They love us. They really need us. They have very little else, and they know we're trying all that we can to help." Christine is not a Native American, but has been teaching a variety of courses at the school for about five years."

By the end of our visit with this dedicated teacher, Kamie and I were feeling pretty depressed ourselves, just listening to the various stories. I asked Christine, "Why do you stay here? What keeps you going?"

"If we give up, they have no one. We're just about all these students have." Then she looked down briefly, and looked up again, with tears welling and streaming down her cheeks.

"I love these kids. They need somebody."

Deceivers are the most dangerous members of our society.
They trifle with the best affections of our nature, and violate
the most sacred obligations.

— *George Crabbe, English Poet*
(1754 - 1832)

Chapter 9
Revisionist History:
Sacajawea is not "Sakakawea"

The love of my life is a tall, fine-looking, gentleman named Grant, of very strong and important Shoshone ancestry. I can see the once young Indian warrior physique gently camouflaged by age in this, serene, silver-haired senior citizen. Grant's mother's name was Margaret Evelyn Mann. His grandmother's name was Kathryn Rebecca Large. His great-grandmother's name was Maggie Bazil. Maggie Bazil was the daughter of Bazil, a son born to Sacajawea's eldest sister, and adopted by Sacajawea when he was four years old. Grant's great-great-great aunt, or grandmother by the adoption of Bazil, was: Sacajawea.

All of the above is a matter of formal documentation maintained by genealogy records of the Church of Latter Day Saints for decades. The night before Kamie and I started our trip, Grant brought me two photographs. One was of his mother as a young woman. She was selected to be the model for a remarkable book by Della Gould Emmons, which was used for the 1955 movie, *The Far Horizons*, starring Charlton Heston as William Clark; Fred McMurray as Merriweather Lewis; and Donna Reed as Sacajawea. Grant's mother was selected in 1946 for her ancestry, her youthful appearance, beauty and obvious Indian features. She was about 30 years old then, older than Sacajawea had been when she joined Lewis and Clark, but Grant's mother had a marvelously youthful and exquisite face.

In the Lewis and Clark Journals is a notation dated August 17, 1805:

After the council was finished the unfortunate woman (Sacajawea) learned that all her family was dead except two brothers, one of whom was absent and a son of her eldest sister, a small boy who was immediately adopted by her.

The adopted "small boy" was Bazil, Grant's ancestor. Grant holds a Ph.D. in Computer Science, teaches for a major university in Washington State, and while tall, handsome, congenial and outgoing, he keeps his deepest feelings very close to his vest. He doesn't say much about things that matter the most. To the world, he would seem a classic academician, a techno-nerd and a notoriously tough instructor, according to his students. To me, Grant has his mother's quiet, stable and wise countenance, and his father's discipline, endurance and love for cards and games with family members.

I had the honor of meeting Grant's mother just before she passed away as a very old woman. Margaret was suffering from Alzheimer's disease and Grant was afraid she would no longer remember him, but she did, and she winked at me, quite frequently. I've yet to see a more attractive older woman with such a full head of silvery, salt-and-pepper hair, very bright, flashing dark eyes and an ever-youthful look upon a naturally aging face.

Margaret's one wish, never fulfilled, was to become re-enrolled with the Wind River Shoshone Indian Tribe. She had been enrolled at birth but her mother later learned that someone had drawn a line through Margaret's name on the enrollment lists, with a penciled notation, "Off." Her mother asked to have her reinstated, but after repeated attempts, she received no answer. Margaret tried on her own to be re-enrolled through 1949. All of the facts were presented to the Tribal Council, but she was declined, with even an uncle voting against her. The only reason that was ever suggested was that Margaret had been born off of the reservation to parents of mixed blood; her father was not an Indian. Her brothers and sister remained on the rolls, but they did not receive an allotment while their parents lived off of the reservation.

Margaret's sole purpose for requesting re-enrollment was because of her pride in her great, great grandmother, Sacajawea. Grant's mother tried very, very hard on many occasions, to formally re-establish her tribal linkage. It just didn't happen before she passed away.

The other picture that Grant gave me was one of the only photographs taken of Maggie Bazil, his great-great-grandmother, and the granddaughter of Sacajawea. I promised Grant that I would go to Sacajawea's grave, and that I would talk to the people at Fort Washakie, if possible, about an experience I will now describe:

I need to step back for a moment to recall an evening about a year earlier, when Grant and I were watching television, or at least channel-surfing for something decent to watch. On the C-SPAN Channel that evening, we spotted very colorful Indian chief headdresses, many of them, at a setting that appeared to be in Washington, D.C. So we stopped for a moment to watch. It was a rebroadcast of an October 16, 2003 dedication of a statue for the State of North Dakota. The Statue was of "Sakakawea." The most prominent feathered headdress on the podium was that of Tex G. Hall, Chairman of the National Congress of American Indians, and also, Chair of the Mandan, Hidatsa, Arikara Affiliated tribes of North Dakota.

After honors to the flag, the national anthem, prayers and acknowledgement of honored guests, Chairman Hall stepped up to the podium to acknowledge "this honor of one of our *own*, a *Hidatsa* woman, Sakakawea." Hall repeatedly defined Lewis and Clark's journey as a "military" expedition. He also stated that President Jefferson knew that Lewis and Clark could not make the journey without the *guidance* of the Mandan, Hidatsa, Arikara tribes, and that the tribal chiefs agreed to *allow* Sakakawea to go with Lewis and Clark.

Chairman Hall did not acknowledge that his tribes had kidnapped Sacajawea from her Shoshone family, nor that she was held as a slave by the Mandan, Hidatsa, Arikara Tribes, until they later sold her to Charboneau, a loathsome old French trapper, three times her age, who would make her his wife. Chairman Hall did not mention that Sacajawea had been sold, discarded by the Hidatsa tribe, and that she was the young wife of Charboneau at the time of her acquaintance with Lewis and Clark.

Now standing in the Capitol Statuary Rotunda, is a statue of *Hidatsa Sakakawea*, an early victim of kidnap, likely rape, slavery and sale, by the Mandan, Hidatsa, Arikara. The new Sakakawea statue now simultaneously honors this egregious conduct upon a young woman, while historically stealing the genetic ancestry of her beloved Shoshones.

An additional irritant of this revisionist history, is that it was a group of today's women—the Women's Federation of North Dakota—that solicited school children across the State of North Dakota, in effect, to *honor* the child abuse, slavery and sale that caused Sakakawea to spend time with the Hidatsas.

A 1998 Bismarck Tribune newspaper editorial, by Ken Rogers, even justified kidnapping of Indian women as a form of *marriage*, claiming that "Life for Sakakawea among the Mandan and Hidatsa people -- food, shelter, living conditions -- was likely better than it was among her own people, the Shoshone." One has to wonder that if her kidnapping was about marriage, why was she then later *sold* to the surly Charboneau?

It is quite true, that but for horrific conduct imposed upon this brave young Indian woman, she would not have been sold to Charboneau, or available to guide Lewis and Clark. There is small comfort to consider that out of even the vilest of things, something as splendid as Sacajawea's contribution to America was spawned.

As of this writing in 2005, nearly eighteen months have passed since the unveiling of the illegitimate statue, and for *all* the claiming of Sacajawea as their *Hidatsa* "Sakakawea," for *all* the historical significance and honor this woman brings to the Mandan, Hidatsa, Arikara tribes, there is absolutely *no* mention or reference to this American Indian woman on the comprehensive historical website of these three affiliated tribes. She apparently merits *no* honor among *them*. There is nothing on the extensive Affiliated tribes of the Mandan, Hidatsa, Arikara website, *http://www.mhanation.com/main/history.html*, about "Sakakawea." However, she is claimed as *theirs* in the Capitol Statuary Rotunda in Washington, D.C.

Grant was outraged. Listening to Tex Hall nearly caused him a heart attack. In eleven years, of loving this man, I've never seen him so visibly and deeply shaken. Grant, the peaceful man, was ranting and bellowing and furious. Neither he nor his direct relatives are finished with this intentional, political theft of his beloved mother's DNA, and that of his descendants.

In fairness, Congresswoman, Nancy Pelosi, and former Senator Tom Daschle, on hand for the statue unveiling, at least mildly referenced Sacajawea's *Shoshone* roots. Such mention is no balm. Congress, the State of North Dakota, the affiliated tribes of the Mandan, Hidatsa, Arikara tribes, the National Congress of American Indians, and most specifically, Tex G. Hall, owe a deep apology to the peaceful and unassuming Shoshone tribal families of the Wind River Indian Reservation in Wyoming.

It is equally important, that during these remaining years when our nation commemorates the 200th Anniversary of the Corps of Discovery, and also for future generations, that the U.S. Department of Education ensure that commemorative events, and that text books for students in grades K-12, reflect the truth of her Shoshone ancestry, and how Sacajawea overcame the atrocities of the Mandan, Hidatsa and Arikara tribes by *surviving* them to guide Captain William Clark and Merriweather Lewis into history. All women's organizations that participated in this mean-spirited, revisionist historical ruse, best find a way to better honor this wondrous survivor of kidnap, slavery and child abuse.

Before one raises the argument that historical or traditional customs of Indian tribes should not be defined in terms of modern social misconduct, let us be very clear that every single misdeed or misconduct of American pilgrims, colonists and settlers *has been* defined as an atrocity in modern terms, and every such misdeed continues to be meticulously inventoried and flaunted by the leading voices of the tribal government industry. No person and no culture have a past that is completely innocent. Some cultures are just more forgiving than others.

Historically, in the 1800s, abuse of women was a non-issue, hardly worthy of mention. But the journals of Lewis and Clark were clear on two critical points. One was an overwhelming occasion for Sacajawea when, along the journey West, she recognized her Shoshone brother, Cameahwait, and went running to him, then dissolved in emotion. It was reported that this reunion was so intense, that a blanket was thrown over the two siblings to give privacy to their feelings.

To be kidnapped by strangers, enslaved and then sold, and to be away from all family and all things familiar for at least six years, had to be traumatic. To be sold to a spouse that was prone to beat Sacajawea, frequently, had to present fresh trauma and indignity to this magnificent young woman. Mercifully, the Corps of Discovery journals report that Captain William Clark put a swift end to the beatings Sacajawea received as Charbonneau's purchased spouse.

Sacajawea was, so very unfortunately, re-victimized in 2004, two hundred years after enduring her continuously painful childhood, and two centuries after her contribution to the success of the Corps of Discovery. In 2004, Sacajawea was, literally, stolen from her Shoshone people again, by the very same tribe. The new North Dakota statue is a deeply unfortunate example of revisionist history. It is a despicable Deja Vu.

Sacajawea belongs to all America. She is the Indian angel that sends the signal for all time, to all women who have ever been treated badly, or to every young girl with a goal or a dream, that hope and self-worth can be found even under the darkest and most dangerous of circumstances. For all of the effort expended to finally achieve Congressional legislation in the form of the Violence Against Women Act, there now stands a statue honoring perpetrators of violence against the most famous Indian woman in history.

There is one additional revisionist historical note to correct, regarding this woman. Sacajawea did *not* die eight years after the expedition, as mentioned in the statue dedication ceremony by Senator Byron Dorgan (D-ND). Charboneau had several wives, one of whom probably did die eight years after the expedition, but it was not Sacajawea.

A monument to Sacajawea is located on Rancher Darrel Smiths lands, a site I visited near Mobridge, South Dakota. Many people think that Sacajawea is buried at Fort Manuel

South Dakota. There are likely several other locations that Sacajawea is believed to be buried. She is buried with her sons and descendants at Fort Washakie, Wyoming.

After the Corps of Discovery Expedition, Sacajawea spent most of her adult life—nearly sixty years—with the Comanches and other tribes in the Southwest area before returning as an old woman to Fort Bridger, Wyoming where she was reunited with her two sons, John Baptiste and Bazil, and met her granddaughter, Maggie. Sacajawea spent her last thirteen years of life at Fort Washakie in Wyoming. She died at an age estimated to be 97 years.

Bazil and his daughter, Maggie Bazil, were caring for her and were with her at her death on April 9, 1884. They were at her graveside, her burial, and they too, are buried next to her, as is her natural son, "Pomp,"—John Baptiste. Sacajawea's longevity of life was passed on to her women descendants, including Grant's mother, Margaret Evelyn Mann.

Grant remembers hearing as a small boy, stories of his great, great, great-grandmother, one of which indicated that, as an old woman, Sacajawea would still wince and stiffen upon hearing the name, Charboneau. No one could speak to her about him. Grant grew up in Fort Bridger and Lander, Wyoming. He played among many other descendants of Sacajawea, including his cousin, Anciel Twitchell, whom I had the pleasure to meet in Riverton, Wyoming, living less than a mile from his famous ancestors grave.

The morning that Kamie and I found Sacajawea's grave was a crystal clear, bright sunny day, when we found a small Indian cemetery on a gently sloping hill near Fort Washakie, Wyoming. Only two or three fluffy, marshmallow clouds were floating on the bright blue sky above Sacajawea's grave. And as good fortune would have it, so was a lone eagle gently soaring around in a large series of circles above us. It felt very real and surreal, simultaneously. Kamie and I got out of the car and I immediately started walking up a small pathway, lined with white-painted rocks, up to the cemetery hilltop to what was obviously Sacajawea's grave, and a magnificent statue. I had Grant's photographs with me.

Some people reading this chapter may not fully understand this experience. Most people will. Historically, before progress in raising crime against women as something not to be trivialized, there was a national culture that accepted that "boys will be boys," or that some women deserved what they got.

I spent quiet time in prayer for Sacajawea and what had been done to her, and to her historical roots. And then I found myself in wrenching sobs for her, and for Grant and his descendants, and for my own Cherokee Indian mother whose childhood was also very difficult, and for Kamie's Paiute grandmother who was sold by that tribe for a sack of flour. I cried for all women, including Naomi Costa, the grieving Crow Indian mother in Montana who has buried two daughters now.

I cried for my childhood knowledge from grade school about this very brave Indian woman who was every young girl's hero. To be in my sixties, at Sacajawea's grave, re-feeling times when I, too, was a victim of domestic abuse; caused an unexpected flood of emotions.

I also felt a deep sorrow for so many prominent national elected officials and women's organizations that, by believing the ruse of the Mandan, Hidatsa, and Arikara Tribes, contributed additional scars upon Sacajawea's life story and memory, by honoring her abusers.

Sacajawea belongs to all America. There should be 101 statues in the Capitol Statuary Rotunda: two for each state, and one for the Indian girl who represents the finest strength of American womanhood, and who made it even possible for thirty-three men to successfully complete President Jefferson's assignment. She made the America we have today, possible. And she's still not even a footnote on the website of the Mandan, Hidatsa, Arikara Tribes.

It is one thing when money buys power. It is quite another thing when money and power steal the fine names and ancestry of other Indian tribes. I say enough is enough. Somebody, please fix this. Do not let new lies become truths in tomorrow's textbooks.

Sacajawea's courage should be honored with our own.

That sovereign is a tyrant who knows no law but his own caprice.

— *Voltaire*

Chapter 10
Lawlessness in South Dakota

The drive along South Dakota's U.S. Highway 12 parallels the border of two states. While Kamie drove, I took the video camera out and played with it. I'd look to the left and say, "Here's North Dakota," then look to the right and say, "And here's *South* Dakota...North Dakota, South Dakota," back and forth with the camera. Literally, the highway is *on* the borderline of these two states. We passed a few old buildings called the town of Keldron, then drove about fifteen more miles, to a couple more buildings called the town of Watauga—tiny towns that meant the whole world to the folks around them. Keldron and Watauga were thriving railroad towns at one time; but are experiencing the last days of economic life.

Life in northwestern South Dakota is a mix of the best of country living—quiet people with deeply ingrained values about work, God and patriotism, living next to and around, absolute lawlessness. Daytime hours are filled with chores of cattle raising, farming, hard work and simple reward, and meeting frequently at a small local cafe, *Joe's Place* in Watauga. The sun was surfacing right after a deep rain in the late afternoon when we got out of our cars at Joe's Place to meet with the locals.

To our sheer joy, for as far as we could see across miles of flat land was a vivid, wide and colorful double-rainbow, so clear and all encompassing, we could see both ends of it. The rainbow stood strikingly high and wide in a stormy sky. I always thought artists exaggerated the majesty of rainbows. They don't, and I will never think that again. Joe's Place, owned for decades by Joe "Buzzy" and Janice Draper, deserves the "America's Most Unique Diner" Award. A full course dinner can be had for $3.00, a cup of coffee is still 25 cents, and welcoming attitudes are free. God bless 'em. Joe passed away last year, and Janice is going to have to close this restaurant by Summer of 2005. Perhaps a new owner will come along to carry on the community warmth.

Keldron, Watauga, and the expansive ranches we were seeing, are located within the boundaries of the Standing Rock Sioux Indian Reservation. The mix of quiet country living with reports of chronic violence and crime, was a contrast that we probed.

After hooking up for dinner at Joe's Place, we headed over to prepare to videotape a larger gathering of South Dakota citizens. What was most disturbing about listening to farm families in this area was the unacknowledged, but reluctance to discuss the sheer violence that borders and affects their very lives. It isn't talked about much; it is just endured. We videotaped a meeting in Watauga of cattle rancher families, farmers, area business folks, and law enforcement personnel.

Rancher Jim Petik, and his family, were among the folks that gathered at Watauga. I've met Jim on several previous occasions, and am struck with something so unique about this man. He is the living model of a man who honors his God, his family, his land and his cattle—likely, in that order. It is impossible for me to stand next to this classic American cowboy/rancher, without feeling a tremendous sense of spiritual shelter and well-being. His devotion to his beliefs, to hard work, and to the power of prayer is so absolutely humble and genuine, it just quietly encompasses those who are near him.

Jim is a quiet, private person, and taught me some gentle manners of the Great Plains. I asked him once, "How much land do you have, Jim?" And he said, "Oh, quite a lot." I believed we were probably talking about thousands of acres or more, so I probed again for specifics. It was then that he smiled at me and said, "Around here, we don't ask people about their land or cattle." Then I realized, that asking questions like this in the Midwest, is like asking an urban dweller how much he makes on his paycheck. If I know not to be nosy with city folks, I learned here, to mind my own business with the cattle ranchers. There's no one better to learn from, than Jim.

Jim expressed concern that citizens who are not tribal members have no voice in reservation decisions, and feel a sense of helplessness. He also noted that many of the large family ranches have been acquired by larger, absentee corporations, or for hunting and sportsmen activities, and these landowners are somewhat disinterested in local conditions.

"Years ago, us rancher kids and Indian kids all grew up together, and worked side-by-side and got along really fine," said Jim. "Not too long ago, I used to have excellent ranch help from tribal members that worked for me; and lived with us here on the ranch; but more recently it seems to have become unacceptable to tribal leadership when tribal members work on non-tribal ranches. I think that's a shame."

The conversation soon opened to discussions of routine murders, teenage suicide and gang violence. Some local sports events between schools required extra security and keeping school buses inside chain link fences to protect the buses from vandalism or being tipped over, as had occurred in the past.

Much of the crime comes at the hands of the young, and is described as "Indian on Indian." We heard about youth gangs that would, to overcome boredom, single out a young boy, beat him unmercifully all weekend, and then kill him. The death would be listed as a "suicide."

Within a 2,600 square mile area of South Dakota is the Standing Rock Sioux Indian reservation. South Dakotans are all too familiar with almost total lawlessness, and the highest incidence of drunken driving accidents in the nation. Only two sheriff's officers who have limited jurisdiction over highway and roads, and no jurisdiction over tribal properties or tribal members. Meanwhile, enormous crime including rampant domestic violence, and child abuse—occur right next door to large cattle ranches and farms where people go about their daily lives, attend church on Wednesdays and Sundays, get together for coffee clutches and essentially exist as though this horror is not happening next door.

These South Dakotans have few options in an area completely governed by the Standing Rock Sioux tribe, which gives no voice or concern to about 4,000 citizens who are not enrolled tribal members. Holding on to legitimately homesteaded lands is quite hazardous to the health on this reservation. The federal government's promises to homesteaders have evaporated.

The same family system breakdown, addictions and abuses that we had heard about on the Crow, the Arapaho and the Shoshone reservations, was here too. It just has to be terribly heartbreaking for tribal families to feel the pull between loyalty to tribal governments, and living in continued hardship. For those who remain on Indian reservations, we simply must implement a process that restores a cherished culture, family systems, and dreams.

We spoke with Keith Gall, Corson County Sheriff, who said, "You know, off or outside of reservations, the sheriff is elected as the chief law enforcement officer of the county. Here on the reservation, it isn't that way."

"Well, how is it?" I asked.

"Tribal members vote in the election for Sheriff, but the Sheriff has no authority over tribal members, or on tribal lands,' said Gall.

"Every four years I have to depend upon tribal members to vote, but the BIA is the actual law enforcement authority on the reservation."

"Does that mean that you have to earn their vote, but you have no law enforcement jurisdiction over them?" I asked.

"Exactly." said Gall.

Several of the ranchers and farmers, as descendants of original homesteaders, have sold their farms and moved on, no longer wishing to live near such a perilous place. So, what happens as this area of crime and lawlessness just continues to grow, as the tribal leaders buy up all of the lands that come up for sale? Answer: large, several-thousand-acre farms are co-existing next to broken down homes, abandoned cars, and even larger ghettos of crime and despair.

One young rancher with a growing family, said, "Reservations should be abolished and that should be the end of it. If you took any one of us—and culture has nothing to do with it—and started us from birth, giving us continuous handouts—well, it is human nature to be lazy if there is no incentive, no reason to do anything. It just destroys you."

Rancher Darrel Smith, who had driven west from Mobridge to join us in Watauga, spoke of uninvited cattle on his land, belonging to a neighboring tribal member, who acts as though Darrel's land should be accessible to him, because of perceived ancestral rights. When I asked Darrel what he did about this routine encroachment, whereby the tribal member just took down the fence, Darrel calmly replied without any type of malice, "Oh, there is not much I can do."

All of these people seemed to act as though not only is there very little they can do, but it is just wiser to ignore, and not think about the horrendous conditions, for so long as they can. More likely, they have learned to just quietly endure, and hope for the best.

Fear over grabbing a hamburger in town, for fear of poisoning by angry tribal members was relayed by some of the young people we met.

Consistently, people in this area discussed what seems to be a sort of mega-violent, ghetto type scenario with young kids running wild and 11 and 12 year olds, writing letters to the editor about being pregnant and how that feels when one is so young. We were absolutely horrified, yet the locals, including the town newspaper, editor, all calmly painted a dangerous picture of this region, as though they were discussing what to have for dinner.

At one point, Kamie said to a local citizen who requested confidentiality, "In my part of the country, this type of lifestyle of having routine break-ins into my home would scare the hell out of most people"

The person laughed and said, "Ah...I'm not scared, there is really nothing to be afraid of...I know these kids," referring to young boys threatening this person with knives inside a private home. The revelation of what is commonplace in local stores and homes, is violent and unpredictable, fraught with danger, should the thin line of tolerance be broken, or should a person ever be caught off guard. After probably 45 minutes of reporting a significant amount of violence, theft, suicide, despair, hopelessness and yes, murder, the citizen calmly told us, "I feel entirely safe." The individual and collective denial was unsettling. Perhaps

there is nothing to be afraid of; but even so, this individual refused to speak without promised confidentiality.

Normal conditions on the Standing Rock Sioux Reservation
in North/South Dakota include perpetual violence, horrendous
statistics on spousal and child abuse, pre-teen and teen pregnan-
cies, murders, burglaries and extreme poverty. BIA statistics for
this reservation indicate that in recent years, less than 10% of all
felonies, where a crime was actually solved and a defendant located, are prosecuted. This is a pretty dismal record that exacer-
bates the lawlessness

We felt as though we were entering into some sort of surreal
world, a palpable war zone, when we entered the actual town of
McLaughlin. It was mid-morning, on a quiet, sunny weekday,
but we were watched and followed throughout our time in this
dusty old Indian town. We parked as close as possible to the
door of the town newspaper, the McLaughlin Messenger, and
scooted in to interview a respected and longtime editor, Merle
Lofgren.

As Kamie was setting the camera up in the Messenger office,
I glanced out the window and saw a young Indian man, standing
across the street, looking into the newspaper office window. A
few minutes later, I looked up again and saw three young men,
and then five. Our presence in town was known, and being moni-
tored, perhaps just out of curiosity. Perhaps not.

Kamie commented to Lofgren, the editor, "We are hearing
that the BIA is understaffed so they are not able to do much enforcement, and the sheriff has no jurisdiction. We're also hearing
that the Standing Rock Sioux tribe wants to remove the State
Highway patrol from the reservation. Doesn't that really remove
all law enforcement?"

Lofgren confirmed what we had been told in the community
meeting the previous evening. He said, "Actually there is no law
on these highways. The tribal government suggestion (no highway patrol) gives the State an excuse not to come. They haven't
set any specific policy yet." Then he continued, "Drunk driving
incidents are much higher here than anyplace else in the United
States."

Just the morning before we had arrived there was a wreck involving a pickup truck that rolled over, killing a young Indian woman and her child. Alcohol was involved.

While we were speaking with Merle, an Indian fellow stepped inside the door. He refused to identify himself, but said, "I know someone that wants to talk to you, but he is afraid to go on camera or give you his name. He has children." Then the stranger added, "My friend is afraid for his safety and his family's safety." Our camera caught only the sound of this stranger's comment. "Word" was definitely out, that we were in town to ask questions.

Kamie attempted several phone contacts with the willing informant, but after two days of efforts, even while continuing on to Nebraska, we assumed that the informant apparently had changed his mind. We should say here, that during our journey on many reservations, we were among tribal members who would look at us with faces that seemed to speak: "We would talk to you if we dared." Or, "I would speak with you if no one could see me, and if no one ever found out."

Tribal families are living with serious fear of reprisal, almost everywhere we went. Enrolled members of tribal governments are dependent upon the tribal government, which decides who gets health care, who gets housing, who gets a tribal job and who may get a small "per capita," (monetary allowance). The tribal government can decide whether you get to keep your children or not, due to the Indian Child Welfare Act that provides tribal governments with rights greater than that of a parent. Reprisal is a very real fear.

At both Watauga and in McLaughlin, several locals encouraged us to video tape the actual reservation housing, as poor as it was. People encouraged us to go see 58 brand new Indian homes, built with state-of-the-art appliances, and well-appointed trims. All 58 homes are entirely boarded up, so some tribal families camp out in the yards. A contractual issue between the Standing Rock Sioux tribe and a building contractor has caused the homes to stand empty for many months, in an area desperate for decent housing.

We decided that we would go film the new Indian homes but then, in doing so, after driving only a couple of blocks, we were followed by BIA police, and getting what was almost an overwhelming feeling of danger or risk.

A local store owner invited us to come and video the interior of the grocery store, fully equipped with metal bars across most products and shelves, much like a prison commissary or something. The owner was proud of systems installed to minimize ongoing shoplifting. Being followed, however, we quickly changed our minds and just left McLaughlin, as fast as our car would take us, really. It was a very odd and uncomfortable feeling to realize that after only two days of hearing all of these stories, we were pretty much scared to death. This, in America?

We left McLaughlin, South Dakota not only as quickly as we could, but hoping we'd never have to go back. We were also grateful that we had decided against a stop on the Pine Ridge or Rosebud Indian Reservations, where conditions are equally, or even more dangerous.

From McLaughlin we headed East into Mobridge, and to Darrel Smith's ranch located on high rolling hills overlooking the Missouri River, just outside of town. Darrel is an impressive contrast of one who is as comfortable seated on a horse with a big hat and grin, as he is in front of a podium talking about federal Indian policy to large groups of people across the country.

On Darrel's ranch, on a high bluff near his home, is a magnificent monument and the grave of Chief Sitting Bull. It's as though Chief Sitting Bull's spirit forever atop the hill overlooking the bend in the Missouri River, keeps a watchful eye.

"A monument to Sakakawea's is here, not far from Chief Sitting Bull's grave," said Darrel. "People think that she was buried near the Missouri river at Fort Manual, North Dakota, about forty miles North of this monument."

I said to Darrel, "Please, Darrel—we just came from Sacajawea's grave in Ft. Washakie, Wyoming, where she, her sons and other family members are all buried together. This woman on your land was likely one of Charboneau's other wives. Don't *get* me started on this again," I said, with a sad smile.

On Darrel's ranch, we were not far South of the Fort Berthold Indian Reservation, home of the Three Affiliated Tribes of the Mandan, Hidatsa, Arikara lands of North Dakota. Another Hidatsa Indian wife of Charboneau is likely getting excellent historical recognition here. But it is *not* Sacajawea.

Darrel has researched federal Indian policy for over a decade and has published writings that garner high marks from legal counsel and historians as well. He is highly respected among his colleagues and among legal counsel across the country. Out of problems arising over the years, Darrel has become nationally recognized as a voice that confronts flawed federal Indian policy, and has testified numerous times before the Senate Committee on Indian Affairs in Washington, D.C. He has also testified numerous times before state Senate and House Committees and a State/Tribal Study Committee in South Dakota.

Darrel's a third generation reservation resident whose grandparents moved to the Cheyenne River Indian Reservation in the mid 1920s. His parents bought the land he ranches in 1946. One used to be able to look in almost any direction from Darrel's home, atop the gentle hill overlooking the Missouri and see miles of river, miles of gentle landscape, and the small city of Mobridge.

More recently, Darrel and his family now step out the front door of home to see the neon-trimmed Class III tribal casino of the Standing Rock Sioux, just across the highway from his lands. The casino's sewer system was so poorly constructed, and maintained, that Darrel has had to contend with sewer runoff coming across the highway and saturating his lands.

One of Darrel's remarkable publications is a comprehensive pamphlet entitled: "Indian Reservations: America's Model of Destruction—A Brief Expose' of America's Disastrous Indian Policies."

Smith has specifically confronted the chronic status of "Have's" and "Have Not's" among tribal families on the Standing Rock Sioux Indian Reservation, and others as well. In his pamphlet, he states:

Americans generally recognize how damaging generations of welfare have been to residents of our inner cities. Few have a similar appreciation for a much more chronic welfare dependency that has decimated Indian reservations. Traditional culture, families, and a work ethic have been destroyed and young people are too often raised without successful role models or positive incentives. Reservation political, economic and welfare systems combine to create feelings of helplessness and hopelessness that lead to other problems such as drug and alcohol abuse. Could people of any culture prosper under such oppressive systems?

Living conditions on South Dakota's Standing Rock Sioux Indian Reservation most certainly fit Darrel's comments above.

One of the problems contributing to lawlessness on reservations is the lack of productive dialogue between law enforcement agencies to establish cohesive enforcement policies and procedures. This works both ways. Tribal law enforcement, often impeded by the political influence of tribal leaders, may not be in position to act as responsibly as they desire.

There are the occasional "rogue cops," but in South Dakota, at least, we learned that this is the exception, not the rule. Local and state law enforcement personnel may not fully understand cultural distinctions in communication that can be interpreted as offensive, causing a breakdown in communication.

In February 2002, for example, the Cheyenne River Sioux Tribal Council adopted a memorandum instructing their tribal police and criminal investigation personnel to route all crimes and official business directly through the offices of the tribal attorney and tribal prosecutor, who would then determine whether or not to inform FBI of crimes. The memorandum recited punishments for officers that contacted FBI first, without going through the tribal attorney or prosecutor.

The tribal memorandum was contrary to federal authority and the Major Federal Crimes act, and created a temporary "standoff" between federal and tribal authority over crimes on the reservation. A very diplomatic U.S. District Court Judge, Charles Kornmann, met with the tribal council leaders and encouraged them to rescind this new, but inappropriate procedure. The Cheyenne River Sioux Tribal Council did rescind their memorandum a few months later.

Kamie and I have also discovered that the Department of Justice is under criticism in 2005 for failing to adequately track millions of dollars awarded to tribal governments, much of which is directed to tribal law enforcement. Apparently there has been a failure factor of 81% for required financial report compliance, documenting proper use of $424 million in grants to tribal governments. This would confirm the frequent comment from tribal members that claim a lack of programs and resources because "the money just disappears."

During our visit with Darrel, he said, "I had a young Indian man with me on the ranch, and he made the comment that 'if all these programs really helped us they would have helped us a long time ago and we wouldn't need them anymore.' And I thought, Man, if the Congress and senators were as smart as that young man was, maybe we'd change something in this whole picture."

There was nothing about the scenario that we saw within the Standing Rock Sioux Indian Reservation that even remotely represented culture, heritage, or tribal people doing well. In fact, it was the opposite. We saw no difference in this place, from any other ghetto in America, except that that in this ghetto there are no police. In consequence, there is no law and the routine loss of human life seemed to matter far less than it should, if at all. The stories of the children alone, broke our hearts. This, all in the name of preserving a culture?

How does one preserve culture, as Smith says, under such "oppressive systems?"

Where government moves in, community retreats, civil society disinte-grates and our ability to control our own destiny atrophies. The result is: families under siege; war in the streets; unapologetic expropriation of property; the precipitous decline of the rule of law; the rapid rise of corruption; the loss of civility and the triumph of deceit.

— *California Supreme Court Judge Janice Rogers Brown*

Chapter 11
Violence and Vigilance in Nebraska

We headed out of Mobridge, South Dakota in mid-day, look-ing forward to an evening off the road, and away from everyone. By this point in the journey, Kamie and I were truly desperate for some quiet, private time to debrief, catch up on family news, and just gather some much-needed down time. We did that at a lovely place in Sioux Falls, South Dakota where, we stayed until nearly noon the following day.

Then we found our way to the Thurston County, Nebraska area, home of the Omaha and Winnebago Indian Reservations, and farmers struggling mightily to be left alone by these two tribes.

"What happened to this little town, Kamie? What happened to Walthill? It's like this town just recently died. It looks freshly dead—like a new ghost town," I said, as we turned off U. S. Highway 77 South, and headed on to State Highway 94 West. Walthill, Nebraska is a small town of less than 1,000 people, and is more than 60% Native American in population. What I was seeing was many town buildings in a row, each of them with boarded up, or papered windows. It was mid-afternoon, and there was absolutely no one to be seen walking around or near the ac-tual downtown. No life happening. The quiet, stillness in this town was startling to me.

Somehow we had missed a turn for the next road we needed, and as we went around a city block in Walthill, sure enough, we had tribal law enforcement behind us again. Out of nowhere. We would learn later what actually happened to Walthill. For the moment, we just needed to find the right road to get to our friends in another small town, Pender.

The contrast of the two towns was fascinating. Walthill looked empty and dead. Pender, just a few miles further West on 94, also has about 1,000 people that call the little town home, and had a colorful, crisp, clean and active little town core. The old historic buildings were well maintained, quite a bit of red-white-blue trims, and people everywhere, going in and out of stores.

We settled in with a wonderful farm family whose home is out among hundreds of acres of corn and soybeans lined with small and hilly gravel roads. Then we headed back into Thurston for an evening gathering with the locals,

Chris Kleinberg, Thurston County Deputy Sheriff told us, "What we worry about is vigilante groups going after tribal members or tribal members going after them. As a sheriff here, that is one of the main concerns—to keep as much peace as possible here without having—you know, rakes and pitchforks."

Kamie asked the Deputy, "Are you afraid that something like that is a potential here?

Kleinberg responded, "I think that with some of the new things coming from EPA and with the State talking about cross-deputizing of tribal members for jurisdiction over non-Indians, that yeah, I think that there are lots of people in this county that are angry enough. There are people out here that are *not* in this meeting that scare me more than the people in this meeting. There are people out here that have lived in these rural areas that haven't had to deal with things like this - not lots of tribal law enforcement. Now we have, on the East side of the county, three times as much BIA law enforcement personnel with which county citizens will have to contend."

When the Nebraska Deputy referred to "cross-deputizing," he was talking about an agreement under consideration between the State of Nebraska and some tribal governments to "deputize" tribal police with authority to enforce state law. The reverse would also be true, in that county sheriffs would be "deputized" by tribal governments to enforce tribal laws. On paper, this policy sounds quite efficient; in reality, however cross-deputizing often authorizes officers with "attitudes" to harass non-tribal members, and in some areas, vice versa.

Vernon Knecht, a third generation farmer in Thurston County, told us that throughout his growing up, even attending school in Walthill with Indian and farm kids, there were few problems.

"Growing up here was good for us, hard work, but good for us all. We didn't have any problems then. We all got along real good," said Vernon. "Some of my best friends, still, are Indians that I grew up with."

Knecht thinks problems started brewing in the late 70s, perhaps with a Congressionally appointed Task Force on American Indian Policy Review. In 1976, the report suggests,

"Provisions should be made for the tribes to undertake an increasing amount of powers and functions as their ability to do so increases. This necessarily requires adequate funding from the United States."

No kidding. Now, in the 21st Century, these words have been fully manifested by enormous funding and powers that two tribes are aggressively wielding over farmers and citizens of Thurston County, who are not enrolled tribal members, and whose lands are legitimately homesteaded, deeded and owned in fee simple, with no "Indian" encumbrances whatsoever.

We had heard about an incident in a farmer's large hay field, and wanted to learn more about what happened. Turns out, the victim was Vernon and Donna Knecht's son.

In mid-Summer 2004, the Knecht's son, Kim Knecht, was on a big tractor and baler out in the middle of his rolling hay fields, when he looked back to see at least three BIA police vehicles plowing through the hay fields, coming straight up a hill, through the hay, to Kim on his tractor-baler. Seems that the Omaha tribe had decided that the Knecht's hay field was really tribal property, not the Knechts.

Kim's first thought was to get up over a hill and headed down where his wife, who was at their farmhouse, could see that he was in trouble.

Donna Knecht, Kim's mother, told us, "In the meantime, his wife came out. Kim knew that she was there because she'd been watching, and the reason he drove over the hill and down near the house was so that he could have a witness. Kim knew he needed a witness other than the officers in the four or five vehicles that belonged to the Omaha tribe."

Kim managed to get over the hill where his wife could watch, but not before one of the tribal vehicles plowed into the side of his baler, forcing him to stop.

Vernon told us, "Tribal officers jumped out of their vehicles, pulled Kim out of the tractor cab by his legs, scraped his back all up on the metal cab floor and steps. They maced him straight in the eyes. They held him down on the ground, and handcuffed him. Then they tossed Kim in the back of one of the tribal vehicles. Of course he couldn't see anything because they had sprayed that stuff in his face."

Kim's wife, who had called 911, ran screaming to him, and was also handcuffed and tossed into a tribal vehicle. Then Vernon got there to help his son.

"I told the BIA when I got there, I want you to call the Sheriff," said Vernon. "You have no right on my property. This is deeded land. You're standing on deeded lands. This is my land and you have no right to be here."

The Omaha tribal police said, "Oh, we have a right to go anywhere on the Omaha reservation we want to go. It don't matter whether it's deeded or tribal. We can go anyplace we wanna go here."

A Nebraska state trooper responded as did a Thurston County Sheriff, but the Omaha officers insisted upon jurisdiction, and hauled Kim off to tribal jail. They released his wife, but charged Kim Knecht with assaulting police officers, resisting arrest, and ramming tribal vehicles (the one that rammed into the side of Kim's baler).

It would be many thousand dollars, and a severe admonishment to the BIA police by a federal judge, before Kim Knecht was cleared of the trumped up charges. However, no counter charges were brought against the BIA officers for harassing a farmer in this manner, on his private property.

As he was telling us what happened to his son, Vernon shook his head, and said, "They (BIA police) have become very ruthless. Some of the ones they had before that were heads of the department were very good. You could work with them. But then the new bunch came here about seven years ago, and those people that came then were trying to promote or increase their power through the Bureau. They aren't there for the benefit of the Indians."

Kamie and I were stunned to hear about this. I could only think of a couple of prominent farm families in my area of Toppenish, Washington—the Elder and Parish families—and wonder what would happen if tribal law police attempted such a horror on one of them. I believe all holy hell would break loose in the Yakima Valley, but all holy hell did not break loose in Thurston County, Nebraska. It is far more isolated and everybody just needed to "get over it."

We were dealing with this information, when petite little Donna Knecht, wife of 73-year old Vernon, says, "Well now, Vernon, tell them what happened to *you*, after that."

A couple of weeks after the incident with his son, Vernon got a call at his house from a childhood friend, an Indian named Louie, who said, "Hey, Vern, I can't find anyone to help me feed the tribe's buffalo and I've got to get some hay out to them. Can you help?"

Vernon said to his friend, "Well, Louie, you know my son was involved in an incident a couple of weeks ago, and our attorney tells me that I should not go onto any Indian land. I'm sorry, but I just better not help you this time."

A couple of hours later, the same friend called Vernon again, pleading with him to help. The friend said he could find absolutely no one to help get hay out to the buffalo. He assured Vernon that everything would be O.K. and asked Vernon to meet him with the hayloader. Vernon agreed.

Vernon and his friend went out to an Indian property where hay was stacked, loaded it with Vernon's loader and got the hay to the buffalo. His friend suggested that Vernon leave his loader at the haystacks since they needed to take another load out the next day. Again, Vernon agreed, and was driven home by his Indian friend.

About a half-hour later, Vernon's phone rang. His neighbor was calling, "Hey, Vern, I believe I see your hayloader goin' down the road. Looks like the BIA are haulin' it away."

Vernon and his son, Kim, jumped into a pickup truck and headed along the hilly gravel roads near their fields, and sure enough, they soon saw the BIA coming, towing Vernon's hay-loader.

Vernon told Kim to stay in the truck since Kim was still involved in *his* legal incident with the tribal police.

The 73-year old farmer stepped out of the truck, and said, "Boys, Louie asked me to help him feed your buffalo this afternoon. That's why my loader was on your property. It needs to stay there because we have to take more hay out to them tomorrow."

Two BIA officers immediately clubbed Vernon on the head, knocked him to the ground, rubbed the whole side of his face in the road gravel, and handcuffed him. Remember, Vernon is 73 years old. His son, Kim could only watch, as he was unarmed and already in trouble with these BIA thugs, but Kim had a camera and took a photo of the two thugs working over his elderly dad.

Vernon pleaded with the BIA officers, for nitroglycerin in his pocket, told them he was a heart patient, and told them he was having severe chest pains. He begged them to un-handcuff him. They would not take the cuffs off, but one of them did get Vernon a nitroglycerin pill.

Apparently, Vernon looked to be in traumatic condition, because one of these BIA officers finally phoned for paramedics. Vernon was taken from the scene by ambulance, into a Sioux City, Iowa hospital, and would spend the next few days in intensive care, recovering from the heart incident brought on by this attack, and from head-to-toe bruises. It would be months before his face healed from being deliberately rubbed in the gravel.

The BIA officers charged Vernon with stealing hay and trespassing on Indian land. That's what Vernon got for helping his

Indian friend, when his friend could find *no* one else to feed the tribe's buffalo.

Apparently the BIA dropped the charges filed against Vernon. And again, no charges were brought against these tribal law enforcement agents. In most parts of the country, this would be outrageous, national news. Thurston County, Nebraska is in the middle of America's breadbasket, rather isolated. It made no news.

So yes, Thurston County Deputy Sheriff, Chris Kleinberg, and Sheriff, Charles Obermeyer, probably do worry about *vigilante* activity. But it is incorrectly characterized as "vigilante," These Nebraska farmers would just be trying to defend themselves, or survive a very aggressive tribal government imposing its authority upon non-tribal citizens and lands. The other pressure point that tribes are imposing upon farmers is authority over pesticides in order to limit, fine, or otherwise harass farmers out of business.

Kamie asked the Sheriff, "So the situation here is that tribal police can actually detain and stop a non-tribal person?"

Sheriff Obermeyer relied: "The BIA can detain and stop a citizen, even though they are not yet cross-deputized by the State of Nebraska, which again destroys the Constitutional rights of every citizen out here. American citizens—they don't have any rights here anymore."

Sheriff Obermeyer told us of other concerns. "There might be sixty kids standing in the street of Walthill, and nobody tells them to go home. We have no jurisdiction, meaning that when kids break into houses and we *do* find out who they are, they are often related to a tribal council member or related to the tribal police. So, the investigation doesn't go anywhere. It is stopped and quashed right there, because the tribal council is like having a governor over us. They basically tell the BIA or tribal police, 'No, you don't do it. Don't cooperate with them.' And if they do cooperate, they get fired."

Kamie then asked, "So if a tribal member actually stands up and says, 'No, this is wrong,' or confronts someone in the tribe, then there's a perception that there will be a consequence of some kind?"

Deputy Sheriff Kleinberg answered; "Tribal members are basically just blackballed if they speak out. We get calls all the time from tribal members begging for help, saying 'What can we do? Give us help.' "

"There are a lot of tribal members who have called us and want to go back to State jurisdiction," said Sheriff Obermeyer, "because many tribal members want to get away from the tribal courts. They believe the tribal courts are not fair, and they want to stay away from the tribal cops because the tribal cops are brutal. The tribal cops don't come when they're called, or won't arrest somebody, or they bully people."

There is BIA and tribal law enforcement on the Winnebago Indian Reservation. The Omaha tribal police who have not accepted BIA law enforcement were recently funded to have *triple* the number of tribal police officers as Thurston County officers. No wonder Thurston County residents live in absolute fear. They are as frightened of the *law enforcement* as they are of the rapidly growing crime in the area.

"People think, 'Well, that's more law enforcement," said Obermeyer, referring to the increase in BIA and tribal police personnel. "But it isn't. It's lopsided law enforcement." The two Thurston County Sheriffs do all that they can to keep peace and provide assistance. But the BIA runs the show here. God have mercy on these communities and the farmers.

Neither the Omaha nor Winnebago tribes have few, if any, current farmers. But that has not stopped them from pursuing EPA authority to exercise tribal control over pesticides (explained in an upcoming chapter) for authority to regulate pesticides over all properties, including private farm properties, within the historical boundaries of their reservations.

Pat and Jo Hoyt just celebrated forty years of owning the "Little Mart" gas station in Pender, Nebraska. Pat has been through thousands of dollars and a lot of anguish dealing with Omaha tribal employees hassling him about placing line leak detectors on submersible pumps at the gas station. The Little Mart gas station is private property. Pat and his property should be regulated by the State of Nebraska, not the Omaha tribe.

"I got a letter giving me 30 days to get this done," Pat said, "But, the letter came four days into the time period, so I only had 26 days. There was no way I could get the job done in 26 days, so they attached a huge daily fine. I think if I'd have taken two weeks past the deadline, they'd have owned my business."

"My wife and I have owned this business and worked hard for forty years. We've busted our tail, trying to make a living, pay our taxes, be good citizens, keep our business up to date as far as laws and regulations are concerned," Pat continued, "And then here comes this joker trying to override the State Department of Environmental Quality. Something's really, really wrong here."

Naomi Brummond is a vibrant, high energy little grandmother, who serves on school boards, farm bureau boards, and stays in hot pursuit of legislators throughout her county, state and federal government when they trample upon her rights or the rights of her fellow citizens—all this while never missing a beat in daily farming chores, canning, frequent travel, and the loving attention she provides as a wife and grandmother to her family.

Naomi has lived most of her adult life in Thurston County, and says, "All members of the tribes are citizens of the United States, and they vote in all the local elections. They vote in all the state elections. They vote in all the national elections. So if tribal members of tribal governments call themselves a separate, sovereign foreign government, what are they doing, voting in our elections? Especially when tribes do not even have to follow our laws! It is almost as if the rest of us are second hand citizens— that we no longer matter."

It's not unusual to get a phone call from Naomi at near midnight in Nebraska. After a full day of meetings, farming, and canning, she'll call to discuss state and national issues and chat for another hour. She is a tiny senior citizen with the energy of a dozen teenagers.

Thurston County Supervisor, Teri Lamplot, explained to us, "The Environmental Protection Agency, EPA Region 7, and federal agencies have written their policies to reflect a trust relationship with Indian tribes which in practice means that anything a federal agency does has to help the tribes in any way they can on their reservations.

Teri Lamplot is a very attractive young farm wife who was a dental hygienist before she and her husband, Joel, started their family. Teri has a brilliant smile, sparkling eyes and is absolute eye candy on the arm of her also very fine looking spouse. The Lamplots have four children. Joel and Teri are highly intelligent and very politically informed Thurston County residents.

Teri continued, "EPA and the tribes are using *historical* boundaries. They are intentionally forgetting about the General Allotment Act of 1887 that allowed Indian allotees to sell land to settlers. They are forgetting about the Burke Act, which sped up the conversion of federal trust land into private (fee simple) status, and allowed settlers to reside here in the first place. But they are using *historical* (not actual or legal) boundaries of 1854 and 1865 to define geographical boundaries as to where tribal jurisdiction should be. And *that's* the problem."

Teri was describing attitudinal changes that have severely escalated over the past five to seven years. Where for over 120 years Indian tribes, tribal families, farm and ranch families have co-existed with mutual respect, this relationship has deteriorated to a very adversarial atmosphere that has almost all citizens of Thurston County on alert.

"Whether we are elected officials or individual citizens," Teri continued, "we are not considered or included in EPA tribal policies or program development. We are quite often the last to know and the first to be affected. I asked EPA Region 7, 'why is this happening?' EPA says, 'It is the *trust* relationship we have with the tribe as a government-to-government relationship,.' So, we are completely excluded from that whole process."

"As County Supervisors here," said Teri, "Most of our questions deal with civil rights and rights of being an American citizen, and rights to freedom. None of those Constitutional guarantees have made it into a publication distributed by EPA, *'Information Repository - Omaha and Winnebago Tribes Handbook.'* But those are the questions that we continue to ask and that they continue to not answer. And in addition to not answering the questions, anytime we have conflict, where federal employees will finally sit down and talk about things; it's about race."

Teri then showed us a Department of Justice Handbook, entitled *"Community Dialogue Guide—Conducting a Discussion on Race."* She continued, "They're trying to make these issues here in our county, not about civil liberties in our county, not about civil liberties, which is what it is. They're trying to make it about race."

"The Thurston County Board of Supervisors has been working on a countywide Emergency 911 system for five years now. We have some very serious public safety issues here, but we're not getting any cooperation from the Omaha Band. Their Tribal Council will not allow the postmaster to release name and address information for their band members."

"Currently in Thurston county, 911 calls go to the county dispatcher who will call Winnebago rescue if the emergency is on that side of the county. I have heard of times that the Winnebago rescue/fire refused to help when the victim was not Indian. I do not know how many times this has happened, but know at least once."

"The Omaha band members cannot dial 911 and receive help," Terri added. "They have to look up and call a phone number for assistance. The Omaha tribe has received numerous grants for fire/rescue equipment, and even recently received a brand new fire truck, but they have no volunteers to use the equipment, and really do not have a department. For some reason, they receive money for that non-existent department, but it is the Walthill volunteer fire department that covers most of the Macy and area fire/emergency calls."

Teri was confirming public safety risks and problems that paralleled the information reported by the Thurston County Sheriff.

"The Omaha Band is afraid the county will use that information against their members," added Teri. "Or use statistics from the information to be competitive in grants that the Band wants. So you see, it is always about the money. It is unfortunate for the State citizens, who are under the tyranny of a tribal council that says public safety is of less importance to them that the possibility of receiving more money."

Like the Knechts, the Lamplots believe that it has been about the past five to seven years, that tribal aggressiveness has escalated to a point that has neighboring citizens apprehensive. "I think it is a real shame for our federal government to keep making policies and programs based on race," says Teri. That is in complete conflict with how this country was founded. It was about your abilities. It was about striving to do your best. It was about hard work. It was not about what your race was, but that's what it has become."

Joel and Teri's frustration grows even more so, not only because of their own struggles to keep tribal authorities from controlling the Lamplot farm lands, but because Teri is the first woman elected to the Thurston County Board of Supervisors, and feels a very serious duty to represent her constituents and neighbors.

"How can my federal government be assisting a tribal government to gain control over me when I do not have any voice or anything to do with that tribal government? It doesn't seem right. Why is this happening?" She goes on, "The answer that I got from a federal government attorney employed at Environmental Protection Agency, Region 7, was: 'Your forefathers should have exercised *Buyer Beware* when they purchased lands on Indian reservations.'" Teri is entirely frustrated with chronic non-responsiveness from EPA Region 7 and other federal agencies.

She then said, "I am thinking that 100 years ago there was no need for homesteaders to worry about *Buyer Beware*. I mean, can you imagine a federal employee, an attorney even, saying something like that to me?"

"I have old newspapers that elaborately advertised the federal government's desire to open up Indian reservations and invite homesteaders to settle. The starting gun went off and people went rushing off in wagons to settle the lands that had not been allotted to individual Indians. Why would those people at that time, when the federal government came in and opened it up— why would those people exercise *Buyer Beware* in 1887?"

It seemed like the Lamplots appreciated a listening ear, someone who finally *heard* them, when Kamie and I arrived, because Teri continued:

"Common sense would say that the General Allotment Act of 1887 was passed and the Burke Act was passed, and there are newspaper articles talking about the rush to settle these areas because the government *did* open it up. One would just assume that the land was free and clear, opened up for settlement— especially when the people that settled that land began paying *taxes* to the State. This land within the Omaha and Winnebago Indian reservation boundaries was not different from any other property in this entire state of Nebraska, until recently, when the tribes and the federal government decided to assert their jurisdiction over geographical, former historical, reservation boundaries."

Teri continued, "Along with this history, I spent about three months in the courthouse trying to figure out how on earth can this happen, because being a County Supervisor, being on the County Board, I will have to say that the most difficult thing I have ever done is answer my back door." She then told us about just one of the experiences she will never forget:

A local farmer, an elderly veteran who fought in the Korean War, was on my back porch, and with tears in his eyes and his lower lip quivering, he asked, 'How can this happen? How can a tribe now tell me what I can and cannot do on my land? We do not bother the tribes. We have nothing to do with the tribes. We've just been here making a living, farming the ground. How can the federal government tell *me*—a veteran who has fought for freedom— that a tribal government can tell me what I can do and what I cannot do on my privately owned property that I pay taxes on? This cannot happen!' The fellow is over 70 years old and I don't have an answer for him.

The Thurston County farmers fully know that if the tribal governments are granted EPA authority to regulate pesticides, they will all know a new hell, not just from an economic stress, but from actual physical threats, such as what the Knecht family has barely survived. EPA and the federal government could care less. They're solely focused on that "trust" relationship with tribal governments, to the complete destruction of any trust or respect earned from American citizens.

We listened to about fifty citizens in Thurston County share their stories and frustration. Before ending the evening, Deputy Sheriff Kleinberg, brought up a couple of other issues:

One serious issue is brewing for Thurston county citizens because the Omaha Band started quiet negotiations with the State of Nebraska for cross-deputizing their tribal police. This would allow Omaha tribal police to have the same authority over private citizens as the Sheriff. The Winnebago BIA and tribal police are seeking the same authority from the State of Nebraska.

Based upon the experiences that citizens like the Knechts are having with tribal law enforcement, no one wants the State of Nebraska to actually deputize Omaha or Winnebago law enforcement personnel. Just the thought of this possibility is keeping people awake at night in Thurston County. But as in many states, tribal leaders and state officials tend to negotiate among themselves, completely failing to make the smallest inquiry or fact-finding efforts as to what is really occurring on a daily basis within Indian reservations. Teri Lamplot has taken a serious leadership roll on the matter of cross-deputizing. She has, after considerable effort, managed to get the State's attention.

Another subject of concern was reported to Deputy Kleinberg:

"A lady that works for the tribal council and makes good money calls me every now and then. She tells me what's going on over there at tribal headquarters. She says please don't give out my name because I'll be out of a job tomorrow. But she says that they are embezzling a lot of money. All this government money coming in is disappearing faster than you can shake a stick. She says that she is appalled at how this money is being handled. She wanted us to come over and investigate it, but I told her I can't investigate it because as a Deputy with the Sheriff's department, I don't have any jurisdiction."

Sheriff Obermeyer then added, "It is *not* tribal people who have caused this. It is our United States government. I don't want to see vigilante members going after tribal members, and tribal members going after local citizens. As a sheriff here, that is one of the main concerns—to keep as much peace as possible without having violence."

Deputy Kleinberg also offered, "After September 11th, we know how busy our FBI is, how important our homeland security is. But I think this is a major issue for Homeland Security. I have sat in tribal council chambers, and I'll give you this, these are radicals of the tribe. They are not the majority of the tribal people and they scare some of the tribal council members. But these radicals are talking like, 'Hey, if the U.S. government doesn't give us money, there's plenty of other countries in the world that would be more than willing to donate to our tribe to house things here, to, who knows what?'" said Kleinberg. He then said very slowly: "In my opinion, that is terrorism. We have to protect our borders, but there are people in tribes here that are willing to take monies from outside of our country to build up their tribal government even stronger, and that's scary to me."

Again, the contrast of absolutely wondrous, spacious lands, rolling fields, and the gentle faces of farm families that were pouring out their daily experiences and fears, to a seldom understanding audience, weighed very heavily upon Kamie and me.

Before ending our conversation with the Lamplots, Joel wanted to ask a couple of questions that trouble him:

In 1924 Congress passed an Act to make all American Indians full citizens, equal to all others. Would that not negate any Indian Treaties, because how can it be possible for our federal government to have treaties with its own American citizens? I would just like to ask Congress and our Courts to answer that.

If Indians have been full citizens since 1924, then what was the need or purpose of the 1934 Indian Reorganization Act, and later, the 1975 Indian Self-Determination and Education Act? If American Indians are full citizens, why do they need to be treated separately? I truly believe that Federal Indian Policy is nothing more than a federally funded and endorsed form of racism and segregation.

Joel's questions lingered in my mind throughout our journey, so upon returning home, I researched the June 2, 1924 Indian Citizenship Act signed by President Calvin Coolidge. The Act includes the following language:

"BE IT ENACTED by the Senate and House of Representatives of the United States of America in Congress assembled, That all non-citizen Indians born within the territorial limits of the United States be, and they are hereby, declared to be citizens of the United States: Provided That the granting of such citizenship shall not in any manner impair or otherwise affect the right of any Indian to tribal or other property." [Approved June 2, 1924]

A short ten years after full citizenship, the Indian Reorganization Act of 1934, promulgated by an avowed socialist, and alleged Communist, John Collier, reinstated and reinforced separate tribal governments, and allowed tribes to create tribal constitutions that deprive enrolled members of their full rights as U.S. citizens. These two conflicting Congressional Acts would seem absolutely confirming of Justice Antonin Scalia's recent comment, in his dissent in U.S. v. Lara (2004), that Federal Indian policy is "schizophrenic." Joel Lamplot is asking questions that go to the very root of the crises in federal Indian policy.

By this point in our journey, the emotional, physical and legal burdens that we were hearing, from where we started in our own state of Washington, all the way through Nebraska thus far, was truly weighing heavily upon us.

And what happened to the once lovely little community of Walthill? The Omaha tribe has moved into Walthill. It is common for kids to run the streets unsupervised. Vandalism, arson, and break-ins are a weekly occurrence. Businesses have left and property values have plummeted. Some people just feel fortunate to get a prospective buyer so they can leave. All of this is a result of confusion of law enforcement jurisdiction and the feeling that their civil rights or even human rights have been stripped away.

In a recent phone conversation with Joel, he reported that three businesses in Walthill were torched just last week (March, 2004). It seems that a favorite pastime is breaking windows and lighting fires. Just outside of town, the USDA manages a Conservation Reserve Program over thousands of farm acres to control erosion and promote soil nutrition. The Walthill Volunteer Fire Department is constantly putting out grass fires; they sometimes respond to three or four grassfires set in one day—and these fires are on 80 acres, and sometimes 200 acres areas.

I asked Joel, "Is there a lot of lightning around this area?" He replied, "No, we get very little lightning around here."

Kamie and I are both quite well educated and informed on matters of federal Indian policy. My doctoral dissertation will be on federal Indian policy; I've completed eleven courses, and will commence the dissertation process, subsequent to completing this book. We are each specifically knowledgeable about the oppressive effects, which federal Indian policies are having in our own regions. What we were learning on this journey, is that across this country, the crises arising from federal Indian policy are coming closer to a serious boil.

The mix of spreading aggressive tribalism within America's constitutional system, is a volatile risk that should not exist in a country that needs to vigorously guard its domestic homeland and is bound by duty to protect its citizens—*all* of them.

The battle, sir, is not to the strong alone;
it is to the vigilant, the active, the brave.

— *Patrick Henry*
American Revolutionary Lawmaker and Patriot
(1736 - 1799)

Chapter 12
Menacing Mille Lacs County, Minnesota

Pastoral, saucer-shaped Mille Lacs Lake is located about 80 miles north of the twin cities of Minneapolis and St. Paul, Minnesota. Visions of lively winter scenes in the *Grumpy Old Men* films come to mind, as small lakes in this region were selected film locations. French for "million lakes", Lake Mille Lacs is most unusual. It is about 19 miles in diameter running north and south, about 17 miles wide, east and west, and 47 feet deep. Yes, that is 47 *feet* deep—a very large, wide and extremely shallow lake, known for it's walleye fishing; or at least, it used to be.

Two strong winds are blowing across this lovely lake: One is the perceived demise of fishing and tourism; the other is a bitter jurisdictional struggle due to an asserted claim made by the Mille Lacs Band of Ojibwe Indians that its former reservation still exists. These two winds have chilled the economy as well as what used to be good will among all cultures. Folks have reason, beyond cold winters, to feel grumpy here.

Nestled around the lakeshore are about seven little towns or villages, with an overall area population of about 23,000 people. Twelve hundred of these citizens are enrolled tribal members of the Mille Lacs Band of Ojibwe Indians whose trust lands include 4,000 acres. The ratio of non-Indian to Indian is 20 to1; however, the tribal political power is nearly reversed.

Sandy Reichel is Mayor of Wahkon, one the small towns. In speaking of the current political climate between Mille Lacs County, its residents and the Mille Lacs Band of Indians, Sandy, worries, "The Mille Lacs Band is saying 'We are no longer at peace.' That is what their Chairman, Melanie Benjamin, said in her annual State of the Band address this year. They are saying this right straight *at* us. They are just coming right smack dab in our face. So, how *can* we feel safe?"

This chapter focuses on Mille Lacs County, Minnesota, but the issues described are spreading across the entire state of Minnesota where tribal governments, made wealthy from gambling revenue, are flexing serious federal and state, political and legislative muscle.

A Treaty signed in 1855 had provided the Mille Lacs Band with 61,000 acres of actual reservation. In subsequent Treaties, signed in 1863 and 1864 by five Ojibwe Indian bands of which the Mille Lacs Band was one, the reservations lands were ceded or sold to the United States. Affected Indians were required to move to the White Earth reservation; however, due to their good behavior, the Mille Lacs Band was not compelled to move.

In 1889, since treaty-making with Indian tribes had been abolished, Congress resolved differences with the Mille Lacs Band by passing the Nelson Act. In the Nelson Act, the Mille Lacs Indians agreed to forever relinquish to the United States the right of occupancy on the former Mille Lacs Indian reservation's 61,000 acres. They received additional compensation for that relinquishment.

In 1913, with continued wrangling between the Band and federal government over reservation land status and compensation for the ceded reservation, the United States Supreme Court ruled on the matter of compensation and in so doing, both the United States and the Mille Lacs Band recognized that the reservation had been disestablished and the lands had been sold.

Despite the Treaties of 1855 and 1863-64, the Nelson Act of 1889, and a U.S. Supreme Court Case of 1913, the Mille Lacs Band has been aggressively asserting that the original 61,000 acres of land is *still* their reservation.

Now in the 21st century, the Mille Lacs County region is struggling with a slow and deliberate tribal government takeover, as are many other areas of Minnesota. The takeover has been greatly assisted by federal agencies, federal courts and the State of Minnesota.

Part of the story of Minnesota citizen struggles with federal Indian policy, and likewise through all the states we visited, includes recording the evidence that one single person, or a small group of citizens, can make a difference. And that difference is strengthened when small groups connect across the country. Even in what seems to be defeat, the educational process, networking and strengthened expertise, better prepares citizens for the next challenge.

Early warning signs occurred in the 1980's when Howard Hanson, a Minneapolis business man and an avid hunter and fisherman, gathered colleagues and formed a group they named, "Proper Economic Resource Management" (PERM). Their mission was to protect the interests of private landowners in a treaty lawsuit filed by the Mille Lacs band against the citizens of Minnesota. State officials had stated publicly that they could not protect private property interests in the case and also used very strong language that they would lose if the case went to court instead of negotiating a settlement.

Hanson's entry in political activism came about fighting the commercial gillnetting over-harvest of walleyes on Rainy Lake where he had purchased a family retreat in 1980. Joining forces with the resort community of Lake of the Woods, a three year battle ensued at the Minnesota legislature, ending with a buyout of about twenty commercial fishing licenses on the two lakes in 1983.

While this fight was ending Hanson started reading about the treaty lawsuit over in Wisconsin and the social problems it was causing. Having learned how powerful the commercial fishing interests were at his state capitol, Hanson quickly realized that they had just been allowed to win a small battle but that the war for the fish was really just beginning.

Hanson connected with a national organization, Citizens Equal Rights Alliance (CERA) and started studying the American Indian Movement and Federal Indian policy. When a treaty lawsuit was filed by three northeastern Minnesota bands in the late 80's for the entire arrowhead region, the state quickly and secretly negotiated a settlement and ran a bill through the State legislature for approval. Hanson was the only citizen that testified against that bill. The citizens were lied to and were also afraid of being called 'racist'.

In 1990, When the Mille Lacs band filed suit, Hanson was better prepared. With the help of the study of anthropology writings Howard then solicited the help of former Vikings football coach, Bud Grant, and they created a plan to oppose the secretly negotiated settlement, and to support the intervention of private landowners into the case so their interests could be protected. Bud Grant is nationally recognized, and is a true hero to Minnesota football fans. He was a star, triple-sport athlete. Bud's an avid hunter and fisherman, has cabins in Wisconsin, but makes his home in Minnesota. He has been a substantial voice on issues of hunting, fishing and citizen rights.

Within the State's settlement language, Hanson noticed a small definition of the Mille Lacs Reservation tucked neatly into a proposed agreement between the State and the Mille Lacs Band of Ojibwe Indians that addressed tribal hunting and fishing rights. The hidden language was an acknowledgement by the State that the Mille Lac Band's former reservation of 61,000 acres *still exists*.

PERM members were concerned that In Minnesota, Indian tribes are attempting to resurrect reservations that were legally diminished or disestablished over 100 years ago and that tribes were very aggressively pursuing special preferences regarding hunting and fishing activities. Along with the hidden language in a State-Tribe agreement, two other colleagues, historian and writer, Joe Fellegy, and Mille Lacs Lake property owner, John Kiehl, discovered a map submitted by the Lake Mille Lacs Band to the Environmental Protection Agency, illustrating an expanded reservation boundary, that included the 61,000 acres. This acreage involves three townships—Isle Harbor, South Harbor and Kathio.

In 1990, the Mille Lacs Band filed suit in Federal District Court for the District of Minnesota against the State, and the Minnesota Department of Natural Resources. Later, several local landowners also joined the suit. Joe and Marty Karpen have owned the Sunset Bay Resort on the lake for twenty-five years.

"I've worked as a union concrete finisher in the Twin Cities some 80 miles away, while at the same time improving and developing the Sunset Bay Resort," said Joe. "I decided to get involved with Howard, other landowners and PERM because I just could not sit back, as the owner-operator of a fishing resort, and watch the reestablishment of the 1837 Treaty Rights destroy the fishing industry around here."

Joe and Marty were vigilant, enduring defendants,. He and his wife were willing to risk their life savings, if necessary, in defense of what they believed to be fair and right. Joe was instrumental in fundraising for intervening landowners, to protect property rights from hunting, fishing and gathering activities of Band members. There were many Minnesotans like Hanson, the Karpens, the Skogmans, the Kiels, the Jevnes, the Fitzs, the Walickis, the Beaudrys, the Reichels—decent hardworking citizens, many now are senior citizens, being abandoned by their state and federal government, and bullied by a newly wealthy private tribal government.

Kamie and I were continuously touched, on each day of this journey, and at each site we visited, by the knowledge, the huge personal efforts and sacrifice, the financial losses incurred, and the endurance that citizens were demonstrating, just to defend themselves against their own federal, and state governments that consistently promoted the desires of tribal governments over other U.S. citizens.

The Mille Lacs Band's lawsuit sought a declaratory judgment that the Band retained their usufructuary (a right to use other's properties) rights, for purpose of hunting and fishing, under an 1837 Treaty and an injunction to prevent the State's interference with those rights, with respect to the 61,000 acres. This litigation moved through the federal legal system to the U.S. Supreme Court.

The Supreme Court agreed to hear only the State's argument, and not the landowners. Hanson had seen Chief Justice Rehnquist on CSPAN talking about the importance of oral arguments on cases before the court so he still felt confident that citizens were still equal parties to the case and would win.

When the Highest Court heard the case PERM's lawyer did a great job citing the bands taking final Indian Claims Commission payments and being forever barred from further claims against citizens of the United States.

The ruling of March, 1999 by Justice Sandra Day O' Conner was a narrow, 5-4 victory in favor of the Band. Justice O'Conner wrote, "Indian treaty-based usufructuary rights are not inconsistent with state sovereignty over natural resources." Justice O'Conner overturned three historical precedents including the only Presidential Executive Order ever voided in the history of our country. Chief Justice Rehnquist and Justice Thomas wrote scathing dissents and cited Justice O'Conner's sleight of hand "legerdemain,"

Former Coach Bud Grant said, upon the defeat in the Supreme Court, "Losing that court case hurt more than losing any one of those four Super Bowls because the negative economic, biological and social effects of losing that case will go on for years."

The citizen group, PERM, raised and spent over a million and a half dollars for legal and professional fees, trying to protect the interest of private landowners against federal Indian policy. Justice O'Conner did, however, leave an opening in her ruling that invites the state to come back to the President for a new Executive Order canceling the treaty harvest if the secretly negotiated settlement doesn't work. PERM is presently working on a plan to make this a reality.

The defeat took its financial toll on the citizen group, and took the wind out of the sails of Mille Lacs Lake's fishing industry. The agreement struck by the State provides the Band with opportunity to establish an annual poundage of fish, and the right to fish with gill nets —some being half the size of a football field—*before* the fishing season opens for other citizens.

Major gillnetting also occurs during spawning season for walleye. In an effort to preserve the fishing resource for the future for non-Indian sportsmen, a process of fishing "slots" was established by the state DNR; these are not the coin-operated slots as in "slot machines." These "slots" on a ruler, that refer to measurements specific to the size of certain fish that can be kept, or must be returned to the lake.

Today in Mille Lacs County, and many other areas of Minnesota, fishermen need to have the skills of a sleuth and a math whiz, to garner any decent catch. For example, each year and for many fish species such as Walleye, Northern Pike, Perch, Muskies and Tullibee, a size "slot" is established by the mutual agreement between the Departments of Natural Resource of the State and the Band, working together.

To illustrate, let's say an annual Slot is 16 inches to 20 inches for Walleye. This means that *after* the band has fished (currently 100,000 pounds to be divided between the Mille Lacs Band and several Wisconsin bands), a non-Indian fisherman may catch and keep only four Walleye, providing the size of the fish is no smaller than 16 inches nor any greater than 20 inches. One *trophy* fish is allowed, if the fish exceeds 30 inches. Under these stringent regulations, a non-Indian fisherman may catch up to sixty fish, and have to throw them all back except for the minimal quantity (usually four) that he is allowed to keep, providing the fish is exactly within the size of the annual "slot" for that species. An Indian fisherman, fishing in the same boat, is allowed to keep whatever they catch.

Very severe penalties can include fines, loss of fishing license for a year, loss of fishing equipment, and if warranted, even the loss of a boat. The Band and the State stringently enforce fishing "slots", to within 1/8th to 1/16th of an inch. Special fishing preferences that provide tribal members with great quantities of fish have a profound economic and recreational impact that is slowly debilitating the sport of fishing in Minnesota.

It is very frustrating for over 90% of the local population, and out-of-area sportsmen, to have to watch a preferred, tribal population, gill-netting with abandon, while setting severe limits upon all other fishermen. The trickle down economic effect has caused numerous resorts to close. When resorts close the loss of business then affects reduced sales at sporting goods stores, hardware stores, bait shops, gas stations and restaurants. This economic unraveling and tribal political takeover began with the Supreme

Court ruling in 1999. The Mille Lacs Band is exercising that usa-fructuary right at every opportunity.

Frank Courteau, Mille Lacs County Commissioner, is likely correct when he recently stated, "I have looked at various tax rates, and I believe that if you look at state and local governments across the country, the ones that have higher taxes, at least here in Minnesota, happen to be states and counties with Indian reservations."

Mr. Courteau, at great political risk, has courageously defended the Constitutional, civil and jurisdictional rights of his constituents and his county government. "I've had personal experience with an apartheid system because of the years I spent in Africa as a student. I was a young man at the time, but I remember the divisions that it caused and the hatred that it caused. I see much of the same thing happening here, for many of the same reasons: different rules for different people, based upon race."

Kamie and I were guests at the lovely home of Al and Mary Jevne's on the lakeshore, and spent a full, long day filming and interviewing dozens of Mille Lacs Lake property and business owners. I had been to this area once before and was so smitten with its beauty, and the warmth and concern of the people, that it was just delightful to be back. Mary is a diligent and tenacious researcher as well as a persistent watchdog and has been invaluable to her neighbors and local governments.

One of my favorite Mille Lacs friends bears strong resemblance to the late Walter Matthau. Truly, Clarence Fitz, a retired veterinarian and resort owner, has Walter's wry wit, his smile, his speech patterns, and gait. Clare has a refreshing mix of absolute intelligence with genuine humility.

"We were active in the Mille Lacs Lake Association for a long time. This group organized initially to promote tourism and economic development, along with protecting property rights, but more recently we opened the Association to others with a shared interest," said Clare. "Then in about 2000, when the Band began marketing and promoting its expanded reservation, from 4,000 to an asserted 61,000 acres, we formed an Ad Hoc Committee of the Lake Association, and called ourselves the Mille Lacs Tea Party."

"Why the 'Tea Party' name, Clare?" I asked. He said, "Because property owners and citizens here feel so threatened with a desire by the Band to govern non-members and private properties, we were feeling much like the original Tea Party colonists must have felt. We were, and will resist being governed without representation," he said. "Except for some brave local elected officials, we've felt quite abandoned by the state and federal government as well."

We then were told of an example of the political pressure exerted by the Mille Lacs Band. In August 2004, at a small annual meeting of the Mille Lacs Lake Association, a full busload of Mille Lacs Band members, led by none other than Winona La Duke, nationally recognized Indian activist, arrived at this neighborhood association meeting. Through the by-laws loophole of "shared interest," some twenty-three enrolled Mille Lacs Band members, including a child, paid an annual $25 membership fee, and filled up the first few rows of the meeting.

These newest "members" were disruptive, insulting, and had a chilling affect upon the Association meeting; the brand new members also elected three Mille Lacs Band members to the Association's Board at that very meeting. Non-enrolled citizens are not allowed to attend tribal meetings of the Mille Lacs Band, but their ability to disrupt other organizations or meetings is another new political tool. Now Mille Lacs citizens have the added concern that their freedom of assembly in public places is an added target for aggression. Even meetings held between the State and Bands Departments of Natural Resource are not open to the general public, although decisions from these agencies affect all citizens and their properties throughout the State.

We learned a good deal from this group of Minnesotans. For many years, strange new boundaries had been appearing on maps—maps appearing in local newspapers, in tribal publications—maps asserting the former reservation as the current reservation—articles in local and state newspapers written "as if" the former reservation still exists. As well, there was extensive tribal leadership chatter and promotion of the expanded reservation. The local apprehension increases proportionally to repeated tribal assertions of jurisdiction. This condition is getting worse;

but apparently, courts await physical damage or personal harm, greater than actual existing economic harm.

"After working almost daily, for several years to resolve or withstand the effects of federal Indian policy, I have come to the conclusion that federal Indian policy is not fixable," said Clare.

"Why do you say that?," I asked.

Clare replied, "I have been reading considerable early American history and Indian history; I have attempted to influence the path of federal Indian policy through both legislative and judicial means, and here is the bottom line: For over 200 years we have as a nation tried to improve on the existing Indian reservation system that arguably should never have been established in the first place."

Then he continued," Conditions on most Indian reservations are deplorable and should be an embarrassment to our elected officials and our nation. It is time to start recognizing the basic problem, that is, unless someone can identify the good—actual *benefit*—that has come from the establishment of Indian reservations, because I cannot think of any; then it is time to eliminate the reservations. "

Clare's wife, Donna, then added, "The effects of federal Indian policy are fracturing our country through both political campaign contributions on *all* levels and political correctness concerning Indian tribes. Tribes claiming to be separate nations is absurd. What happened to One Nation Indivisible?"

In 2003, to defend against perceived and threatened tribal government takeovers, Mille Lacs County, joined by a local affected bank, initiated litigation against the Mille Lacs Band, seeking a declaratory judgment seeking the legal status of actual boundaries of the Mille Lacs Band of Ojibwe Indian reservation.

Pete Allen, a local banker, told us, "We have to operate under all federal regulations." He expressed the bank's concern about having to answer to a tribal court, when he continued, "If there are violations or questions or claims relative to our functioning under those regulations, those would be decided in a tribal court. Bear in mind, that I don't know if the tribal court even has any legally trained judges, but whether they do or not, it would still force us into a court where we have absolutely no involvement, no connections, no authority, no protections. For those reasons, we just felt that our bank has different concerns, on behalf of our customers, than the county, nonetheless; very real concerns. These were things we felt worthy of becoming an intervener in the Mille Lacs County suit against the Band."

By March 2004, the case had moved from dismissal by the federal District Court to the Appellate Court, which ruled:

> *The County and the Bank argue that they have standing because they have suffered threatened injury caused by the Band's alleged ownership of certain parts of the Mille Lacs Indian Reservation. We disagree. . . . The County presented no evidence that its ability to enforce state or local law on the reservation has been usurped or even affected by the Band's alleged intentions. In order to demonstrate standing, a plaintiff must demonstrate that he has suffered an injury or a threatened injury. Neither the County nor the Bank has shown that it is in immediate danger of sustaining threatened injury traceable to an action of the Band. Therefore, they are unable to demonstrate standing." [Mille Lacs County v. Melanie Benjamin, 8th Circuit; No. 03-2537; March 9, 2004]*

The County, the bank, the community group of Mille Lacs Tea Party and PERM, all had expended thousands of dollars for an urgently needed decision to stop the assertions. But the 8th Circuit found no harm had occurred from just "talk," and later the U.S. Supreme Court would also decline to hear the case. This case was never heard on its merits.

The irony is that the *talk* is backed by huge money, extensive land grabs, and more recently, vigorous publicity and advanced notice of the Mille Lac Band's Sesquicentennial, acknowledging its reservation of 61,000 acres. Since the County's case was never heard on its merits for lack of standing, and for not being "ripe" with actual damage, the actual damage continues. And the Mille Lacs Band is even more aggressive and more brazen.

While at Mille Lacs, we were pleased to visit with two prominent writers, one a journalist, the other an author. We spoke with spoke with Bill Lawrence, an Ojibwe tribal member from Red Lake Indian Reservation. Bill is publisher of an award winning "Native American Press/Ojibwe News" newspaper.

We were visiting with Bill in September, 2004, little knowing that we would be learning of the horrific school shooting that just occurred this March of 2005 at the Red Lake Middle School. I asked Bill to describe conditions on the Red Lake Indian Reservation. He said, "We have about 5,000 people living on about a 830,000 acre reservation, and some decent resources, which have been abused to a certain extent. I just don't feel that we're on the right track."

"I've been to Washington D.C. and I tried to talk to all the senators, at one point," Bill continued. "I knocked on every door in the senate—all one hundred of them. I think I got two letters back."

"The culture has been so diluted we don't know what culture is anymore. I grew up in Red Lake and the things that went on then, and the things that are going on now are as different as night and day."

"Is there a sense of hopelessness?" Kamie asked Bill. "What is going on, that all these young kids on the reservations we have been to are so hooked on alcohol and meth? I mean, these are really *young* kids, Bill."

Bill responded, "It is at a point where once a kid gets to be thirteen or fourteen, they just run wild, and I don't know how much control a one-parent family has. With the drugs and alcohol, and now the gambling, it's just like throwing gasoline on the problem. I know there was a program on Red Lake about suicide and there is an awareness of it, but I don't see a huge effort by the tribe or federal government to address it."

[Recent Associated Press articles report statistics that include 81% of ninth-grade girls, and 43% of the boys had contemplated suicide; nearly half of the girls said that they had actually tried to kill themselves. Much like the deeply depressed Arapaho Indian student in Riverton Wyoming who had marked "*Reservation Bound*" on his binder, a truly distraught and conflicted tribal boy, Jeff Weise, described himself in internet postings as, "nothing but your average Native-American stoner." The same Associated

Press article reported that before taking 9 lives and his own, Weise described life on the reservation as, "every man's nightmare. This place never changes and it never will."]

"In most cases, I go back to Red Lake," Bill Lawrence continued, "and that was a good, average school district. The kids got a good education in my generation and before, and probably up through the 70s. When I look at the beginning of the Great Society of Lyndon Johnson, the Indian Self-Determination Act and all the stuff that happened, and I helped implement some of it in some of the tribes out West—well, I just see a change within Indian life, and a revival of what was supposedly the culture. But in the 80s when there was a massive effort to turn education over to tribal governments, the tribes really started to deteriorate."

"What does the future hold, Bill?" I asked. He thought for a moment, and then said, "I guess you are asking if the reservation system is viable any more. I've often thought it was a huge failure, but I guess I more or less believe that it has probably been a bigger success than I realized, because it has driven most of us off the reservation. When I think that only about 20% of Indian people still live on the reservations, and 80% have left; well, that's got to be some measure of success."

But what about those who are left on the reservation?" I asked. Bill responded, "When I look back at the group that still lives on the reservation, I think you'll never get them off. They come back and forth. It's all they know. They believe that they are owed everything for infinity, and so I don't see anything less than a policy of ending the reservation system down the road at some point, that would make a needed change."

Bill has noticed a recently observable migration trend that he discussed, based upon statistical changes in his newspaper circulation. "There seems to be a trend of Native Americans leaving the large metropolitan areas and settling in small communities near, but not within, their reservation boundaries. There is also a migration of several tribal families leaving the reservation and settling nearby, but outside of the reservation." Bill went on, "at first I thought this may be attributed to tribes with casinos, but I now think it is not that, it is something even more important to Native Americans."

He then said, "It may be that more and more Native Americans want to be close to their homelands and close to their culture but do not want to be under the thumb of the corrupt tribal governments."

The migrations Bill was referring to would support a couple of concepts—that American Indian culture need *not* be intrinsically locked to a tribal governance, but could be transitioned to some other cohesive system such as a nonprofit corporate structure or fraternal organizations that would help preserve and sustain cultural traditions and cohesiveness.

Another irony is that getting out from underneath oppressive monarchies and corrupt governments was the driving force that brought early Europeans to this continent in the first place. Perhaps that freedom to practice our beliefs and cultures is a mutually shared one, among people of all cultures in this country. It would support the urgent need that American Indians be provided the full protections of the Fourteenth Amendment that are denied with tribal enrollment.

We also visited with David Price, author of "The Second Civil War —Examining the Indian Demand For Ethnic Sovereignty," a book addressing federal Indian policy. Price is an accomplished federal Indian policy researcher.

David said, "I've coined a term for the system of government on Indian reservations. I call it *Tribe-ocracy*. I think it is a very accurate term. It is a good word to describe what goes on, because where democracy is 'of, by and for the people,' and that is just about the best description of democracy you can make—the government on reservations is 'of, by and for the tribe.' The Tribe does not want anybody who is not a part of that tribe, and the priority is placed on the needs of the tribal government, before the needs of individual tribal members."

Then Price continued, "We are really arguing about those two ideologies, and it could just as well not be a tribe. You could just as well say, 'Well, there are a bunch of Presbyterians living around here; and they should run the government because they have lived in this area for a long time.' Nobody would think that was rational. But when you have a tribe, such as the Mille Lacs Band here, saying, 'Well this whole 61,000 acres—we want to have political control over it, with taxation, criminal jurisdiction, tribal courts, but you people are just going to be *subject* to us; meaning, that if you were living within these historical boundaries that were disestablished a long time ago, that you would be subject to tribal rule. What tribes are doing is going back; turning back the tables. They are taking advantage of a system that used to exploit them, and now they are using it to exploit other people, including sometimes, their own tribal members."

"David," I asked, "When you come across people that are concerned about what you just said, are they blatant racists?"

He answered, "For the most part, no. But I do run in to some people that you could describe as being racist in some of the things that they say. The idea that it is racist to talk about equal rights is first of all, absurd. This is about two political ideologies and I do not think this has been well defined because people tend to think that we have democracy in this country, and that there is also democracy on Indian reservations. There is not."

"Tribal people, the first time you meet them," Price continued, "will often tell you that you are sort of a bad white person, that your ancestors came here and stole this country from the Indians, and that somehow you owe them. I hear that from a lot of Indians in the beginning; but then once they get to know you a little bit, they then begin to talk about how corrupt their own system is, how terrible it is, how you can't trust anybody in the tribal government, and so forth. So I think even Indians themselves are very confused about what is happening and what to do about it."

Much like the North and Central Idaho economies reported in earlier chapters, we discovered another common denominator here at Mille Lacs Lake. As a result of its gambling casinos, other enterprises and hefty federal subsidies that are not reduced as a result of gambling wealth, the Mille Lacs Band of a mere 1,200 members is very wealthy. The combined annual revenue resources of the Band dwarf the cumulative, and very limited annual budgets of Mille Lacs County and its small towns and villages. The Band's two casinos are the second wealthiest in State of Minnesota. The Saint Paul Pioneer Press newspaper noted on March 27, 2005 that the Mille Lacs Band spent

$460,000 in a single year, just lobbying the State of Minnesota; one has to wonder how much additional money was expended for lobbyists and political actions occurring in Washington D.C. What this tribe spends in political contributions and lobbying expenses alone is greater than the annual budgets of neighboring towns—the governments charged with all public service deliveries to the area.

So, where the population is lopsided—one tribal member for every twenty other citizens—the available financial resources are lopsided in reverse. The problem is that Mille Lacs Band does not provide area infrastructure, law enforcement, education, libraries, hospitals, highway and road system maintenance, except only minimally as needed for its small enrollment. All of the other local governments provide the area resources, with a pittance of funding in comparison to the Mille Lacs Band. And the local governments have nothing budgeted to lobby Washington, D.C. about local economic and political distress that is ever increasing.

On at least nine of the reservations visited so far, the net effect of economic disparity rolls out into a predictable pattern:

A tribe gets a casino(s)
A tribe buys political and legal power
Surrounding counties, towns and citizens are bullied
A tribe buys or economically forces out landowners/ businesses
Elected officials get quiet, or get purchased.
Non-tribal lands and economies dwindle quickly
Thousands of American citizens, lose—sometimes everything.
Tribalism as a governing system replaces democracy.

In addition to the few brief subjects addressed here, The Mille Lacs Band, has incrementally inserted itself into additional numerous conflicts with county and local governments, in matters of water quality, underground tanks, injection wells, sewer and wastewater treatment and other public resource and public service areas. An intentional strategy to disrupt and overpower local government authority is clearly under way.

The Mayor of Wahkon is absolutely correct: "They are just coming right smack dab in our face. So, how *can* we feel safe?"

The sacred rights of property are to be guarded at every point. Call them sacred because, if they are unprotected, all other rights become worthless or visionary.

— Judge Joseph Story,
U.S. Supreme Court Justice
(1779 - 1845)

Chapter 13
Wisconsin Farm Land Grabs

We stayed in a dairy barn near Gresham, Wisconsin. No, we were not among milk cows and hay. The talented Curt and Marty Knoke have transformed an historic dairy barn into a magical place to live. I had the pleasure of previous visits with the Knokes and could not wait for Kamie to experience the wondrous landscape of their 80 acres, a small lake, and the exquisite architectural thinking that creates an open, but multi-floored space for comfortable living in a large old dairy barn. Curt is a consummate entrepreneur and a gifted photographer as well. Marty has played the piano at their local church for years, and provides a strong home foundation for her talented spouse.

Pastoral Gresham, a town of just under 600 residents, is about 60 miles northwest of Green Bay, Wisconsin and is located in the townships of Red Springs and Bartleme. These communities are located in Shawano County that includes approximately 40,600 residents, 2,500 of which identify themselves as American Indians in the 2000 U.S. Census.

Subsequent to the Treaty of 1856, the Stockbridge and Munsee Indian bands moved to the townships of Red Springs and Bartleme in Shawano County, and, since 1937, have exerted tribal jurisdictional authority over, initially 2,500 acres of reservation for the "Stockbridge-Munsee Band of Mohican Indians." Their land holdings have substantially increased over the years.

As well, an even larger, Menominee Indian Reservation, is adjacent to and just north and east of the Stockbridge-Munsee Indian Reservation. Menominee tribal headquarters are just a few miles away from Gresham, in Keshena, Wisconsin. The

Menominees are known for a highly successful timber industry, and are pioneers in sustained yield forestry practices.

The Menominee Warriors figured nationally during a period of time from 1969 to 1978, known as the "Red Power Period." The Menominees were determined to reclaim lands lost, beginning with the extensive lands and buildings of a once peaceful Roman Catholic school for novitiate priests. Very close to the Knoke's home is the former Alexian Brothers Novitiate, where a siege begun on New Year's Day of 1975, lasted 34 days in a standoff between the Menominees Indian Warriors, and federal, state and local law enforcement officials.

The Menominee Warrior Society takeover was a result of a Congressional act that terminated the Tribe. The takeover attempt claimed the Novitiate property but was in reality, an attempt to draw publicity to their efforts to have the Tribe's federal recognition restored. The Menominee Warriors were radicals associated with the American Indian Movement (AIM), and the psychological scars of this event that occurred thirty years ago, still hangs like a thin veil over the areas of Shawano and Menominee counties.

This hostile land takeover attempt has been replaced in recent years with facilitated federal assistance in placing Indian acquired lands into federal trust. Nationally recognized Indian activist, Ada Deer, was the Menominee Tribal Chairwoman at this time.

Ada Deer later took a key BIA position at the Department of Interior in Washington D.C. during a period that provided numerous additional tribal recognitions, and elevated tribes which lacked certain sovereignty or governmental authority with an equal level of authority as the primary Indian tribes. Ada Deer commented in 1975, "We have learned to use the (federal) system to beat the system." That has become quite an understatement.

The 1980s throughout Wisconsin were replete with tribal Treaty demands for off-reservation hunting and fishing rights, as Wisconsin, like Minnesota in the previous chapter, relies upon a strong sportsmen and tourism industry. Without belaboring details of these protracted battles, the victories went substantially to tribal governments, which acquired significant control of Wisconsin's fishing industry.

Citizen community groups formed throughout Wisconsin, and fought noisily and valiantly for equitable management of Wisconsin's fish stock, much like PERM, the group that organized in Minnesota. Former Vikings Coach, Bud Grant, with land and cabins here in Wisconsin, was helpful in the process, too.

The power of the federal government, and ambiguous language of Indian Treaties, interpreted generously on behalf of Indian tribes has taken its economic toll in Wisconsin, in the same manner as its neighboring state, Minnesota. Voices such as Bob Manske in Milwaukee, and Constitutional researcher, Vic Bellomy, in Crandon, Wisconsin, remain vigilant in their efforts to protect the Constitutional and property rights of Wisconsin citizens, and never cease to seek equality and relief from federal Indian policy that has become far too lucrative for elected officials.

In 1989, the Wisconsin State legislature and then Governor Tommy G. Thompson, signed a bill giving the Governor sole authority to negotiate tribal gaming compacts. This would be predictive of serious problems in 2003.

The Knokes and many private landowners within and near the Stockbridge-Munsee and Menominee Indian Reservations, and do all they can to minimize, but defend themselves against jurisdictional conflicts between local towns, townships, county government, and state, federal and tribal governments. An example, at one small intersection of two country roads there are no less than three signs. The first one says, "Stockbridge-Munsee Community has adopted a Land Use Code. Permits are Required." Two feet away from this sign is another: "Town of Red Springs is Zoned. Permits Required." Directly across the road from these two signs is a third: "Menominee County & Reservation."

In 1997, concerned Wisconsin property owners formed the Shawano County Concerned Property Taxpayers Association (SCCPTA—affectionately pronounced "Skip-ta"). SCCPTA's original mission was to oppose a tribal reservation boundary dispute, but the organization has remained continuously active, most recently with fee-to-trust land transfers and other jurisdictional problems.

According to the BIA in 2002, when 278 acres known as the Beyer Farm were removed from the local tax base and placed into federal trust for the Stockbridge-Munsee Tribe, there were 17,679 Indian "trust" acres within Shawano County alone. About 6,900 trust land acres are within the County and Town of Red Springs. The acreage has been increased since 2002. Only 1% of Menominee County remains taxable and the County must rely upon aid from the State of Wisconsin to fund meager County services.

While I caught up with laundry and emails at the Knokes, two SCCPTA members took Kamie and her camera for a drive around the area to capture on film the picturesque Wisconsin farmlands and what is happening there. Kamie came back from the tour, very upset.

"Elaine, you would not believe the sheer number of farms that stand completely vacant. I mean I took film of storybook buildings, nestled in among abandoned corn field after cornfield. The farms are empty! There were barns with windows broken out, dark homes, neglected front yards, and acres upon acres of fields standing fallow. I was absolutely stunned."

"What explanation are you given for what you're seeing?" I asked.

"The Stockbridge-Munsee tribe is buying up all the land, regardless of the fact that the farms used to be productive, had been fully functional, or farms that had been in families for five or six generations." She continued, "They also showed me a local golf course that the tribe bought—nice place, beautiful grounds, completely darkened windows—vacant."

Kamie talks fast when upset and kept on, "I saw where a local property owner had purchased lands to provide a barrier between his land and tribal lands, so that if the tribe built a huge development, area residents would have some control over keeping somewhat of a rural atmosphere for the small, picturesque community. The neighborhoods looked like you would expect Wisconsin farmlands to look, except there were no happy cows, no tractors in the fields, just empty buildings. It's so strange, Elaine.

It's so strange. I was imagining that if you put these places we're visiting on mainstream news, they look completely normal. Who would guess that a battle was taking place. Would anyone notice the dark windows and neglected fields? And if they did, would they understand what's happening to America's heartland?"

"It was the same in Nebraska, Kamie, and the same in South Dakota, Montana and Wyoming," I said. "And it's the same where I live in Washington, and the same in Idaho. America's farmers are getting forced out by tribal government water claims, or forced out by tribal pesticide programs or other EPA-Tribal control programs, or they are being bought out at a low dollar, with tribal gambling money."

"I hate this trip, Elaine. I really hate this trip," Kamie whispered. Again I was seeing that face; that face that refuses to cry but is full of anguish and outrage. "I mean, I'm really glad we're *doing* this, really I am. But, God, it's so hard, and it's so sad. These are just plain good American families, great little towns, beautiful regions, and look what's happening."

It wasn't a meltdown she was having, because Kamie's the kind of tough, strong cookie that just won't melt down when someone's looking. "We're more than halfway through, Kamie "From here, we head into Michigan and on into three stops in New York so we're getting there, Kam," I said. "But I have to tell you, that the stories we'll hear and the issues we'll discover will not get easier, moving East."

We had reached a mental point that was beginning to answer questions we had at the front end of this journey. Some were silly questions, like "Are we out of our minds?" No, but we were certainly feeling the burdens of others about now. Other questions were, "Are we wasting our time?" No, not at all. "Will we find anything worth recording on this journey?" We were finding more than we ever even anticipated, and most frightening of all were the political patterns, replicating in waves across one state after another, sweeping silently across the land. It is best to not say anything. It is best to not do anything. Just pretend things are really O.K. Maybe it won't get worse.

The Stockbridge Munsee Tribe has a profitable casino, the "Mohican North Star" tribal casino in Shawano County, and has negotiated an agreement with New York's Governor Pataki for a future Class III tribal casino in Sullivan County, New York. The Menominee Band has a Casino-Bingo-Hotel complex in Keshena, Wisconsin, and is pursuing an $808 million dollar gambling complex at the Dairyland Greyhound Park in Kenosha, Wisconsin. The gambling revenue for these two tribes is facilitating land acquisition in the quiet farm country that is Shawano and Menominee Counties.

The broad themes that provide continuous friction in this region of Wisconsin, are not unique to just this region of Wisconsin; these struggles are playing out in about thirty-five other States across the country, as well. Law enforcement, loss of local taxable parcels, boundary disputes, and land use are the most significant jurisdictional disputes. In the region of the Stockbridge-Munsee and Menominee Indian reservation, the problems are doubled by the presence of two, sometimes competing, Indian reservations co-located with local and state governments.

The most recent fuel that has ignited expanding local conflicts was the election of Wisconsin's 44th Governor, Jim Doyle, who brought a new day for Indian tribes in Wisconsin in 2003. He accepted $700,000 in campaign contributions from Wisconsin tribes, and is known by many as "Navajo Jim" because of his former legal services provided to the Navajo Indian Nation. Governor Doyle seldom denies a tribal request that reaches his desk. He even negotiated lucrative gambling compacts with Indian tribes in *perpetuity*, denying the State legislature or succeeding Governor's opportunity to effectively control tribal gambling in Wisconsin.

In 2004, the Wisconsin State Supreme Court ruled that Governor Doyle's "perpetuity" of tribal gambling compacts was invalid, but not before tremendous gains were made by the State's Indian tribes. Wisconsin receives over $200 million in gambling revenues from the tribal gambling compacts, but there has been no serious fiscal cost-benefit analysis that would illuminate the actual price Wisconsin pays annually to receive these compact contributions. The taxable land base loss, the taxable disposable income loss, the loss of sales and business taxes—all from accelerated tribal gambling—is the invisible "red ink" for Wisconsin, as well as numerous other States.

Wisconsin's enrolled American Indian population is 1% of the State's population. The political clout of this group is enormous.

Scott Seaborne speaks with intelligent, measured thought. Scott is a Neenah, Wisconsin, businessman and local property owner, who told us, "With generous proceeds from the casinos, the tribes have hired more attorneys than they ever had before. The tribes are buying up more farmland around the community." Scott is a quiet presence in any room, the kind of fellow who listens intently to a range of perspectives, then sorts it all out in his own head, before sharing his view.

"The tribes have hired more lobbyists," he continued, "And are making larger political donations to state and federal political systems. It also seems like some of the tribal leaders are living a lot better financially, but the average tribal member does not seem to have benefited from this change."

Kamie asked Scott, "Are tribal members able to hold their leaders more accountable for gambling revenue distribution?"

Scott replied, "Tribal members have to tow the political line in order to receive any funds or preference for a tribal job. That is why they have no voice. It's because the political and the economic system are in bed together under tribal governments."

To understand the frustration of local citizens it may be helpful to remember that most American citizens are accustomed to governmental processes that include public notice, public hearings, open public meetings, citizen input, full disclosures, environmental reviews, and compliance with local and state land use and zoning regulations approved by elected officials serving the constituents that elect them. Tribalism as a governing system does *not* embrace these routine activities of a democratic, republic form of government.

Tribal governments have no duty or obligation to notify local governments or citizens as to their short or long-range goals. Tribalism as a governing system often operates in *secret*. Tribal leaders elected in most tribal governments are elected by a physical show of raised hands of enrolled tribal members in a room, rather than a secret ballot.

This visible public vote affords tribal leaders the ability to wield a powerful, and often-oppressive authority over tribal members. Absent a secret ballot available to enrolled tribal members, leaders see and know exactly which members support them, and which oppose them. This knowledge can often result in serious consequences to "dissident" tribal members. The Cherokee Nation and a couple of other tribes do offer a secret ballot to their members, but only a few tribes do this, and these are clearly the exception to the rule.

Now imagine these two entirely opposite styles of government, trying to communicate reasonably to do local problem solving. It seldom happens, again, because tribal governments have no political obligation to neighboring governments. The "trust" relationship between Indian tribes and the federal government offers almost no opportunity or consideration for other governments or citizens, when constructing generous new federal Indian policies. The payback is generous contributions to both political parties and elected officials. The end result is that federal Indian policies developed between the federal government and Indian tribes are too often sprung upon local governments with no consideration as to the effect such policies may have. And those who dare object are called *racists*.

There is one other critical piece that poses continuous problems for local governments and Indian tribes across the country; that is zoning. Historically, zoning was forged from the fiery tenements of New York at the turn of the century. Zoning is a boring subject to many readers, but it should be understood that zoning is absolutely critical for two reasons: the first is public safety, and the second is orderly management of municipal, county and state growth.

As example, zoning ordinances fall into four general categories: commercial, residential, industrial and agricultural. Why is this important today? If a homebuyer expends many thousand dollars to acquire a quality home in a quality neighborhood, what would happen if the next door neighbor could just arbitrarily open a car wash, or tavern, or rendering plant? Property values, land use conflicts and public safety are all critical issues managed and resolved by local zoning ordinances.

Now imagine federal land taken into "trust" for Indian tribes that have *no* obligation to comply with local zoning. If a tribe acquires a parcel in a lovely residential neighborhood, has the land taken into trust to construct a "small cultural resource center," there is no regulation that requires considering the impact on adjacent property owners. This very situation occurred in Florence, Oregon, except for one tiny "bait and switch" that the Siuslaw Indian Tribe pulled on residential property owners in that quaint coastal town.

The Siuslaw tribe indicated that they simply wanted a small cultural center, until the neighborhood land was formally taken into trust. Then, Voila! the tribe implemented plans for a Class III tribal casino, in direct violation of the Indian Gaming Regulatory Act (IGRA), but today that casino is open and running full steam. This infuriated local property owners and put an entire town into full legal battle armor to keep the character of their community from becoming another "casino town." The battle goes on. People Against a Casino Town (PACT) a group in Oregon is running full steam with litigation, but it will be years before they see justice, if they ever do. Are there consequences for tribes that violate IGRA? There are none yet for Oregon's Siuslaw tribe, and very few consequences for others that frequently bend, stretch or break IGRA statutes.

The point here is, that in Wisconsin, the predominant land base is agricultural, and the townships struggle to ensure that tribal activities on federal trust land maintain some semblance of public safety and compatibility with surrounding areas. A secondary impact of so much acreage falling out of farm production is the impact upon the local economy; there are fewer farmers making purchases at feed and hardware stores, or farm families purchasing goods and services in local businesses. And this too, is a pattern sweeping across Wisconsin, Nebraska, South Dakota, Wyoming, Montana and all the way across to the Western States of Washington, Idaho, and Oregon.

Scott Seaborne states another obstacle when he says, "You can't solve a problem until you admit that you have it."

"Congress and Indian activists continually promote the fact that what they are doing is good." He continued, "They made a political decision to promote sovereignty. In order to promote the recognition of Indian governments by the federal government, they continually promote the fact that what they tribal governments are doing is good. Now, in order to promote continuous good, you have political reason to minimize and ignore the problems."

We had two more experiences that would prove unsettling for Kamie, perhaps because she has not had the experience of living within an Indian reservation, or interacting daily with tribal members, as I have. We were put in contact with two Stockbridge-Munsee tribal members, willing to talk with us. Their names and genders are, for obvious reasons, omitted here; suffice it to call the Member 1 and Member 2.

Kamie asked, "How do you see things going here these days?"

Member 1 explained, "I think the tribe already has the ultimate lands here. It doesn't need to buy up any more farms." This member then said that the real solution to federal Indian policy would be for the tribe to encourage members to farm the purchased land. Member 1 acknowledged the tribe's intent to "buy back" all the lands in the area, as they are systematically doing.

I asked, "If the tribe buys all the farm lands up and no crops are produced, and if this is happening across many states, what does America do for its food supply?"

Member 2 said, "We have commodities, and there are grocery stores." The term actually used quite frequently here was "Commods," meaning staple foods provided from tribal and state food banks.

Neither tribal member was pleased with current tribal government goals and activities, but then neither member was highly critical either. A very strong sense of loyalty came through from these members. But to Kamie, something was missing.

After we left the tribal members, Kamie said, "You know, the whole time they were talking about all the lands the tribe is buying up, all the farm lands out of productivity, and all the farm families leaving, there wasn't the slightest concern about how this is affecting others—none at all."

"I think that's an unintentional, perhaps, but entrenched pattern," I responded to Kamie. "Tribal governments do not concern themselves with the well being or needs of other cultures, and that concern is hardly ever encouraged among their members either. It took me awhile to understand that persons living an isolated lifestyle within one culture, think very seldom of other cultures or consequences. It is not necessarily unkind or meanspirited; it strikes me more of the reality that we all live what we learn. We're all a product of our environment and beliefs passed along to us."

We caught up with Scott Seaborne again. for a videotape interview. Kamie and Scott were discussing Class III tribal casinos and the impact of the Indian gambling monopoly.

"I recall an article by a prominent Indian journalist, Tim Giago, noted Scott. Giago was writing about some of the newly recognized Indians tribes that he had visited. One tribe held a powwow but they had no dance ceremony. They had no traditional dance, no traditional language, and here you have a group of people that have very minimal Indian lineage and they are making huge amounts of money.

We all agreed that the new Wannabe tribes seeking their casino were tarnishing the reputations of legitimate Indian tribes. California gets the grand prize for this new trend, but Southern and Eastern states are beginning to experience shiny new "aboriginal" tribes seeking recognition.

Kamie then asked Scott to talk about possible solutions for resolving failed federal Indian policy.

"In searching for solutions, I've thought of one idea that may seem a little radical, but maybe it's worth considering. It might be a drastic but a final and complete solution. It would begin with ending the federal trust relationship with tribes. One of the ideas that I have looked at would be to reconfigure tribes into a different legal entity," said Scott.

"For example, perhaps a tribe could become like a county, a subdivision of a state. It would be integrated into state government and the reservation would become a county within state, and any tribal assets would be owned by a corporation in which the tribal members would be shareholders, and share in the resources of their tribal assets, and maintain community and jurisdiction as though they were a county—use zoning, set speed limits, set school standards—all that a county could do, but integrated into our federal, state and local system. That would eliminate a lot of conflicts that we see all across the country.

"People might ask pro-tribal government voices, 'What would be lost?' Earlier today I heard a tribal member say that if the tribe had to give up its sovereignty, it would just mean one less unresponsive government to deal with. Perhaps we ought to look at that. "

Scott then added, "Part of the problem is that there's a significant difference in economic systems between tribal and mainstream governments. It is actually pretty simple to explain: Mainstream governments rely on funding from their citizens through the raising of taxes by consent of the governed. This is government "of the people," from the bottom up to the top. Tribal members rely upon their governments for social services, land assignments and reservation jobs. In this way the power comes from the top down, and not from the bottom up, as good government should."

"It appears to me that the current system has not benefited the people as a whole," Scott Seaborne continued. "The people that seem to benefit by the current system are the bureaucrats in D.C. who support federal Indian policy. The other people that benefit are tribal members who are on the Tribal Council or in strong leadership positions.

The last difficult experience for Kamie during this visit was when we all headed into town for lunch in a local restaurant. It was suggested that we not speak of federal Indian policy or anything controversial. Kamie looked over at me, very puzzled? Later she would ask, "What was that all about? Why couldn't we say what we feel?"

"It's the same in my town. I understand it fully, Kamie." Then I told her that if we are within or near the boundaries of an Indian reservation, or within a range to be overheard by tribal members, it is taboo to speak of things like equality, or what's good for the town or community." These are subjects viewed as disrespectful to the tribal government or worse, anyone speaking of equality is targeted as a *racist*, and when those conversations occur in restaurants, or businesses, those businesses soon lose their tribal clientele. In low-income areas that have small businesses, every customer counts. So we stay silent, to help the businesses.

"God, Elaine, is this America or what?" she said.

The fog comes on little cat's feet....it sits looking, over harbor and city, on silent haunches...

— Carl Sandburg
American Poet (1878 - 1967)

Chapter 14
Sneaking Up on New Buffalo, Michigan

Cheryl Lynch would look great on the cover of any hot fashion magazine. She is a tall, slender, ageless woman whose flaming crimson hair announces her presence everywhere she goes. Mike Lynch is a handsome complement to this woman, and they're terrific business partners, as well as husband and wife for the past ten years.

If somehow you failed to notice her, Cheryl's vigorous mind and motivating voice will not be ignored. Of Old Irish and German descendants, she lives life in the high moment, and truly believes that today is not a dress rehearsal; things must be said and done right now! These two are passionate thinkers and implementers. Of Irish and Swedish ancestry, Mike is a licensed builder. Cheryl's a designer, and they are both real estate professionals who own their brokerage firm. What is most important to these two fireballs is that country life runs in their veins. Michigan is their love. They are worried sick, and are furious about an imminent, devastating change in their town's character.

Here in what is called "Harbor Country," we spoke with the Lynches' about their involvement in a community group that is confronting the construction of a Class III tribal casino in New Buffalo, and we discussed taxation aspects of federal Indian policy. Our conversations were quite illuminating.

Cheryl opened our discussion with, "I was born here in Michigan. I am a Native American and I resent others calling themselves Native Americans, as though I am less so. "

"My family enjoyed traveling and we camped everywhere in Michigan when I was growing up. I love the outdoors. That's why I get furious when I see people desecrating this beautiful land in any way. This state is *my* ancestral homeland."

Cheryl added, "Federal Indian policy is ethnically discriminatory. We have not been able to vote in this community on what happens here. We have not been considered by the federal government as having the individual sovereignty that all Americans have been constitutionally guaranteed."

As a builder and broker, Mike pointed out, "As people begin inquiring about investing here, the subject of the potential casino inevitably arises. I have noticed great concern about property values and taxation. I can't totally respond to that. When local revenue generation includes relying upon subsidies from a gambling venue of this nature, it amounts to a proverbial crap game."

New Buffalo is nestled in the farthest southwestern corner of the State, on the shore of Lake Michigan. It is a part of a cluster of small, quaint resort communities along the Lake, established during the mid-19th century. The classic beauty of this small harbor town compares with Santa Barbara or New England harbor villages. New Buffalo is a resort community whose primary property tax is derived from high-value, second-home properties. Urban dwellers buy second homes to spend all of their available free time in New Buffalo, since it is only an hour from Chicago.

Vacationers, and the summer day-trippers do not come to New Buffalo to get involved in the community, or in politics, and they did not purchase property in New Buffalo to experience suburbia. They are in town for the summer to unwind from work and urban tensions. That is why New Buffalo is reeling from a sneak-attack, and the economic takeover of the tourist economy developed by people like the Lynches over decades.

Six counties in Michigan and four counties in neighboring Indiana are considered the ancestral "roaming lands" of the Pokagon Band of Potawatomi Indians, a tribe that received its federal recognition in 1994, as restored by then President Clinton, in the final hours of his administration. The Band headquarters are in Dowagiac, Michigan, about fifty miles northeast of New Buffalo. The Band claims an enrollment of approximately 2,700 members; however, none live in the New Buffalo area, and they are not planning on establishing residency once the casino is opened.

On December 3, 1998 former Governor John Engler, signed a Tribal Gaming Compact between the state and the tribe, that was approved by a "midnight" resolution, not a legislative act or bill, of the Michigan legislature. The majority of legislators had made it known that they would oppose the bill. The Pokagons acquired 675 acres near heavily traveled Interstate 94, at the edge of the town of New Buffalo, and dedicated 51 acres for a planned tribal Class III casino. The purchased land included many homes that have since been removed.

The Gaming Compact has a 20-year life, and includes a contribution to the State of Michigan of 8% of the casino's "net win," (total amount wagered on each electronic gaming machine, minus total amount of winning wagers paid) contributed semi-annually to the state. There is an additional provision to compensate the State for direct costs associated with administering the gambling compact, for an amount not to exceed $50,000. There is provision for a 2% of "net" casino revenue to be made to the local host county.

Although the immediate area of New Buffalo, township and city, includes only about 5,000 permanent residents, this gambling market location for a proposed class III tribal casino will draw from about an hour west, including Chicago, to a short drive south, South Bend, Indiana; and then as far north as Grand Rapids, Michigan—literally millions of gambling customers in the immediate region.

Tribal casino developers are quite sharp, and do extensive market studies. Once a prime location is selected, the courting of elected officials begins. The message is a sparkly one, especially to communities such as New Buffalo, whose employment and economic base is seasonal. "We'll create full-time jobs and increase your tourism significantly." Part of this spin is true: Class III casinos create a lot of jobs and stimulate tourism. The footprint of tourism shifts from local taxed facilities that are competing at significant disadvantage, to the untaxed tribal casino.

Cheryl notes that, "The tribal casino promoters are also skilled at intimidating small town officials, who were not elected to deal with community changing issues like casino gambling. In New Buffalo, officials actually operated as 'lobbyists' by signing a document agreeing to be the tribe's promoter during legal proceedings against the town's casino opposition. Casino promoters do that because they know that only the elected officials, not the citizens of a community, are acknowledged by the BIA."

What local leaders fail to see when dazzled with the hope of such an economic stimulant, is that these massive local revenue vacuum cleaners, literally suck up the disposable income from a wide area, into a private tribal government revenue stream, with almost nothing coming back into the state and local tax base. Or worse, with actual written promises of financial commitments to state and local governments, that remain unfulfilled.

Dollars that once went into a local dress shop or restaurant go into the tribal slot machines. Dollars that made purchases at quaint little "Harbor" boutiques, antique shops, sporting goods, and novelty shops, are flushed down the tribal slot toilets. Small proprietors are generally the first to hang up the "Out-of-Business" sign, followed quickly by local restaurants that cannot compete with the cheap, All-You-Can-Eat tribal casino buffets.

Previous disposable income that once went into tax-paying businesses located on taxable parcels, shifts nearly immediately into private, non-taxed tribal revenue coffers. Much like a leech on an arm, the economic lifeblood of surrounding communities is drained. Tribal governments claim, "Look at all the jobs we've created. Look at the tourism we've generated." Yes, they sure have. The entire character and quality of life of impacted communities are changed. "Harbor Country" as New Buffalo is known, will never be the same.

No one is saying it, but many local communities are enduring increased poverty from low-wage casino jobs that do not support family needs. Another impact resulting from large tribal casinos is an influx of language requirements that fall upon area public schools receiving the children of immigrant, [mostly non-Indian] imported workers to accommodate staffing tribal casinos, resorts, hotels, marinas, and other tribal enterprises that quickly blossom around the gambling monopoly, purchased by the tax-exempt gambling profits.

The Lynches see an even darker national pattern emerging.

"There's a sense of apprehension, almost like a mob influence," said Cheryl. "We cannot even get our local newspapers to report an opposing point of view about the planned tribal casino. We have to purchase advertisements to get our views out. Even the Chicago Tribune has several of their own reporters who live here. This is a very liberal city and State. Our Governor is from Canada. So we look to national groups as an oasis of hope."

"How are you handling this feeling of being a voice in the local wilderness?" I asked.

Cheryl continued, "As I have said to our local organization, we just have to reach out. We are just going to have to coalesce in America—all of us—even people who are not aware, or have not been hit by a coming tribal casino. People are going to have to realize that we must connect the dots. This tribalism is not unconnected with many other socialist pressures on America to set aside our nationalism, to set aside our patriotism. You are seeing this throughout our American society."

Mike Lynch shared another perspective: "You hear about the ACLU or something as if, say, "The Russians are coming." The Russians couldn't have *done* a job like this. They couldn't have invaded us with gambling, vices, prostitution, an idea of increased crime and organized elements and spread it so quickly across this country."

Cheryl then affirmed Mike's analogy, with, "These are distractions, and the more distractions we have to contend with, the more disjointed we are in America, the better for socialism and those who would undo this country."

In April 1996, concerned residents of New Buffalo formed the Taxpayers of Michigan Against Casinos (TOMAC) community group to insist that the federal and state governments receive and consider local community impacts when processing a Pokagon application for a Class III tribal gambling facility on 675 acres of land acquired by the tribe.

TOMAC outreached to other citizens, and conducted educational workshops. In May 2000, TOMAC published results of a survey that their local State Representative mailed to out-of-state

New Buffalo area property owners: Some 279 completed surveys provided the following results:

1. As a 2nd homeowner in Harbor Country, do you support the development of a casino? *95% said No.*

2. If you had known that a tribal casino was proposed for Harbor Country when you invested in property, would you still have made your purchase? *72% said No.*

3. Do you believe a nearby casino will have a negative impact on your property value? *85% said Yes.*

4. Would you spend less or more time in Harbor Country if a casino was nearby? *69% said Less Time.*

New Buffalo's second home owner respondents then ranked the following items in terms of importance as matters of interest or concern:

35% Character of Community
29% Crime Threat
16% Traffic Congestion
15% Property Value
14% Problem Gamblers
13% Impact on Local Economy

The TOMAC group, as so many others have, began the arduous task of becoming familiar with the Indian Gaming Regulatory Act of 1988 (IGRA), and with their State's role in the process. Within IGRA, they found very little opportunity for the voice of affected citizens.

TOMAC members also discovered that the Pokagon land, claimed that "ancestral roaming land" of the tribe, could be taken into trust as "restored" lands, eliminating the federal obligation to consider local community impacts. TOMAC disagreed with the tribe's asserted land status. The group evaluated its options, and decided that a legal action, always so costly to citizens who are intentionally disenfranchised from the approval processes for Class III tribal casinos, was their best hope.

The community group then pursued a path very familiar to frustrated citizens across the country. It gathered legal funds and went to court. In 2001 TOMAC, filed suit in Federal District Court in Washington D.C. *TOMAC v. Gale A. Norton.*

TOMAC asserted that during the last days of the Clinton administration, a process for taking land into federal trust for the Pokagon Band of Potawatomi had circumvented administrative processes of the Indian Gaming Regulatory Act, denying citizens and local government rightful input into the process. Near the end of the briefing period, TOMAC moved for discovery pursuant to Rule 56(f), asserting that the Department of Interior had failed to provide a complete administrative record and had acted in bad faith.

TOMAC prevailed in a small, but very important piece of their legal battle. Early in the case, a ruling that established the legal *standing* of locally affected community groups or individual citizens was a minor victory in comparison to the larger land status challenge. However, securing judicial recognition of citizen standing, that is specific to IGRA, provided a major tool for groups across the country that are confronting off-reservation Class III casinos.

IGRA includes a statute that requires tribes who are trying to construct Class III casinos off-reservation to comply with the National Environmental Policy Act (NEPA). NEPA includes the *right of a citizen* to participate fully in the environmental review process, and provide affected citizens with legal *standing*. This is an absolutely critical tool for communities that do not desire a Class III tribal casino in their community.

Unfortunately, in February 2005, the U.S. Supreme Court declined to hear TOMAC's appeal of a 2004 Michigan Supreme Court decision that four tribal compacts did not violate Michigan's constitution.

The State of Michigan offers another important insight arising from federal Indian policy—the matter of how taxation is addressed. It is quite likely that most readers of this book are unaware that racially based tax exemptions are available to individual enrolled tribal members, but unavailable to other citizens.

On December 20, 2002 former Governor John Engler signed yet another very interesting Agreement between the Pokagon Band of Potawatomi Indians and the State of Michigan: a Tax Agreement providing the tribe and its individually enrolled members a wide range of Michigan State tax exemptions. There are several such agreements with other tribes in Michigan, and similar tax agreements with tribal governments and states across the country. The Tax Agreement provides that the Michigan State Treasury is authorized by the State legislature to accommodate the provisions of the State-Tribal Tax Agreement.

Tribal governments, as is the law with other government entities across the land, are exempt from taxation, because they are a government. Extending numerous tax exemptions to an individual, enrolled tribal member is a different matter.

Imagine being able to say, "I am a resident of Johnson County, and Johnson County doesn't have to pay taxes, so because I am a participant in this tax-exempt government (county), then I do not have to pay taxes either." U.S. citizens may not say or do this. Enrolled tribal members, by their enrollment, *are* exempt from a good number of taxes imposed on other U.S. citizens, especially as Governors and state legislatures so generously cooperate with federally recognized tribes within their state.

Below is a partial list of tax exemptions provided to Pokagon tribal members who are "Resident Tribal Members" in Berrien, Cass and Van Buren counties of Michigan, and other specified tribally held lands:

Exemptions for Resident (Pokagon) Tribal Member

- Personal property, other than motor vehicles, purchased or acquired by a Resident Tribal Member for his or her use.

- Resident Tribal Members are exempt from both the sales tax and use tax on the following items *regardless* of where purchased or used:

  - Passenger vehicles including automobiles, pick-up trucks, recreational vehicles and motorcycles;
  - Recreational watercraft;
  - Snowmobiles; and
  - Off road vehicles.
  - Modular homes. mobile homes used as principal residence.

Tax Exemptions for Affixation to Real Estate:

- Materials that are purchased, used or acquired in the performance of a contract entered into by the Resident Tribal Member for real property.

- Materials that are purchased, used or acquired in the performance of a contract for construction, renovation or improvement to the principal residence of a Resident Tribal Member are exempt from both the sales tax and use tax.

Treaty Fishing

- Tangible personal property purchased or acquired by a Resident Tribal Member for use in exercising a personal or commercial treaty fishing right is exempt from both the sales tax and use tax regardless of where the property is used.

Other Tax Exemptions:

- Restaurant food and beverage sales at casino operations located within the Tribal and Trust Lands are exempt from both the sales tax and use tax.

- Sale of Electricity, Natural or Artificial Gas, Home Heating Fuels, and telecommunications and Internet Services.

- Sales of electricity, natural gas or artificial gas, home heating fuels and all transmission and distribution charges are exempt from both the sales tax and use tax.

- Telephone (intrastate and interstate), telegraph leased wire, internet, cable, and other similar communications rendered to and paid for by a Resident Tribal Member are exempt from both the sales tax and use tax.

Remember voices from the previous chapter that commented on problems spreading across regions when there is one set of laws for one class of persons, and a different set of laws for another class of persons. Using the State of Michigan as an example, there are 68,501 enrolled "Resident Tribal Members" who are provided one set of special-preference laws:

- A tribal government that receives federal funds provided by taxpayers for free health, education, child welfare, cultural and recreational services for its members.

- Extraordinary hunting and fishing preferences.

- Tax exemptions for tribal members.

All other Michigan residents must fully comply with all federal, state and local tax laws and regulations. The proceeds derived from American taxpayers, not only subsidize tribal governments but must offset the lack of taxes collected from enrolled tribal members.

Federal Indian policy has racially divided this country into two distinct classes of person: taxpayers and preferentially-treated taxpayers. For additional information on this subject, simply go to the website of the federal Internal Revenue Service (www.irs.gov), and keyword "Indian," and watch the tax exemptions come rolling up on the screen.

Another net effect of federal Indian policy is that the tax-paying class of persons must supplement taxes unpaid by a special-preference class of persons. This has been the case since about 1934 and it is certainly burdensome upon American taxpayers that this should remain the case for *time immemorial*.

Any appeasement of tyranny is treason to this republic
and to the democratic ideal

— *William Allen White*
U.S. Editorialist, Publisher
(1868 - 1944)

Chapter 15
The Salamanca Sixteen

Susan Swiech said, "They followed me into the bathroom." I asked her why? She then looked up and said, "They were afraid I was going to kill myself." Susan was referring to her attorney, Jennifer Coleman, and a U.S. Marshal.

This was a specific day in the life of Susan D. Swiech, one member of sixteen American citizens evicted by U.S. Marshals from homes they had lived in for decades. For twenty years, Susan was a highly regarded Special Education teacher for intermediate grades in the Salamanca schools. Over 2,400 City of Salamanca citizens were forced to sign the title and deeds of their properties over to the Seneca Nation of Indians. They were put through the humiliation of having to videotape every room inside their home to assure no vandalism, so as to not reduce the home's value to the Seneca tribe.

After leaving Michigan, Kamie and I had driven as far as Elyria, Ohio, on the way to Little Valley and Salamanca, New York. We knew we needed to rest and regroup for the next stop, but we had no idea how intense and how tragic this visit would be.

The sunny, crisp October afternoon drive from Elyria was peaceful, and Kamie and I were quiet in the car. As we exited Interstate 86 and turned onto State Highway 242, we were in for an inspiring sight. The autumn leaves of the Northern Allegheny Mountains are splendid—as awe-inspiring as the marvelous rainbow we saw in South Dakota.

Salamanca would be the only stop in which we had never previously met at least one of the locals. We would be among total strangers, but not for long. New York colleagues in other areas of the State had told us, "You just *have* to go talk to those people in Salamanca. They got shafted so badly." So with some telephone contacts and email networking, we were invited to stay with Virginia Banner, a gentle widow whose graying hair is sprinkled with hints of what probably once was a lively auburn hue.

We got to Virginia's in the early evening, but it was dark. She had prepared a guest room for each of us, and we went through the little moments of introduction, getting squared away as Virginia's guests, and then sat at her kitchen table for some great pie and coffee. It was the evening's quiet conversation, coming from a very soft-spoken woman that alerted us to an upcoming rough day of capturing the story of one of the first major casualties of the Indian Gaming Regulatory Act (IGRA).

Before moving through the process that caused American citizens to be abandoned by their federal, state and local governments, a little background about the Seneca Nation of Indians (SNI), and especially their lands, is in order:

The SNI includes three separate reservations—the Allegany, the Cattaraugus and Oil Springs Indian reservations. The City of Salamanca is located within the Seneca's Allegany Reservation that essentially follows the Allegheny River from New York's border with Pennsylvania, north to Vandalia, New York. The wooded hills and valleys of this region are just lovely to behold at any time of year, but especially so when the brilliant autumn leaves are on parade.

A historical researcher, Paul R. Frederick, has described SNI land interests as follows:

Legal title to the three reservations of the Seneca Nation of Indians remains in the possession of the Seneca Nation and has never been relinquished to either the federal government or the state of New York. Individual ownership of surface portions of land "a plowshare deep' is recognized on the reservations, and allotment in severalty was never accepted or applied to any of the New York reservations. Individually held plots of land may only be sold to another enrolled member of the Seneca Nation, and leases to non-Seneca individuals or groups must be formally approved by the tribal council.

New York Indian reservations differ from other Indian reservations in that the lands have never been under federal superintendence, or in "federal reserve," hence the term "reservation." New York Indian reservation lands are a result of Treaties enacted between Indian tribes and the United States, on behalf of lands previously negotiated between Indian tribes and the State of New York.

So in New York, there is the oddity of *federally* recognized Indian tribes controlling Indian reservations resulting from prior arrangements between tribes and the *State*. The SNI occupies lands set aside for it in the Canandaigua Treaty of 1794, statutorily known as the Pickering Treaty 7.Stat 44.

Virginia and others would tell us about a 99-year lease executed in 1892, between the Seneca Indians and non-Indian settlers for Indian land upon which, ultimately, approximately 2,400 property owners (many being descendants of early settlers), had built homes and businesses. Non-Indian lessees relied upon the "automatic renewal" for an additional 99 years, when the first least expired in 1991. The language of the lease was clear. All parties agreed that the land belonged to the Senecas, and the improvements upon the land belonged to those making the improvements.

Based upon the strength of the language in the lease, the State of New York invested in the area to create Cattaraugus and Allegany counties, and to incorporate the City of Salamanca. Private citizens and property owners actually pay municipal, county and state taxes upon lands owned by the Senecas. These governmental agencies provide education, public utilities, infrastructure, and traditional governmental services to all Seneca tribal members and properties, as well as Salamanca citizens located on Indian lands.

Investors, lenders, mortgage and title companies also believed in the clarity, legality and long-term commitment proscribed within the 1892 lease. Financial institutions were instrumental in the development of what would become a lovely rural community of mostly non-Seneca tribal members, confidently and comfortably residing on Seneca Indian lands.

Remember that Congress passed IGRA in *1988*. Tribal governments were into serious strategies to obtain investment income and bankable assets to get doors open on shiny new casinos. The Seneca Nation of Indians was definitely on the move.

Prior to its expiration, the Senecas determined not to automatically renew the original 99-year lease. See how fast the political timeline, below, flowed for the process that ensnared Salamanca citizens and took their Constitutional protections completely away:

- In May of 1990, the Seneca Nation refused to negotiate a new "Master Lease" with the City of Salamanca, a lease that would have protected individual home and business owners. Citizens were forced to negotiate with the Senecas; however the tribe would not negotiate with individual citizens. This was the proverbial Catch-22, that forced citizens to accept a new, 40-year lease, at higher annual lease rates, and one that arguably transferred title of "improvements on the land" to the Seneca Nation of Indians.

- On July 25, 1990, Congressman Amory Houghton (R-NY) Introduced the *Seneca Nation Settlement Act of 19*90, (H.R. 5367). Congressman Houghton would later be acknowledged with an award equivalent to "Honorary Membership" in the Seneca Nation of Indians.

- On October 10, 1990, in Washington, D.C., the House of Representatives approved a new lease arrangement, entitled the *Seneca Nation Settlement Act of 1990* in which the SNI would be given $60 million dollars and the right to a *new* lease—not the old 99-year lease that ensured private ownership of "improvements"—a 40-year lease at substantially increased lease rates. The $60 million would be provided as follows: $35 million from the federal government; $25 million from the State of New York. Source of funds: U. S. taxpayers.

- On October 16, 1990, the Senate approved the deal.

- On November 3, 1990, President George H.W. Bush signed the *Seneca Nation Settlement Act of 1990*.

Salamanca citizens had formed an organization called Salamanca Coalition of United Taxpayers (SCOUT), and headed into courts as affected individual property owners, and as an organization.

Despite the provisions of Section 9 of the Settlement Act that an action could be maintained in the United State District Court of the Western District of New York to challenge the constitutionality of the Act, the Court found that the defense of "sovereign immunity" raised by the SNI, was valid and therefore dismissed the action.

"We exhausted every legal means available to SCOUT, up to and including the U.S. Supreme Court, but were never heard. Legal fees amounted to more than a quarter of a million dollars paid from 1992 through 1997, raised by the people of Salamanca who were trying everything they could to preserve, and later to restore, title to their "improvements".

On January 25, 1990, United States District Court Judge Richard Arcara dismissed the SCOUT legal action by ruling that the Seneca Nation of Indians was an indispensable party, and that acting upon their sovereign immunity, they declined to be sued.

Further strengthening the tribal government position was language within its Treaties with the United States that required the federal government to defend the tribal government for any and all "disputes or disturbances" upon the land. Apparently, the Salamanca homeowners were "disturbing" the SNI, and the federal government jumped right in to assist the tribal government and, thus, to directly oppose and abandon U.S. citizens.

The odious trap had been set for the home and business owners in Salamanca. A tribal government refused to negotiate with individual citizens, and refused to negotiate with the City of Salamanca. The tribal government also refused to consent to be sued, leaving affected citizens with no judicial recourse. Then Treaty language *required* the United States to assist the tribal government, leaving the citizens with no legislative or Executive recourse either.

The next timeline involved coercive efforts to force individual residents and business owners to sign the arbitrary leases, being foisted upon them. The Salamanca folks were telling us about "The Signings" and the increased emotional, psychological and financial pressure exerted upon over 2,400 U.S. citizens to sign over title to their homes and business, whether they chose to remain in Salamanca or not.

The SCOUT organization had been diligently encouraging the citizens to hold together as a large group and refuse to sign. But the majority of the local residents were quite elderly, living on limited fixed income, and were afraid to hold out, because of threats by the SNI to have them evicted. Many held out for a while. There were four formal "Signings:"

September 1990: Two hundred property owners signed. These were the citizens with the limited incomes and great fears of financial ruin in their retiring years.

April 1991: Two hundred more property owners gave in.

December 1991: Rumors were rampant; the psychological heat was on, and about 1,800 property owners stepped forward and signed the arbitrary leases.

September 1994: About 120 remaining Salamanca home and business owners had held out as long as they could, along with the political and psychological pressure, so that all but 16 Salamanca families signed on this occa-

sion—hence, what would become known as "The Salamanca Sixteen."

<u>May - August 1997</u>: Having exhausted every legal ave-
nue to no avail, the sixteen Salamanca families were
served the Eviction Order by the District Court.

Somehow, these sixteen Americans just firmly believed that
as United States citizens, a remedy to this nightmare would be
available to them. And if no help were forthcoming, they would
stand up for their rights for so long as they could.

On one occasion out of numerous court appearances, elderly
Nathan Frank, a veteran himself, and now deceased, inappropri-
ately stood up in the courtroom and said to Magistrate Carol
Heckman, "Your Honor, we have never, ever been heard. I want
to speak." Bailiffs immediately approached old Nate, but the
Magistrate allowed him to briefly speak. He tried to tell her of
the stonewalling they had all faced by every elected official, and
the federal government. He was able to get a few brief state-
ments in, but that was the only occasion and the only "word" that
these victims would get to speak in a courtroom session. Nathan
died very shortly after his eviction.

The "Signing" events were not without significant psychological moments for Salamanca citizens. Property owners were
not allowed to accomplish the relinquishment of their homes by
mail. They were ordered to appear in person, to physically line
up with their old (99-year) leases in hand. Each "lessee" had to
sign a "Declaration of Surrender." During the 1994 Signings,
they could be represented by legal counsel. The Salamanca City
Attorney received Powers of Attorney from many at this time,
because they could not emotionally bear the trauma of their
Signings.

The Signings were manned by members of the SNI, who
were less than gracious, and described as arrogant to long lines
of hundreds of property owners, giving up their homes. The financial loss was now compounded with a psychological humiliation later celebrated by the SNI in a major "Victory" party, well
publicized in local media. The lead attorney for the U.S. De-

partment of Justice, Barry Brandon, was rumored to be a grandson of a Seneca tribal member, and would frequently meet after court appearances with Seneca tribal members.

In an undated editorial, the SCOUT attorney, Jennifer Coleman, wrote: "In the local media, this complex lease dispute was often reduced to another 'white man stealing Indian land' story."

Virginia Banner noted, "We were told that *60-Minutes* was interested in *mass* evictions, but apparently what was happening to just sixteen U.S. families was not politically significant enough for prime time viewing."

The next steps involved the SNI engaging federal courts, the Department of Justice, the Department of Interior, and the Bureau of Indian Affairs to serve the sixteen citizens with eviction notices requiring that "back lease fees" be paid, that any damages to property be paid, and that these citizens be liable for all court costs, if evicted by federal Marshals.

The Salamanca Sixteen stood firm.

They received their notifications from the U.S. District Court. They videotaped the interior rooms and exteriors of their properties. Most of them started the process of finding another place to live, and moved some of their personal possessions. But each of them stayed firmly in their homes until evicted by Court Order of the federal government, as requested by the Senecas.

One morning the citizens awakened to find large numbers, an orange fluorescent "X" or obscene graffiti spray-painted on the fronts of their homes. They believed and always will, that the SNI was sending a message to the larger community that *these* citizens were in for trouble. This had a chilling effect, but the citizens stayed in their homes.

We asked Bob Johnson, whose kind eyes, white hair and rosy cheeks revealed a pleasant disposition, "What caused you to fight for yourself?"

He said, " I have heard a lot of stories about different patriots, where they stuck up for what is right, and I feel that way too." Then he added, "But we were told that we had to abide by all rules and regulations of the Seneca Nation, and go to their tribal courts because we are under *their* jurisdiction, because we do not live in the United States. We live in a country within a country."

"The Senecas claim they are not U.S. citizens," Bob continued. "They denounce their citizenship. They claim that they had to sign something to be citizens and that they never signed anything so they do not consider themselves U.S. citizens. The government says they are, but if you talk to most Senecas personally, they'll say, 'No, I'm not a citizen. I'm a Seneca.' They should not have the power that they have; they misuse it."

Kamie asked Bob, "How can they get away with this?" to which Bob responded, "The Constitution does not apply on the Seneca Nation's Indian land."

I then asked Bob, "Do you think we ought to have nations within this nation?" He answered, "No. We're all equal. They shouldn't have any more power than we have."

The Salamanca story was so shocking to us that I then asked Bob, "Why does the City of Salamanca exist on this reservation if it has no authority? How can they collect taxes if they cannot provide you protection? They have no enforcement capability on this reservation. They have no governing authority on this reservation, but there is a city, a county and the State of New York that collects taxes from homeowners and businesses here."

Bob replied, "They collect taxes because the State of New York said that they can do so, but the State has no jurisdiction to say that. Only the federal government and Senecas have authority here."

"But Salamanca citizens have to pay the taxes anyway, right?

"Right." Bob was confirming the pattern across the country. Taxpayers contribute to the funding for the general operation and needs of tribal governments, such as the SNI, and also for the public utilities, infrastructure and public health and safety components of Indian reservations. Tribes contribute little or nothing. And this tribe was now taking title to the properties of over two thousand taxpayers.

"Will the Senecas have to pay property taxes on your homes and businesses?" I asked

"No." Bob whispered.

"So, the State of New York and City of Salamanca says to the citizen here, 'We are helpless to help you, but oh-by-the way, you will pay us taxes!'" I said. "But the Senecas, proud owners of all of your properties, and improvements on properties of 2,400 other citizens—they won't be paying any future taxes."

I was outraged, listening to these truly wounded people. "You were truly kicked to the curb by your own United States government, weren't you?"

The sorrow in Bob's eyes came full force into our camera, when he calmly said, "They just passed jurisdiction from one department to another, from one court to another..."

Nancy O'Brien was a part of the group we met. Nancy is also a senior citizen and had owned a home and business. When she was initially invited to meet with us, she told Virginia Banner that she just didn't think she could go through exposing her feelings again, even if it were to help tell their story. But she came along, and had been sitting quietly for some time.

The group explained to us that for many of them, these events were so personally painful and financially devastating, that even now, eight years later, the heartache and the wounds still run very, very deep.

Nancy first started to speak, then she stopped, turned to Susan Swiech, and broke into deep quiet sobs, "See? I just don't think I can *do* this." But she gathered her composure and listened for a while.

As Bob was talking with us, Nancy suddenly commented, "I don't know what's happening to our country. I don't know if we're getting to a point where we just say "oh well, we can't do anything about it..." Then Nancy told us that she went through the trauma of being forcefully evicted from her home and business. She complied with all requirements of the U.S. Marshal, including videotaping her properties. The tribe had required a lease fee of several thousand per month for Nancy's home and business.

"I just couldn't pay that...so I lost everything," she said.

Nancy would later tell us that on the day of her eviction, she took two of her children and walked to a bridge in town. Then joined by other evictees, she and others all threw their keys into the river, in a somewhat last act of quiet rebellion. In a voice cracking with emotion, Nancy said, "I remember it all very well. I was very proud." Members of the Salamanca Sixteen had created a large poster-board "Cashiers Check" in the amount of all back lease payment demands. "We carried the Check to the river, and quietly tossed it in," said Nancy.

"We made our protest very quietly, lawfully and orderly. We didn't burn tires on the Expressway," said Jerry Titus, alluding to previous violent protests by Seneca Nation of Indian members.

Jerry Titus is a stocky fellow, served with the U.S. Navy Seabees from 1963 to 1967, including a tour in Viet Nam. He's has a very quiet manner about him. Jerry and his wife, Liz, grew up in the area, and had owned their home in Salamanca for thirteen years. Jerry brought a good deal of documentation to us, and walked us through much of the political process described here. Jerry and Bob Johnson seemed to be a source of quiet strength for the women.

The Salamanca Sixteen also suffered serious health problems, and the passing away of spouses and longtime friends, not long after the evictions. John Brahaney and Nathan Frank died soon after their eviction. Marjorie "Midge" Schubert passed away not long after, too. She was a highly respected and caring foster parent (of many Seneca Indian children) and a local beautician for years. Also, Virginia Banner's beloved activist spouse, Chet Banner, passed away on June 1, 2002 of lung cancer, likely exacerbated by years of stress. But Chet never quit fighting, nor did he ever stop helping other New Yorkers in their struggles with federal Indian policy. Marie Brahaney passed away in 2004.

Susan Swiech was the youngest of the Salamanca Sixteen, probably in her mid-'50s at the time of the eviction. Susan is an attractive woman, smartly dressed, a false bravado that shows up as a cheery disposition, under the circumstances.

Kamie asked Susan, "How did you even handle it?" referring to the eviction.

"I faced it like—and she paused for along time—a death. When you die you leave your home and all earthly possessions behind." Susan is a deeply spiritual being, and said, "I just relied upon my Father to walk me through this, to help me stay calm, help me stand tall, and show me what I must do."

"On the day the Marshal came, our attorney, Jennifer Coleman was with me. She was very comforting, and she felt so badly for all of us. Jennifer had done everything she possibly could. I had decided to just simply walk away from my home, leaving everything in it. Everything. My furniture, my piano, computer, appliances, clothing, important documents, family photographs and memorabilia, purse—I simply walked out. What was happening to me was so egregious that it was in a sense a holocaust. Everything in my world was turning to ashes," she told us very slowly.

"The Marshal and Jennifer could not believe that I would do that - not even take my purse," Susan continued, "But I treated this eviction from my home as if a whole piece of my life had died, because it had—you can't take anything with you when you die—I just walked away from it *all*, in faith, in peace, as a patriot, and I was convinced that somehow God would take care of me." And He has, but it has been very, very difficult.""

"So when the U. S. Marshal gently took my arm, I walked out onto the front porch and saw a crowd of people, including television reporters. As we approached the Marshal's car from where I would view the eviction, one of my friends yelled out, "God Bless you, Sue." Spontaneously, I burst out singing "God Bless America," joined by my friends and many of the spectators. In effect, I was blessing those who were cursing me.

"Once inside the marshal 's vehicle, I viewed something I took as a sign or omen of the day's events. Two moving vans with the name 'Mayflower' arrived, and the movers had words, 'Good and Fair' written on the back of their uniforms. It seemed to me to be a metaphor of how the first colonists arrived, and now my life was being loaded on to vehicles of the same name; however, it did not feel either 'good' or 'fair' to me at all."

This trauma occurred to Susan just before Labor Day, and school started immediately afterward. Susan resumed her teaching while staying with a friend, as all of her belongings, and her personal teaching materials, were gone.

U.S. Marshals came to Susan's school twice with bills for money owed the federal government. She received a moving and storage bill for $9, 959.29.

"I told the Marshal that I wouldn't pay a penny. I did not order the moving vans, and I believed that the federal government did not have my permission to take my home, or my personal furnishings and goods," she said, softly. When she declined to pay the storage fees, her belongings were later auctioned, and the Marshal returned again to her school, this time with a "deficiency" bill for $11,000 owed to the Department of Justice, subsequent to the auction. She has declined to pay that also.

When the gentle Salamanca senior citizens kept telling us, "This (Salamanca) isn't the United States. This is the Seneca Nation of Indians," as stunned as we were, Kamie and I had to find some way to emotionally grasp what they meant. To us, we were clearly in the State of New York within the United States. To the people we were listening to, we were in a separate "nation," totally apart from the United States.

These citizens had no one, and lost title to their homes and businesses, with *no mitigating compensation*, in the waning years of their lives, except for the youngest, Susan. This separatist mentality hangs like a dark cloud, and sometimes a large hammer over *this* community, and thousands of non-tribal citizens in many other communities across the country. It's a huge cloud now spreading across all of Western and Upstate New York.

"I had to give up teaching," Susan said, "I just couldn't teach American History ever again, not after what I lived through was so very different than what I had been teaching. And my son gave up a 12-year career in the Air Force, after what happened to his mother." Incidentally, The Seneca Indians fought on the side of the British against George Washington and the colonists.

Virginia Banner was a quiet host during our conversations. Chet, her spouse, had been one of the group's key leaders, and was the "activist" of the family. Virginia was his strength and comfort. The Banners' home (in which Virginia was born) was in the name of their son, who was also career military, a Lieutenant Colonel, serving in Bosnia at the time his parents were evicted. The Banners had life-use of the home. Their son was fighting to bring freedom to Bosnians while his own parents were being evicted from their own home in the United States.

On May 5, 1996, Chet Banner, along with then Seneca Nation President, Dennis Bowen, were guests on "Native American

Calling," a national Indian radio talk show. During the broadcast, the Seneca President said that he felt sorry for the Salamanca citizens, but that they just got "bad advice." In a polite on-air debate, the Seneca President reinforced the notion that the United State's *first* duty is to the Seneca Nation of Indians, not the non-tribal citizens. Then he offered, "I feel sorry for the senior citizens in this group. They have lived there two and three generations." He then alluded to the possibility that they were listening to the wrong people. "You should listen to us," the Seneca Nation President said.

Chet said to Bowen, "Apparently, my son is over in Bosnia fighting for *your* rights, because I don't have any."

It is worth noting that on the same radio talk show was a representative of 24 non-tribal, long-time Indian-land lessees, who were being evicted from *their* homes on the Blackfeet Indian Reservation that straddles the Montana-Canada border. The Blackfeet had decided that renting to non-tribal members violated their tribal constitution. The legal issues were quite similar.

It was a bit eerie for me to be sitting in Chet's home in 2004 with his wife, Virginia. Chet passed away in 2002. I never met him, but I also heard him when he spoke on July 17, 1999, by way of a videotape provided to our local Toppenish, Washington community group from the Upstate Citizens for Equality (UCE). Chet had been invited to speak at a large motorcade rally that ended at the Schuster Farm in Seneca Falls, New York. The rally was a protest against Seneca-Cayuga Land Claims in the Union Springs area of New York. Our local group in Toppenish, Washington was hungry for resources and information from New York to help us with federal Indian policy issues in the Pacific Northwest, so we appreciated everything we could learn from people like Chet and the UCE folks.

Now, over 875,000 New Yorkers, and perhaps more, are facing Indian land claims, and had heard what happened in Salamanca. Chet went to Seneca Falls to warn them, and to help however he could. In his memory and to further inform readers about tribal government actions, here is what Chet said to thousands of New Yorkers who drove 1,200 cars in a motorcade to protest the Cayuga-Seneca and Oneida land claims. This brief speech was six years ago:

Chet Banner, at Schuster Farms in Seneca Falls, New York: July 17, 1999:

You remember when I was with you folks in Albany—one of the things I told you then was that you should not leave here today hoping *THEY* can do something for you, because what THEY (elected officials) are going to do is negotiate a Settlement and shove it down your throats before you can say "teepee." That is what they did to my family and me. If something is going to happen, YOU have to make it happen. I don't care if you are part of the land claims or not. You, as New York citizens are heavily involved. As this thing (Indian land claims & settlements) is coming down, you are going to see (tax-exempt tribal) gas stations, and you are going to see smoke shops. You are going to have a loss of property revenue and school revenue. You are going to have losses of sales tax revenue because all of this stuff (tribal government enterprises) is non-taxable. It is a huge factor to support your local governments in their tax issue.

I asked Connie Tallcot see if there had been any discussion about power lines in your area. She said none that she knew about. Folks, if they (Cayuga-Seneca's) get this land you are going to find *out* about your utility lines, because they are going to want a *fortune* for them.

I was a Commissioner for the Board of Public Utilities in Salamanca for some eight years so I was privy to some information. After our Seneca Nation lease came down in 1990 the SNI started checking all the lines within the reservation boundaries. They found a couple of miles of Niagara Mohawk transmission lines coming across one corner of the reservation, coming over a mountain—absolutely nothing there—the lines made a junction, then went off the reservation. The SNI approached Niagara Mohawk and said, "You don't have a lease on those power lines." Niagara Mohawk offered a settlement to save themselves what they thought would be a lot of court battles. They offered them a million dollars and a lease. I'm not going to say this but once: The Seneca Nation demanded $60 million dollars—*$60 million*. Right now (1999) after eight years, the SNI is down to $30 million, Niagara Mohawk is offering $17 million but the SNI won't take it. I don't know where the SNI is going from here, but that is just one problem with a couple of miles of power line. I understand that you have water lines, telephone lines, cable lines, and electric lines. You are going to pay for it, BIG time. Not just the property owners in the land claim, but all the people in the county. The people in the County—YOU New Yorkers are the ones that will pick up that tab.

I think you all know that I was one of the 16 property owners that was evicted from our home in Salamanca. Jerry Titus, here with me, was another one. We went to Federal Court in Buffalo, but all this is *not* about law. We thought we had law on our side, all along. We think we *still* do. But because of their ("sovereign") immunity, our case has never been heard. Never. The Courts have dismissed everything because the Seneca will not *consent* to be sued. One time in Federal Court in Buffalo, our attorney presented a Presidential Executive Order to Federal Judge Richard Arcara. The Executive Order was in 1964, and it said categorically that the Interior Department had three years to settle all land claims and the BIA would no longer exist. The Judge asked the attorney from the Department of Justice, "What about that?" The Department of Justice attorney said, "I don't know anything about it." The Judge then said, "We'll recess for fifteen minutes."

After fifteen minutes we came back, and the Judge said, "Well, what about it (referring to the Executive Order)?"

The Department of Justice attorney said, "Well, there were a lot of Executive Orders along about then, that read more or less the same way." Then the attorney for the Department of Justice said, "They (Executive Orders) don't really mean anything."

The Judge then ruled that the Presidential Executive Order was *irrelevant* and he dismissed our case again. It was never, *ever* heard on the merits of a Fifth Amendment taking of our private property. This (federal Indian policy) is not about *law*, folks. It is about *politics*—188 percent *politics*. If you don't get involved and get the politics on *your* side, I have some news for you. You have been had! Good luck to you all, and if there's anything I can do for you, I'm available.

Chet Banner was available until June of 2002. He served a 20-year career with the Air Force from 1948-1968, including two tours in Korea, retiring as a Master Sergeant. He knew what struggle and hardship was all about. For his patriotic service, the federal government assisted a tribal government to force Mr. Banner out of his home.

It is worth remembering that all of this was happening to the residents of the City of Salamanca, and the Salamanca Sixteen *immediately* after the passage of the Indian Gaming Regulatory Act. It should be no surprise that the thriving Seneca Allegany Casino is located in Salamanca. The Senecas also have a second prosperous casino in Niagara Falls, New York. The Seneca-Iroquois National Museum is also located in Salamanca.

As we were leaving, I put my arm around Virginia Banner. I hugged her and told her, "We are here so late. There's nothing we can do to help you, but some how, some way, Virginia, I think the United States government, should make amends to all of you and your families, and I hope to return to Salamanca one day, for an unveiling of a large bronze memorial to the Salamanca Sixteen. Perhaps there will be a piece of American ground upon which it could stand."

When we arrived in the Little Valley and Salamanca area, Nature was painting the leaves and a clear, bright sky was showcasing the fall changes. We left Salamanca in tears. I think the sky was crying too, for it had become a very dark and quiet, rainy day for our departure. Neither of us could even speak for several hours.

Kamie and I absolutely could not absorb the contrast in our heads that we were actually *in* the United States but we had just talked with six of 16 surviving family members, U.S. citizens whose Golden Years had been so horribly tarnished.

Kamie reminded me about what Nancy O'Brien had said. Nancy said, "It's really, really hard to put my hand on my heart and say, I pledge allegiance to the flag of the United States of America...but I still do."

*The battle, sir, is not to the strong alone, it
is to the vigilant, the active, the brave.*

*— Patrick Henry
American Revolutionary Lawmaker and Patriot
(1736 - 1799)*

Chapter 16
Champions of Activism:
Upstate Citizens for Equality (UCE)

It was only 175 miles between Salamanca and the Village of Union Springs, our next stop in New York, but it seemed like an endless drive. Kamie and I were physically exhausted—this was the 24th day of our 26-day journey. We were emotionally drained from capturing on film the sheer amount of heartache, betrayal, and shattered dreams of so many families all along our way.

We are both true believers in the United States, but this road trip experience was instilling a numbing realization that our level of trust in our government was in acute pain. It was a relief to turn south off of the New York State Thruway, and slowly wend our way over to Route 90 that follows the Eastern Shore of Cayuga Lake.

Where the Salamanca experience was a horrendous injury inflicted upon a few, the Central New York experience demonstrates the *massive scope* and potential injury of federal Indian policy upon millions. It seems to be a never-ending story with so many in-state and out-of-state Indian tribes seriously on the political move for land and gambling territories. The tribes compete against each other now for "ancestral lands" long ignored, and have caught the undivided and deplorably willing attention of all New York elected officials, but for a very brave few.

The game played in New York is similar to the recent offer made to Colorado by the Cheyenne and Arapaho Indians. These tribes suddenly developed a longing for 27 million acres of *their* "ancestral lands" in Colorado, nearly half of the State, but were simultaneously willing to forego its land claim in exchange for

500 acres near Denver and a behemoth Class III tribal casino. New York tribes set the model, and tribes across the country have rushed to imitate this game and to capture the booty that might come with it.

We knew we were nearing Dick and Connie Tallcot's place in the Village of Union Springs when we started seeing large signs along the roadway announcing that we were definitely in the Seneca-Cayuga Land Claim area. Some were big, some small, but they were everywhere—in front yards, at intersections, and there was even an enormous Red-White-Blue sign that filled an entire barn wall. It said:

NO SOVEREIGN NATION!
NO RESERVATION!
CAYUGA-INDIAN LAND CLAIM!
UPSTATE CITIZENS FOR EQUALITY!

It truly looked like the Fourth of July all year long, along the road into Union Springs. We knew the signs were the efforts of the Seneca-Cayuga Chapter of Upstate Citizens For Equality (UCE), of which Dick Tallcot is the Chairman. For years, Dick and Connie Tallcot owned the quaint little "Tallcot Bookshop" on Cayuga street, the main street of Union Springs. They've recently closed up the bookshop since both of their lives have been so consumed over the past eight years with just defending their little community and its right to exist and never be governed by a tribal government. I was sorry to hear that the bookshop was closed because the Tallcot bookshop was, for a long time, a great resource for information on federal Indian policy for many groups across the country.

When I think of Dick, I think of two things—a man who loves his pipe, and the slogan, "Fight Like Hell." The first time I received an email from the UCE group in New York, Dick had signed his email, with "Fight Like Hell!" a statement I initially felt was a bit aggressive. But six years of research and 6,000 miles wiser, I more fully understand. Literally millions of New Yorkers are losing sleep at night, worrying about the future of their businesses, homes and communities, and some of these folks are keenly aware of what happened to their neighbors, not far away in Salamanca.

While Connie was fixing dinner, Dick took us on a tour of the local area. With video camera in hand, we drove to a site where the local tribe wishes to build a massive casino. He showed us the wildlife refuge right next door and explained how allowance of such a monstrosity would surely cause irreparable loss. Kamie related to Dick that in her community in La Center, Washington, the Cowlitz tribe and Mohegan Sun Casino have proposed the very same kind of super-sized casino on a site directly between *two* pristine wildlife refuges there. The mother's milk of Mother Earth seems to play a sad second fiddle to the casino cash cows.

Dick and Connie were among thousands of people threatened with possible eviction notices when two tribes began to lay claim to what the Tallcots describe as "most of Central New York." Neither tribe had indicated any interest in the area for over 200 years, did not live in the communities, and were essentially mimicking other tribes pursuing land claims.

Dick then drove us to a site for a second proposed casino, just a few feet from the parking lot of the local high school. Union Springs is a small, and very old, health resort town, of about 1,000 people, only 2 of whom claimed to be American Indian in the 2000 U.S. Census. The Village was settled before the War of 1812 and has survived over 200 years, with storefronts and homes scattered along Cayuga Street (Route 90), and a very few side streets. It was turning dusk so we ended the local tour and headed back to the Tallcot home.

Connie is an attractive, petite woman with a great capacity for major community event planning and organizing. But what we thought she did best on this particular evening was a simple home-cooked pork chop dinner that perked our spirits up considerably. We asked Connie when she and Dick first got into the grassroots activist efforts.

"I think it was about August of 1998 that I heard a BIA administrator, Kevin Gover, at a hearing, announce that property owners in the Cayuga Indian land claim could either leave the area or lease from the tribes," Connie said.

Considering that we had just come from Salamanca that gave Kamie and me the shivers.

Connie said, "We discovered that discussions were under way for a settlement whereby property transfers could possibly take place at the courthouse and the landowners losing their property really wouldn't know anything about it until it was too late, or at least that was the strong rumor floating around then, and that fear got us into action," she continued.

"We've always been active in campaigns and elections, but since 1998 we've been seriously focused on federal Indian policy," said Dick. "A few of us locals started meeting in the back room of the Tallcot Bookshop. I attended only because we lived upstairs, and then I got elected secretary at the first meeting because nobody else would do it, " he continued. "The group decided that it was best to take Executive notes with no details of when and where we met, and to only list motions passed, no names, no discussion, because we weren't real sure what we were up against. Paranoia over the feds was obvious."

"We had no money, but passed the hat. One of our members donated time and money to send out post cards to veterans in the area, asking for memberships and donations. Another member, Russ Wheeler, suggested we join another group that had already formed in the Oneida Indian land claim area; that way, we would be part of a group that was several thousand strong."

The Upstate Citizens for Equality chapters have been tireless and truly dedicated in their insistence that citizens be heard and property rights protected. The Tallcots told us that in 1999 they held the first public informational meeting on the Seneca-Cayuga land claim in twenty years, and signed up 1,200 people at that meeting. The citizens were the last ones to know that the Court had appointed legal counsel to represent them, as well as some larger business and utility clients, so this first public information meeting surfaced a conflict. The corporate client interests were strictly financial, and many were willing to quickly settle with the tribes; however, local homeowners whose very futures were on the line, wanted no settlement whatsoever.

Dick filled us in on some background that keeps the Tallcots so seriously attentive to current events in their area. "In March of

1999 Connie and I took a road trip through the Onondaga Indian reservation, near Syracuse, then we went on to the Mohawk reservation at St. Regis, NY and saw the swamp lands that were being filled in for a casino.

"From there we went on to northern Vermont to ask about the Abenacki Sioux attempts at recognition and land claims, and then on to Connecticut.

"In Connecticut we asked questions of the business owners, people on the street, and politicians. We met the Wadecki's, the Knights, and Wes Johnson, then Mayor of Ledyard, Connecticut."

Dick continued, "Both of us came back from that trip more depressed than either of us had ever been in our lives. Looking back I would have to say the depression came from discovering the depth, the extent, and the high level of widespread corruption and deceit in politics. Federal politicians and the Governor, if not several of the governor's staff, and many local politicians were heavily involved in sacrificing the people in exchange for a buck or a favor. The Town of Preston came close to having a pristine neighborhood, built in the 1700's, taken by eminent domain and razed in exchange for a super highway to the Pequot casino.

"Several landowner lawsuits against the state resulted with one group discovering an endangered species bird along the route, and the state finally gave up. Although several people organized to do what they could, more felt hopeless as the only buyers for the properties they owned were the tribe. Some ended up owing a mortgage to the bank that was more than their property was now worth. That's how one gets evicted without being evicted.

"We came home. I reported our trip at the next UCE meeting and basically broke down. I told our Union Springs friends and neighbors that we just *had* to stop these settlements at all costs— no matter what the cost."

I, too, had met Ledyard's former Mayor Wes Johnson, and place him, much like the local elected officials in rural communities in Idaho, among the most honest, ethical and courageous elected officials I've met. It is getting increasingly difficult and rare, to find elected officials like Wes.

Being from the Northwest, Kamie and I were just stunned to learn of the apprehension, fear, depression, and financial losses from legal fees—years and years of, literally, thousands of people doing absolutely everything they could to get local and state elected officials to consider their rights. Their efforts fell then, and still do, on the deaf ears of those ignominious "casino coin-operated-elected officials. The sheer scope and enormity of the political and gambling-revenue influence that tribal governments have over elected officials in many states, and most certainly in New York, is near catastrophic, and the spawn of the Indian Gaming Regulatory Act is just getting rolling in 2005.

The Tallcots have a quiet home above the bookshop, as in the old spirit of "shopkeeper quarters" upstairs, in an historic little building in the heart of the tiny Village of Union Springs. We actually relaxed and watched a little television that evening, for one of the first times on the whole trip. Or, I should say, we stared at the television, probably oblivious to what was playing, while thinking of what the Tallcots were telling us, and about the upcoming day of filming conversations with several Union Springs, and Town of Aurelius officials and citizens.

Dick is a Union Springs Public Works employee, but after his 40-hour work week, he spends countless hours in research, letter-writing, networking with peers across the country—he has been a large part of the networking that has built the UCE organizations and connected them with similar organizations throughout the land. I asked Dick whether citizens were experiencing individual pressures or harassment, as had been the case in other states.

"Tribal officials have not harassed citizens here," Dick said. "They just absolutely ignore us. We don't matter to them at all. They spend the bulk of their time and money lobbying local, state and federal politicians, and it has really paid off for them. Now our politicians ignore us too."

Are you still "fightin' like Hell, Dick?" Kamie asked. He replied, "We *have* to; we've got tribal casinos going in next to schools, local businesses giving up or folding up, and tribal land claims springing up like tics on a dog. We just have to hold on, somehow."

Upstate Citizens for Equality has three separate chapters—the Madison-Oneida chapter organized in August of 1997 to give landowners faced with a major Oneida Indian Land Claim a voice in what will determine their future. David Vickers is its current President and has been outspoken and frequently quoted in area newspapers.

Then in 1999 the Cayuga-Seneca chapter was formed for the same reasons, to contend with the Seneca-Cayuga land claim. Dick Tallcot is Chair and Russ Wheeler is Vice-chair of this chapter. Both of these New Yorkers are also active in the national voices that struggle with federal Indian policy.

More recently in 2002, the Niagara Frontier Chapter of UCE formed, also focused on land claims. Daniel Warren is the President of this Chapter.

The three chapters of UCE create a broad, grass-roots base upon which citizens can monitor New York elected officials that are all too willing to hand over Upstate New York to Indian tribes. UCE is as equally frustrated with state and federal elected officials as they are with aggressive tribal government activities.

UCE has truly matured, established a credible track record and insists upon a voice in federal, state and tribal decisions that so dramatically affect their homes and communities. Their position on Indian land claims is posted on their website, and states:

It is the position and opinion of Upstate Citizens for Equality and its members that any purchase by the State of New York of Indian land that occurred prior to 1790 or between 1793 and 1834 are valid notwithstanding any court decisions to the contrary. For the following reasons the State of New York was not prohibited from acquiring such lands and extinguishing Indian title thereto.

Speaking of land claims, here are a few, but not nearly all, of the Indian Land Claims currently hanging over the heads of business and property owners in approximately 38 affected counties of the State of New York. Scanning through the list should quickly illustrate the absolute intention of the federal government, with generous assistance of Governor George Pataki, and most New York elected officials, to spread *tribalism* as a replacement governing system throughout all rural areas of the State:

Oneida Indian Land Claim. Ray Halbritter recently testified before a State Judiciary Standing Committee in March 2005 that the Oneidas filed the first and largest Indian land claim in 1970. Halbritter vigorously opposes out-of-state tribes from Wisconsin and Oklahoma, entering either the land or gambling business in New York. The Oneidas claim includes 250,000 acres of land, and was upheld by the US Supreme Court by a 5-4 decision in 1985. The Oneidas initially wanted to name 20,000 families as defendants within this area near Fort Stanwix, and 15 miles away from the Oriskany Battlefield—two sites of historical Revolutionary War events.

Mohawk Indian Land Claim. In May 2003, Governor Pataki partially settled this claim that allows the Tribe to acquire as part of its reservation up to 7,005 acres of lands, within designated areas, by purchase of contiguous parcels from willing sellers utilizing the proceeds of the settlement. In addition, the Power Authority shall convey to the Tribe the "Long Sault" and "Croil" Islands and ninety-five acres of land identified as the "Massena Point East Parcel." And for good measure, the tribe receives $30 million to be paid, one-half each, by the federal and state governments, along with a guaranteed state-tribe gaming compact for a Class III casino, and numerous tax exemptions and advantages.

Oklahoma Seneca-Cayuga and New York Cayuga Indian Land Claim. Filed twenty-five years ago in 1980, this claim includes 7,000 (taxed, deeded) parcels that are home to 21,000 residents. The Cayuga Indians claim to have about 450 enrolled members, 150 actually living in the State. Tallcot says that he's unaware of any tribal Cayugas that live within a hundred miles of Union Springs. The tribes have received a judgment for $250,000 for the loss of 64,000 acres, in a ruling by Judge Neal P. McCurn, a ruling being appealed.

The Cayuga Indians fought on the side of the British when the colonists sought freedom from England in the American Revolutionary War. They also fought with the British and against the Americans in the War of 1812. Yet the roots of their substantial land claims lie in lands the tribes claim from original land sales that *pre*-date these historical events.

Stockbridge-Munsee Indian Land Claim. The Wisconsin Stockbridge-Munsee land claim – six square miles – is surrounded by the Oneida Nation of New York's 250,000-acre land claim. The Oneida Indian Nation that does not desire to have an out-of-state tribe co-located in its neighborhood disputes this land claim, of course.

Onondaga Indian Land Claim. The most recent Onondaga Land Claim is 10 miles wide, 40 miles long, includes 4 million acres upon which 875,000 New York residents live and work, in 11 counties: Broome, Cortland, Cayuga, Chenango, Jefferson, Lewis, Madison, Onondaga, Oswego, Tioga and Tompkins. The area takes in land in New York from its Pennsylvania to Canadian border, and includes large cities such as

Syracuse. Sid Hall, the Onondaga's spiritual leader, has been quoted in local newspapers saying that the tribe does not want money or to evict landowners, it simply wants to control "the water, land and air." These are the three essentials of life itself.

These are just *some*, but not all of the "lets-swap-land-for-casinos" game disrupting and dismantling Central New York State, and towns that had been quiet, and believed all was well for over 200 years. Once the casino is on the ground, then the revenue to acquire more land is Phase Two. We'll look more closely at this phase in the next chapter.

Seneca County Supervisor, Richard Ricci, who serves as Land Claim Committee Chairman, reports that 38 counties in New York are under Indian land claim clouds, including bordering counties affected directly by land claims.

In April 2005, Keller George, president of the United South and Eastern Tribes (USET) recently testified in an Albany, New York hearing, "In at least 12 states Indian tribes are seeking to move across state lines to take advantage of lucrative gaming markets. In most cases, these efforts are being funded by 'shadowy' developers who underwrite the litigation expenses, lobbyist fees, and even the cost of land in exchange for a cut of the profits."

There is no better confirmation of Keller George's statement than the actions of another "George" referred to by his rural New York constituents as "King" George Pataki, the Governor. In November 2004, Governor Pataki announced a proposed settlement with four Indian tribes—the Wisconsin Stockbridge-Munsee, the Oklahoma Seneca-Cayuga, the Wisconsin Oneida, and the New York Cayuga Indian tribes—all to be granted a casino in the Catskills, Sullivan County, in exchange for claimed lands.

Then in February 2005, Governor Pataki announced an additional proposed settlement with the New York Mohawks, adding a fifth future casino in tiny Sullivan County, whose population is 73,600 residents, of whom only 197 (.002%) report to be American Indian in the 2000 U. S. census database. Resolving these land claims would remove the tribal sovereignty clouds over an additional 300,000 acre in New York, at the expense of imposing five (5) tribal casinos into Sullivan County. Sullivan County citizens have been completely overwhelmed as to where to even start to oppose such a socio-economic calamity foisted upon them.

Sullivan County is described as "idyllic," having "unsurpassed quality of life" on its website. There's a gentle photo of an old rock-based, covered bridge. One has to wonder how well the old bridge will handle up to 45,000 cars daily, and what will happen to "idyllic?" In an April 2005 news article, the strongest local reaction among elected officials and the county residents is "how many jobs will the five casinos bring, and how much money can we all get for our social services, animal control, county nursing, the hospital, and so on?

A likely answer is that tons of money redirected from the local Sullivan County tax base into private tribal government coffers will also correspondingly, overwhelm and replace the voice and authority of local government in Sullivan County. The change will be slow, but sure—from the traditional, "of the people," representative form of government, to a closed, tribalism system, to which Sullivan County residents will be subject, but not participatory.

In the long term, the few remaining taxed parcels in Sullivan County—those *not* acquired with revenue from five tribes with five casinos, and placed into federal (tax-exempt) "trust,"—will experience substantial tax *increases* on the remaining privately-owned parcels, as well as likely increases of local sales taxes and other levies to compensate for the siphoning off of Sullivan County's existing tax base. Yes, the casinos will certainly create jobs—but at what long term price, and under whose future governance do Sullivan County residents wish to submit?

The land claim tribes receive an amazing amount of assistance from what the UCE chapters call a "Wheel of Influence" in a handout that they distributed in mid-2004. The flier replicates a roulette wheel with "King" (Governor) George Pataki at its center. Around the wheel is a description of alleged *influences* so helpful to the land claim tribes:

- State Senator Michael F. Nozzolio (D-54th) is an affiliate of Harris Beach, the law firm representing the counties. William Dorr, attorney for Harris Beach LLP, represents the counties in the land claim.
- Congressman Sherwood L. Bochleit (R-NY) was approached by former President Clinton for his vote for passing NAFTA. Congressman Boehlert was promised that Ray Halbritter would be named as the recognized spokesperson of the Oneida Indian Nation by the Bureau of Indian Affairs, even over to objections of the Oneida Indian Clan Mothers.
- Jane Rossi, wife of Ray Halbritter has been one of Governor Pataki's top fundraisers.
- Tom Wilmot, owner of Wilmorite Corporation is the developer for the Seneca-Cayuga Tribes and utilizes Harris Beach for its representation.
- Ray Halbritter, CEO of Oneida Indian Nation has loaned $1.3 million to the Cayuga Indian Nation. The Seneca Tribe ranks third in the State for funneling monies through lobbyists for political influence.
- John O'Mara has a consulting agreement with a Syracuse law firm Hiscock and Barclay, which has a state contract to handle Indian land claims. Mr. O'Mara serves as Chief Commissioner to Governor Pataki, and represents the Governor in casino negotiations. John O'Mara has a lobbying firm with former Senator Al D'Amato, a firm that lobbies on behalf of Indian tribes.

One more point: Business owners, landowners and residents throughout central New York are legitimately concerned about their future; however, there are tendencies among media, especially those located near such lucrative advertising clients as tribal casinos, to describes persons who oppose government decisions, as "anti-Indian" when the issue has nothing to do with race, but simply is about jurisdiction, governance and economy. The general effects of the tribal land claims can be reported as follows:

- Loss to municipalities of state and local sales tax revenue. Taxation of non-Indians from tribal businesses is a confrontational conflict between the tribes and the state.
- Loss to taxpaying businesses and loss of incentive for new tax paying businesses to start up because their is no way to compete with tribal businesses.
- Loss to municipalities and school districts of property tax revenue. No federal reimbursement to municipalities or state for taking of land. Tribal contributions, if any, to municipalities & school districts are a small fraction of what property tax revenue would be.
- Loss in quality of life and increase in animosity between tribal and non-tribal citizens due to double standards created by Federal Indian Policy.

Dick had arranged for several people to drop by the Bookshop the next morning for informal interviews. Among them was Edward J. Ide, Jr., Aurelius Town Supervisor, who confirmed what Tallcot had mentioned the evening before about being ignored by elected officials.

"I talked to my State Senator once," Ed said. "I asked him what happened to equal rights under the law, or the whole civil rights movement? I asked him if the State Legislature stands for equality or not? The Senators response was, 'Well, it ain't perfect,' and then went back to eating his lunch."

Ed then added, "The tribes keep going back a couple of hundred years. We were not there a couple hundred years ago. Why are we responsible for what happened then? And nobody that was there then is alive *now* so why do the Indians keep bringing this stuff up?"

Dick's voice would sometimes tremble with emotion, when he pointed out more than once that many tribes in the eastern states do not consider themselves to be American citizens. We had heard this about the Senecas in Salamanca, and were hearing it again. Dick said, "American Indians have the same declaration of citizenship that was passed by Congress in 1924 but they renounce their citizenship. They are a good neighbor but they refuse to pledge to the flag; they will not lower the American flag to half-mast when it's called for in the rest of the country, and they continue to fly their own tribal flags higher than the U.S. flag."

Kamie commented to Dick and me during a break that she always thought New Yorkers were stereotypically *tough*, that they would not put up with things like eviction notices, unfair tax increases to support tax-free enterprises, unconstitutional discrimination, or forceful placement of tribal casinos in unsuspecting communities.

Dick responded, "we're staying tough and tenacious, and UCE is growing in numbers, strength and credibility, but we can't line the pockets of our own elected officials like these tribal governments do." Then he added, "The horrible irony is that it is *my* tax dollar funding tribal governments who then line the pockets of our political system to receive *more* funding, programs and tax-exempt lands, that is also funded by *my* tax dollar; then the net effect is that my own taxes go *up,* as my civil rights and ability to be legitimately heard by an elected official goes *down*. It's a win-win for tribalism, and a lose-lose for democracy, as I see it."

"Dick, you can vote those elected officials out of office," I said. "That just has to be done by an educated voter population in Central New York." I no sooner said this, than I realized what an uphill battle New Yorkers have to do some serious political house cleaning.

"Well, we're trying like hell to educate voters," Dick responded, but families are busy, or just plain apathetic, or would rather not think about these dark futures, or worse, have terminal cases of apathy."

"It is so very, very frustrating," he continued. "We are promoting tribalism here and trying to create one nation out of tribalism in Iraq. Go figure."

That last statement caused me to remember an article published in September 2002, when Ed Ide, Jr. had written a letter to then Homeland Security Director, Tom Ridge. That land we had toured, near the pristine wildlife refuge and now being proposed as a casino site, contains important, regional infrastructure. Ed was calling to the attention of Homeland Security that a 36-inch transcontinental natural gas pipe line owned by Tenneco originates in the Gulf of Mexico, then goes right through the land being claimed by the Seneca-Cayuga for a casino area, and extends northeasterly all the way to Concord, Massachusetts.

Also, the Niagara Mohawk Power Corporation has two high-voltage transmission lines running through the parcel, and the Buckeye Pipeline Company has a 10-inch liquid petroleum pipe nearby. National security is not the only concern. Cayuga county ratepayers and others throughout the service industry of these utilities can expect to see monthly bills skyrocket when the tribes impose their "franchise fees" for allowing utility infrastructure to pass through their lands.

In the news article about Ed's letter to Tom Ridge, it was pointed out that Ed reminded the Homeland Security Director of past incidences where the New York State Thruway and Interstate 81 were closed because of "armed disputes" between the state and tribal governments. The article quotes Ed as saying, "I see no reason why these sovereign territories could not be a threat to national security." In light of Tallcot's comments regarding tribal members disclaiming American citizenship, and frequently expressing adversarial attitudes toward Americans of other cultures, there may be cause for concern in New York and many other states.

Later in the afternoon, Ed would say, "Everybody feels that they are trying to make amends for the injustices that happened centuries ago. Is not the resolution of those injustices just as unjust or more, than the original injustice?

As Aurelius Town Supervisor, Ed is probably relieved to hear that in April 2005, a Seneca-Cayuga tribal decision was made to pay a back property tax bill pf $68,000 plus interest and penalties, in Cayuga County and to drop its plans for a high-stakes bingo hall in Aurelius. The tribe's decision follows a March 2005 U.S. Supreme Court decision, the *Sherrill* case that will be a key focus in the next chapter. The Village of Union Springs is hopeful that tribal back taxes of $67,000 owed on four properties there, will also be paid.

There are a few thousand tribal members in New York claiming nearly half of the State's land base, and affecting the lives and properties of millions of New Yorkers. There are a few hundred tribal members claiming nearly half of the land in Colorado, affecting thousands of Colorado citizens and properties. Perhaps this illustrates what Ed is alluding to when he asks if more injustice today is the solution to yesterday's injustice.

"Dick, what are the biggest obstacles that UCE faces?" Kamie asked. "We have educated ourselves and find that we have also had to educate elected officials of every level, because when we would initially speak with our legislators, they would initially assume, from their own lack of knowledge, that we were just anti-Indian, and that is wrong. It is sort of like people with a life-threatening disease quite often become more knowledgeable than the doctors that are treating them. We're *there*."

We did not meet Scott Peterman, another prominent UCE member, on this visit, but he recently sent a letter to the Republican National Committee, in response to a funding solicitation. Federal Indian policy is bipartisan. His letter could just as easily have been directed to the Democratic party, or corporate non-profit funding solicitors. Peterman's comments illuminate the mood of many New Yorkers, and probably many other American across the country. Here's what he said in March 2005, when asked for a financial contribution:

Dear Mr. Reitzer,

In today's mail, I received a request from you to confirm my RNC membership and make a donation. I am sorry to report that I am unable to do this because the present administration has turned a blind eye to the serious problems facing millions of American citizens because of profoundly flawed "Federal Indian Policy.

I live in the Oneida Indian land claim area of Upstate New York and have seen my federal courts revive 200 year old claims against New York Counties that weren't even in existence at the time that the state supposedly violated federal statutes prohibiting the purchase of Indian lands without federal approval. Moreover, I have experienced having my own Justice Department join the Indian tribes in an attempt to sue me and thousands of my neighbors for eviction and damages for something the state may or may not have done over 200 years ago!

Numerous New York Indian land claims based on alleged violations of federal statutes known as the Trade & Intercourse Acts continue to destroy the social, economic, and political fabric of our communities. Our congressmen and senators sit mute, sucking up tribal campaign donations, while our citizenry divides more and more with each passing day.

I, as well as a number of my friends and neighbors, have written to President Bush concerning this problem. To the best of my knowledge, none were even acknowledged let alone answered.

When I write to one of my federal representatives about the Indian land claims, my requests are passed on to some "Acting" official of the BIA who is usually a "Native American" and has no interest in me or my constitutional rights.

I now hear that the Hawaiians want to be federally recognized as "tribes of indigenous peoples" so they too can have casino monopolies, special federal handouts, and exemptions from our taxes and laws. Where is this to stop?

If you have bothered to read this far, I'm sure you can see why none of my hard earned, after-tax money, is going to go to those who could, but refuse to do something about this catastrophe.

Send any further requests for donations to CEO Raymond Halbritter of the Oneida Indian Nation of New York. He's the one you seem to be working for.

No respect left in me,

Scott E. Peterman

The UCE chapters are diligent fundraisers through community can-and-bottle recycling drives, barn-sized yard sales, protests, frequent picketing, and community education presentations. UCE people know that this *is* an endurance contest and that increasing an informed registered voter base is crucial. These folks stay in motion. They stay in constant motion, as is required when citizens are the last to be informed and the first to be affected by the secretive liaisons between our federal government and their new *political money machines*. The *trust* relationship between the federal government and Indian tribes as their dependent *wards* has come at the cost of alienation of the ability of American citizens to trust what remains of its own government.

Ed Ide, Jr. noted, "These policies start to breed on a lot of the basic civil rights issues. You have a group of people whose sole basis for that group is their ethnic origin, and then you create a special set of rules to go with them. I don't see that ever *not* being a source of friction. I mean that if you take any group of people and start treating a select group differently than the rest, there is going to be a problem."

Ed's perspective comment goes to the heart of this issue. This is not about ethnicity, as much as it is about human behavior, and general fairness. We have a federal government behaving badly.

Swinish gluttony ne'er looks to heaven amid his gorgeous feast, but with besotted, base ingratitude, crams and blasphemes his feeder.

— Milton

Chapter 17
City of Sherrill and Turning Stone Casino:
David and Goliath

Located almost in the center of New York State—half way between Syracuse and Utica—the City of Sherrill is recently the center of national attention in 2005, for its valiant efforts to preserve its community integrity. The diminutive town has a little over 3,000 people, and no less than *ten* lovely, manicured parks to serve them. The cheery and helpful quarterly newsletter from City Hall reminds their residents, "If you are going to be away for a week or more, notify the Police Department so a check of your residence can be made."

Ongoing summer concerts are held in Reilly-Mumford Park, named for two beloved local police officers killed on duty in 1969. The expansive lawns of the park surround a large red-roofed, and white-railed gazebo. Skating rinks, athletic fields, football and soccer fields, tennis and basketball courts are well appointed and scattered throughout this smallest (two and one-half square miles) City in New York. Sherrill's Knot Hole Club, active for over 25 years, is solely focused on delivery of incredible athletic and recreational programs for approximately a thousand young people, fortunate enough to call Sherrill home.

The town history includes such special little claims to fame as the fact that "George Herman 'Babe' Ruth," pitched a baseball game in one of their parks in 1910, and in the 1940's Carmen Basillio, a former two-time welterweight and middleweight champion, had numerous fights at Sherrill's Noyes Park.

"You know, we have a commitment to our people, that when they move here, they see what they have, they know that this is a quality community, and that there is zoning, and they know that we enforce our rules and regulations," said David O. Barker,

Sherrill's City Manager since1994. "Our residents have expectations, and we meet them."

By some measure, Sherrill is one of the younger communities in New York, incorporated as late as 1916, and less than one hundred years old. Its origins derive from mid-1800, however, with the Oneida Community founded by a utopian religious leader, John Humphrey Noyes, and his followers.

The Oneida Mansion is an historic site in the community and offers beautiful apartments, overnight lodging, a library, historical tours of the mansion and the lush 33 acres within which the mansion is showcased. This historic group of religious "Perfectionists" lived communally and was renowned for production of canned fruits, animal traps, silk thread and silverware—the root origin of Oneida Ltd., a leading name in tableware.

The community is not a particularly wealthy area, with a median household income of less than $50,000, but the 2000 U.S. census reports that only seven families live below the poverty line. Sherrill is a town that takes good care of itself. This is immediately observable to a total stranger, just passing through. Sherrill is the *David* of a true legal battle of *David v. Goliath* proportions.

In early October 2004, when Kamie and I were given a tour of Sherrill, we were struck by a large, 4' x 8' white, wood sign, located on a well-tended front lawn of a bright yellow home, with crisp white trim. The sign said, in bold black letters:

MY HOME
MY LAND
MY GOD
WHAT HAPPENED?

What happened is the *Goliath* of this story. Not far from Sherrill, about three miles as the crow flies, standing 253 feet in the air, with 19 floors, about 200,000 square feet of space that offers over 2,400 slot machines, and over 100 game tables, stands the Turning Stone Casino—the millennium *castle*, the manifested dream of Oneida Indian Nation Chief Executive Officer, Ray Halbritter.

The glistening, glass and mirrored exterior of the Tower that is the Turning Stone Resort-Casino absolutely dwarfs everything around it, with the next nearest tall building for a radius of 40-miles being the 10-story Madison County seat.

In 1979, the Secretary of the Interior published the first list of federally recognized tribes, which included the Oneida Indian Nation (OINNY) of New York. Today the OINNY, has an enrollment of approximately 1,000 members, many of whom are traditional Oneidas who not only do not recognize CEO Halbritter as a legitimate chief, but have vigorously exerted efforts to have him disclaimed as their Chief, to no avail thus far.

By 2002 the OINNY had acquired 14,000 acres of land adjacent to the Turning Stone and non-contiguous parcels scattered throughout Madison and Oneida counties. By 2005 the OINNY acquired 18,000 acres within these two counties. All of these parcels are situated within the 250,000 acres subject to a 1970 Oneida Indian Land Claims compensation action that is yet to be resolved.

Annual revenue figures for this Class III tribal casino vary from $70 to $167 million in recent years, with rumors of 50% profit margins. In its 2004 Annual Report, the OINNY reported that its "total expenditures on consumable goods and services totaled over $342 million, "almost one and a half times more than the amount New York State budgets annually to run its State Legislature, $200 million." This is an enormous amount of goods purchased annually upon which little, if any, sales tax is collected or paid.

The position taken by the OINNY when acquiring properties on the current tax rolls of these two counties, is that once acquired by the OINNY, these former "ancestral" lands become new "Indian country" and are therefore not subject to tax or regulation by local, county, or state government. Halbritter takes this one step farther. He has refused to place any of the 18,000 parcels into federal "trust," either. Thus, CEO Halbritter has established a veritable *kingdom* within the two counties that is answerable to no one—not the counties, nor the State of New York, nor the United States—a separate, sovereign nation that makes its own rules as it goes along, and follows no one else's.

Only two of the OINNY parcels were acquired in Sherrill. The City of Sherrill determined that OINNY *was*, in fact, answerable for property taxes. Sherrill believed that if a couple parcels could be purchased, more could surely follow, and its community could become seriously disrupted by properties that fail to comply with local tax or zoning regulations. Sherrill wasn't about to sit idly by while *patches* of "sovereign Indian country" dismantled what they work so hard to preserve—a quality community where everyone knows the rules, respects them and abides by them.

In 1997, Sherrill sent a property tax bill to OINNY, as they would every other property owner in the City. OINNY declined to pay the annual property taxes. As this debt to Sherrill continued in delinquency, Sherrill filed tax liens on the parcels. The City Commissioners as well as the entire community stood firmly behind the City Manager in all actions respecting this dilemma.

In February 2000 the OINNY took Sherrill into federal court, seeking to prevent the City from collecting property delinquent or future property taxes on OINNY properties. In a casual, serendipitous, encounter, Dave Barker chatted with a prominent New York legal counsel, Ira Sacks, explaining the city's legal issues. Mr. Sacks, of Esther S. Trakinksi, Gursky & Partners, LLP, so believed in the merits of the case and the needs of the local government that he agreed to take the case on behalf of City of Sherrill, on a *pro bono* basis, charging for direct, out-of-pocket expenses only.

The litigation proceeded through the federal judicial system, with the City losing in the U.S. District Court in June 2001. Sherrill also was defeated in the 2nd Circuit Court of Appeals in July 2003. Courageously, the little City had pursued appeals to every decision, including its last hope—an appeal to the U.S. Supreme Court that was filed in 2004.

The Supreme Court proceeded to ask a former Solicitor General, Ted Olson, for an opinion as to whether the case should be heard by the Highest Court. Even Senator Charles Schumer and New York Congressman John McHugh encouraged the U.S. Solicitor General to support consideration of Sherrill's case. But in early June 2004, Olson advised the Supreme Court *not* to hear the case.

On June 28, 2004 the Supreme Court decided otherwise, and *accepted* the case for review. This would become "the little City that could."

It was this incredible story of a tiny town and a politically overwhelming tribal power in Central New York that was flying under the radar across country, except for those who closely watch federal Indian policy. The issues involved with the case held substantial consequence for both the victor and the vanquished.

This is why Kamie and I put Sherrill on our route. It was the last stop of our journey. We were guests of the Bachmans who live in a neighboring community, Vernon, New York. Judy Bachman is not affiliated with any New York organizations, but is locally vigilant, and serves as Vice-Chair of a national organization, Citizens Equal Rights Alliance (CERA).

Something happens to me when I'm spending time on the grounds of the Bachman home in Vernon, New York. The high, deep and thick foliage around the perimeter of their eight acres replicates my childhood visions of historical spaces and events. I have visited the Bachmans twice before and this strange "Spirit of '76" just encompasses me when I'm there.

I look out among the thickets and expect to see a colonial soldier or an Indian step out of the brush. Corny as it seems, I am a child of the West Coast, and it is 200 years younger than the East Coast. The lands of all of Upstate New York just whisper history at me and I revel in our country's formation and struggles that occurred in New York and the original Thirteen Colonies.

Kamie had never been to New York so the beauty of the rural landscapes and historical spaces were a special treat for her too.

Fred and Judy Bachman's home was built in 1854. They've beautifully preserved the original home, and so gracefully expanded upon it. It was once a rural farm, and now, through years of effort and loving maintenance it seems to be a very special private park. The Bachmans constructed a large, lovely pond on the property, an ideal setting for morning coffee or just quiet repose.

Fred just baffles me. He seems so genuinely at ease, rather carefree and ever available to help someone or chat, and yet it's clear by the home and the grounds that he also must work tirelessly, including a hobby of several antique cars stored in a spotless barn-garage. Honestly, you *could* eat off of the floor.

The Bachman's property is within view of the Turning Stone Casino, and is rapidly being surrounded by lands acquired by Ray Halbritter and the Oneida Indian Nation.

Fred and Judy were high school sweethearts. They grew up in Oneida County, New York during an era when belief and trust in the federal government was well placed, or so they thought. They married in 1961, raised three children, worked very hard, participated in their community, served their church, saved money and retired early with high hopes of enjoying the "last third" of their lives. Their goal was to live the American dream, with travel and leisure being the order of the day.

Kamie asked Judy, "When did you and Fred realize that something was happening to your community? When did you and Fred first get involved in jurisdictional and political processes?"

"Somewhere in the '90s, slowly at first, we became aware of land being purchased near us, that it was being called "Indian country," and taken out of the tax base," Judy replied. "That piqued our curiosity and here we are today—no vacations, no leisure—no such thing as pleasant, or stress-free retirement years."

We had a lovely dinner and evening with Fred and Judy, and were told that a full day had been planned of meetings with elected and administrative officials, and a substantial tour of the Madison County area. The following morning we loaded into the Bachman car and were driven by an extraordinary number of vacant homes, and an equally large number of sizeable construction projects under way, all of which were OINNY enterprises.

As we passed one of the local businesses, Fred commented, "That guy opened up his business less than a year ago, but he just couldn't compete, and he's gone already. Nobody can beat the low prices the tribe can charge for just about anything."

Fred also noted, "They're buying up our neighbors so fast, and all the stuff around here. We're feeling like maybe we should just give up and move on, but we've got forty years of our life and a ton of hard work in our home." Their home and grounds truly reflects all forty years of wondrous landscaping and ongoing home improvement.

"Oh, you cannot give up. I hope it never, ever comes to that, Fred," I said.

"But the politics are just overwhelming," Fred said. No one hears us. It's getting to be that I'm thinking, what's the use?" That was another familiar phrase we were hearing at every stop on our road trip. We knew the Bachmans would never give up, but discouraging days do linger, sometimes.

"Ray Halbritter, appointed and sheltered by Congressman Sherwood L. Boehlert (R-NY) and assisted by federal Indian policy, is developing what can only be described as a "Monarchy." Judy went on, "Halbritter ignores the State of New York, ignores his own people, and refuses to place his properties into federal "trust," so he literally answers to no one."

Judy is nothing, if not straightforward. She's a dynamic and tenacious woman, very principled and fair-minded. Judy has been as upset with the way the Oneida Indian Chief treats his own tribal members as he does other people in the community. She's also a combination of classic Mother Hen with a professional demeanor that comes from years of work in title and property businesses, and nearly twenty years serving local government on planning commissions or boards of adjustment. Judy deeply worries about what's happening to her community and to the people of Oneida and Madison counties. She worries about the future of their seven grandchildren too.

"Ray's an equal-opportunity adversary," she said. "Traditional Oneida tribal members have truly suffered at his hand, while his kingdom grows, and now entire communities— Vernon, Sherrill, and Verona—are also feeling the results of his, literally, unchecked power run amok."

> *"A Nation is not conquered until the Hearts of its women*
> *are on the ground. Then it is done, no matter how brave*
> *its Warriors, nor how strong it's Weapons"*

> *—Cheyenne Saying*

The hearts of elderly Maisie Shenandoah, an Oneida Wolf Clan Mother in her 70s, and her daughters and their families, are not yet on the ground. Their hearts are also looking to the U.S. Supreme Court for justice. The traditional Oneidas have struggled bitterly with CEO Halbritter, and have paid dear consequences. Joanne Shenandoah was a 2005 Award Nominee for "Best Native American Music Album." She is a nationally revered American Indian singer and composer.

The traditional Oneida members, supported by the Six Nations of the Iroquois Confederacy, do not acknowledge Halbritter as a legitimate tribal leader. The Shenandoahs report on numerous websites that "in 1993 the Grand Council (of the Six Nations of the Iroquois Confederacy) sent notification to the Bureau of Indian Affairs of the procedure taken and the removal of Ray Halbritter," as chief of the Oneidas:

> The Grand Council of the Iroquois deposed Halbritter as Representative of the Oneida Nation and the decision was ratified by the Department of Interior. One day later the ratification by the Dept. of Interior was rescinded on the urging of Halbritter supporter and gaming advocate U.S. Rep. Sherwood Boehlert, and Halbritter was reinstated.

> In 1995 Halbritter closed the Longhouse to the residents of the Oneida Territory and gave the order to arrest anyone trying to gain entrance.

> Meetings of the Oneida Territory residents were moved to the Wolf Clan Mother's home, Maisie Shenandoah. There it was decided to remove Ray Halbritter from his position due the numerous injustices and violations against the People and the Great Law. Halbritter retaliated by labeling

the traditional Oneida dissidents and unenrolling them from the Tribal Rolls and therefore denying them jobs in the Nations Businesses, and tribal benefits.

In 1996 the traditional Oneida filed suit in Federal Court to have Halbritter removed from his position. The case was dismissed, but upon appeal at the Second Circuit, enough evidence was found to warrant an investigation by the U.S Department of Interior about Halbritter's status and the case was dismissed without prejudice.

The traditional Oneidas have been evicted from their homes, the homes demolished, the families forced to move away from their Oneida lands. A sister, Danielle Shenandoah, was treated particularly rough by Halbritter's regime, tribal jail and "court," and the voices of these families have been rendered "silent," disallowed to speak on any matters within the current OINNY administration. They are called the "Dissidents" which is a name frequently given to any enrolled tribal member that disagrees with current tribal leadership, legitimate or otherwise.

Danielle pursued legal action in the U.S. District Court, but that court ruled in August 2003 that the federal government recognizes Halbritter as "the official representative of the Oneida Indian Nations of New York," and that she had not evidenced sufficient violation of "substantial deprivation of liberty" as required in the Indian Civil Rights Act of 1968 (ICRA)—Danielle lost *this* battle.

In December 2004, the case of *Maisie Shenandoah v. Arthur Raymond Halbritter*, was submitted to the U.S. Supreme Court. On March 30, 2005 the Briefs of all parties were distributed for an anticipated Conference of April 15, 2005. If the U.S. Supreme Court calendars this case, it will ultimately determine the effectiveness, or not, of the Indian Civil Rights Act, and will address the issues occurring between the "federally recognized" OINNY Chief, Halbritter, and the traditional Oneidas who completely disclaim him as their Chief.

In the meantime, the Shenandoah women stay strong, Joanne Shenandoah continues to produce amazing music, filled with soul that reflects the courage of these few brave Oneida Indian women who have dared, at deplorable personal and financial risk, to speak up for their civil rights and for legitimacy of their people.

Traditional American Indians, such as the Shenandoah family, honor, practice and preserve the cherished heritage and traditions of their culture, with or without the federal government, and in this case, in *spite* of their own tribal government. The Shenandoah family pain reflects two critical points:

- Individual American Indians find little recourse within federal Indian policies that protect them from even corrupt tribal governments, as legitimately aggrieved tribal members.

- The Indian Civil Rights Act of 1968 lacks any enforcement and provides no viable protection to individual American Indians.

As Judy had mentioned, the communities of Sherrill, Vernon and Verona have all been significantly affected by acquisition of patchwork properties claimed to be "Indian Country," and accountable to neither Madison nor Oneida Counties.

Kamie and I met with Paul Miller, Madison County Planning Commissioner, and Rocco Di Veronica, Chairman of the Madison County Board of Supervisors. Initially, the OINNY had informed the county that it was just going to build a small bingo hall.

"Obviously, the size was considerably underestimated, but then again, so were the impacts," said Paul. "Individuals (tribal) who own those businesses are in large part, the elected leaders of the tribe, so you have the tribal government and the business people, being the same people." He then noted, "We need a balance to this. If it is a tribal government then act like a tribal government, but do not allow corporate entities to hide behind the veil of being a tribal "sovereign" entity. Tribal sovereignty was never intended for that."

Paul and Rocco were telling us about the serious fiscal impacts to Madison County occurring from a depleting property tax base, simultaneously with a depleting sales tax base.

Paul started giving us some background, as he said, "In 1998 before the Oneidas started vigorously expanding their purchases there were 32 gas stations in the land claim area. So now today, when it is all said and done, there are only 16 of 32 stores that are open, collecting and paying taxes. In addition to having only half of the stores remaining, these stores have lost significant business because they compete at a great disadvantage of 50 cents a gallon on taxes and $17-20 on a carton of cigarettes. That affects us."

I asked Paul to talk about the Oneida Indian Land Claim, and its affect upon Madison County.

"Paul said, "The land claim includes about 250,000 acre, which is about one-third of the west half of Oneida County and the northern half of Madison County. They started buying property and immediately declared the parcels to be a "sovereign nation," even though no sovereign nation had existed here for nearly 200 years. When this all started, the Oneida owned a small 32 acre site. Since then they have purchased thousands of acres of lands. So as this OINNY land purchase process grew, the idea of who has jurisdiction over these properties and over this land has become a real concern for us."

He then continued, "Because of the *checkerboard*, and because of the expansive nature of their acquisitions, it really is affecting us. It affects us today to the tune of about 1.2 million in annual property taxes. Over a century ago, the Oneidas sold their land to New York State. They were paid for it. Most of their people moved away, many to Canada, many to Wisconsin, yet now they try to assert ownership of these 250,000 acres as if nothing ever happened. Something *did* happen."

"Oneida (the city) is the biggest, most populated area in our county, a community of about 11,000. In Oneida you can no longer buy diesel fuel except from Indian gas stations. If you own a boat, the Oneidas, in addition to buying gas stations, have purchased a number of marinas on the eastern end of Oneida Lake. You cannot refuel your boat on the eastern half of Oneida

Lake, except at a tribal gas station. There are other marinas but they no longer have gas facilities because they have left the business, unable to compete, and they have to comply with extensive federal regulations about fuel around water. That is not a problem for the Oneida Indians because they only have themselves to answer to." Paul noted.

"The Oneidas manufacture gambling machines. They have purchased most of the competitive motels; they have purchased many golf courses that would have been competitive." Paul then continued, "They built a topnotch entertainment venue; so now places like Albany, Niagara Falls, Buffalo, Syracuse and Utica—that used to be able to host convention business—are losing a great quantity of that business to the Turning Stone Casino."

Rocco said, "To make sure that this county, and the county next to us get treated right we need some help from the federal government, as well as help from the state and local governments. If we could get all of that together, well, we'd live happily ever after."

"Here's another thing," added Rocco. "We have international boxing organizations. Right now, I have heard that they are going to bring their big dinner—which is 1,0000 people that we used to host in our community—to the Indian casino. I mean Turning Stone's a gorgeous place, there's no doubt about it. But this is just one more event taken away from our community resources. We used to have people come in and spend some money, spend some time in our community, stay at our hotels, but it does not happen anymore. Once they move the boxing over to the casino, we lose that too."

The OINNY really put forth a full campaign," Paul noted, "with full page ads in the New York Times, and probably elsewhere around the country—very emotional ads. Some would say, "Break a treaty, break the law," ignoring completely the Supreme Court precedent that was set because of Seneca businesses, and instead, going back to an obscure and questionable term in an ancient treaty."

Madison County's Planner, Paul, continued, "There have been attempts at the federal level to help states collect tax revenues, but they have all gone down to defeat at the hands of strong tribal lobbies that exist around the country."

The OINNY now owns 90% of the fuel stations, including diesel. They have captured the Marina industry, including propane as the sole vendor, and in certain areas, one out of three farms or homes stand vacant as residents sell or move.

Kamie asked Rocco if the Turning Stone Casino actually generates additional tourism traffic to existing businesses as is being claimed."

Rocco responded by saying, "That does not happen here. What happens here is what I call "footprint" traffic. A guy drives his car to the tribal casino. He'll get anything he wants there. He'll get gas. He'll get food, and he'll get gambling. He doesn't come to our community and stop and say, 'O.K, I want to buy something.' That's one of the major downfalls that people do not understand."

"The tourist coming into the community is coming in to gamble. The tourist is not coming to visit our community anymore. It doesn't happen." Rocco continued, "The Oneidas have the hotels, they have the restaurants, they have everything a tourist needs to support whatever they want to do. Pretty soon, they'll have the Turning Stone set up so gamblers can bring their families there, just like they do in Las Vegas. If they keep going the way they are, tourists will never see or visit our communities. They just drive through it."

"What are some of the impacts that trouble you most, Rocco?" I asked.

"The casino to us is a drag on our communities; not only because we have to take care of the roads, the lighting, the protection and all that, but even local people that have extra money go to the casino." Rocco went on, "Then they lose their homes, they lose their marriage—that's a true statement, right there—they lose everything. I know some big business people that lost their business because of the casino. These are just dragging communities down, and I think the quality of life has changed somewhat too, because of the casino."

We also asked the Madison County officials if stories we had heard about loss of jobs were true. We asked if the replacement jobs were equivalent as far as same pay and benefits.

Paul commented, "We hear those same stories and that is true for a lot of businesses that they have bought up. They're just replacing somebody. Perhaps they can add more people because they have such a tremendous competitive advantage, but I think the net result is that it is not a good foundation upon which to base your economy."

"The National Governor's Association has a Policy Statement from their Economic Development Commerce Committee with respect to Indian gambling, Paul added. "That policy asks for a balanced approach. States have been called to task to negotiate in good faith, while tribes do exactly the same thing. Tribes are so aggressive in their negotiation, and give almost nothing to the states or local governments; however, because if the "negotiations" break down, the decision goes to the Bureau of Indian Affairs, who will support the tribe."

"So I think what local government and local elected leaders should ask for, from their state governments and their federal government, is that same balance, so that local issues are resolved *before* a tribal gaming compact is approved—*before!*" With a tribe's ability to then use "sovereign immunity," there is just no equality in the situation."

"We're not opposed to the casino, per se," said Rocco. "We're opposed to all the other tax-free businesses that the casino gives them—the gas stations, the marinas, everything that money can buy—and every competitive advantage that our other business just do not have. These tribal businesses should have to follow the same local, state and federal tax laws as everyone, to keep a fair marketplace."

The competitive advantages Rocco is speaking of extend far beyond tax exemptions. Tribal businesses do not incur the same building, planning and permitting process or fees, do not require extensive environmental review and associated permitting, and other various licensing requirements by cities, counties and states. Startup costs and ongoing operational and overhead costs are considerably less than that of non-tribal businesses.

A more obvious competitive advantage is the ability to offer goods and services to consumers at a considerably lower price, absent most, if any, sales tax.

As we drove around the Madison County area, we were completely amazed at two things: the massive grading, earth moving and construction projects going on everywhere—all OINNY projects; and the fact that little to nothing else was happening in the area. We saw what has been reported as one out of three farms standing vacant as residents sell and move away. It truly appears that large areas of Madison County are going to pieces.

Throughout our tour, and later on the following day, we were told about, and then experienced "the white trucks." These are the OINNY tribal law enforcement vehicles that keep a sharp eye on everything and everyone. As Kamie would raise the video camera up inside the car to film the Turning Stone Casino, or other OINNY properties, there would suddenly appear a white truck behind us. At no point in time did we take any risks on having the camera confiscated, by getting out of the car or stepping onto OINNY property.

At a property near the Bachmans is a lovely old home with acreage that borders a newly installed OINNY golf course. The tribe had helped itself to a portion of this neighbor's land in order to build a road along the side of the course, and had dumped debris on her lands. We walked along the roadway in front of her home and then along the property line next to the golf course road. The neighbor showed us where drainage fields from the golf course were draining into fresh streams, and we saw open pipes with rags stuffed in them, installations that would not likely pass ordinary inspections.

A maintenance truck from the golf course came by, and the woman said, "You watch, they saw your video camera, there will be a white truck here in five minutes." There was. The lady concealed Kamie's camera and we made certain we were on her private property. These are chilling experiences to have in the United States. We did not feel secure, even on private property.

In this once lovely and prosperous area, now economically lucrative for OINNY, and depressed for counties and their non-tribal enterprises, we saw many vacant buildings, including homes. Some of the buildings are bought by the OINNY, and then bulldozed down. The vacant homes dotting the countryside are those of residents who were offered money to move, or did not want to live next to the large-scale commercial developments springing up throughout the areas surrounding the towering Turning Stone.

At this local government level, the evolving economic take-over, or at least transference of the economic base in these two counties, precisely illustrates a *national* discussion on "Dual and Dueling Economies," later in this book.

Kamie noted, "Elaine, this is what will happen in Marysville (Washington) soon, with the Tulalip Tribe's "Quil Ceda" Village." Kamie was speaking of a major shopping center acquired by the Tulalip tribe and converted into an alleged federally authorized "municipality."

[The Quil Ceda Village is home to a Wal-Mart, Home Depot, and will soon boast over 400 stores in an enormous land space that adjoins their Class III casino. This tribal enclave is immediately across Interstate 5 from Marysville. A marketing study performed for the City, to assess future fiscal impacts upon Marysville, reports that Quil Ceda Village will capture 100% of the neighboring town's retail business within ten years or sooner. Marysville's Mayor publicly denies any impacts; yet the studies paint a different picture. The similarities between the Madison County area and Marysville, Washington area are far too striking.]

The Bachmans had arranged for Kamie and me to meet with Sherrill's City Manager, David Barker, and the Clerk/Comptroller, Michael Holmes. On the drive to City Hall, we noticed a couple of other large, really great, hand-made signs. One said, "For a Few Pieces of Silver." The other said, "Sherrill, New York—The City With Integrity."

When we got settled into a conference room at Sherrill City Hall, we asked about the City's position regarding the two OINNY parcels and their position regarding tribal businesses.

Dave responded, "I have no problem as long as the tribal businesses play by the same rules as every other corporate citizen. If they want a longhouse, if they want a museum, I have no problem with that being tax exempt. But when they have a commercial enterprise, that is a whole different ball game."

The lawsuit stems from Sherrill's determination to treat a tribal business and property in the very same manner as its other businesses within the city. We then asked about what kind of support the City of Sherrill has been receiving regarding the litigation.

The City Manager replied, "We were asked at various stages of the legal road, to back off, by state and county officials, when we first got into this lawsuit. We were involved in a meeting in Syracuse where they asked us not to proceed, and this was even before—this was very early on. We were told that the county and state are already involved in this tax dispute. So I said, 'Well, we will be putting that much *more* pressure on it." he said, with an impish grin. "We all recognized the fact that if we lost that would strengthen the Oneida position, and when we lost in District Court it certainly *did* strengthen their position, and they became much more aggressive. But we took the case to the next step, and we lost there too, but it was a two-to-one vote there, so we were getting closer."

Judy added, "We had the County Executive of Oneida County, going to every town board meeting in the county, publicly saying that Sherrill should not have filed this case; that it cannot win, and when they lose, that we are *all* going to lose."

None of us wanted to contemplate that kind of an outcome. So I asked, "What will you do if you win, Dave?"

He smiled again, "We will expect that the Oneidas will pay their taxes, and if they don't, we will treat it just like we do every other property. We will treat it just like we did in 2000 when we filed tax liens on their parcels."

Dave Barker then provided us with some background and his perspective about things happening within his community.

"We lost, about $60,000 the first year in sales tax money," he said. So to cover that means a 10% tax increase—I mean that's 10% - each *year!*

"Then the Oneidas opened another facility, a smoke shop and Tee shirt factory. They have a retail outlet out front. Normally, when something like that goes in we would see our sales tax revenues go up, and it absolutely didn't. We really can't put a handle on that because we don't know what their revenue is. We can speculate on that but it is an annual loss of revenue from the property to the city.

Dave then went on, "I'm sure you have heard the term "cherry-picking property." That is what they are doing. They are going around picking the cherry—the *cream* of the properties.

You know the convenience store in Sherrill—the previous owner had just put a lot of money into it. It was a gorgeous facility. And the Oneidas came along and offered to buy it. The owner said, 'No, we don't want to sell it.' This story was told to me by one of the vice-presidents out of Pennsylvania with this company. They were told by the Oneidas, 'either you sell it to us today, or we are going build one right next to you and we will put you out of business. In two years you're gonna be beggin' us to take it.' "

"Did they sell?" I asked.

"United Refinery sold—at a good *price*. They got a *very* good price for it, " Dave noted. "But still, it was one of their better Upstate New York facilities, so over the long run it was *not* a good price."

Dave then continued. "You might mention the fact that we had only one convenience gas station here, and that is gone. We lost a little bit of property tax by their refusal not to pay. The bigger picture for us is our sales tax issue. And our state leadership will not collect the sales tax as they are supposed to. The people in Boonville, Camden and Rome and all these surrounding communities don't realize that they are helping to pay the public school tax. They are saying 'Jeez, he (Halbritter) just gave you a million dollars that's a lot of money.' Had he *paid* his school taxes bills, there would have been 10, 12 or 15 million dollars or more. So I mean, Halbritter is getting a whale of a bargain."

The Oneidas just went through a $300 million expansion, according to what I read in the papers, and I see the evidence of a lot of it. That is supposedly going to create another 1,000 jobs. It is going to add another $15 million to the payroll in Central New York. If you take $15 million and divide it by a thousand, that's

$15,000 a job. You know, that is *poverty* level. So, the quality of jobs—and in that 1,000 jobs there *are* some good paying jobs. I am talking about an average pay. You cannot raise a family on the majority of jobs that the Oneidas are providing."

"We have talked about taxation, but we have another very serious concern, and that is zoning. Our zoning ensures that adjacent uses will be compatible and that property values will be stable. The OINNY ignores our zoning. Our people move here, buy homes and businesses and they have a right to feel secure. What happens if an entity moves in next door to them and you don't *know* what's going to happen. They could go into one of the finest residential districts, and the Oneidas have *not* done this and I don't expect they *will*, but they *could,* go in and put a rendering works in there, right next door—or put in God-knows-what, and these people have bought the properties, have maintained the properties with the idea that Sherrill is going to remain Sherrill."

Kamie asked if there had been any improvement in the local economy arising from casino tourism or other enterprises.

Dave replied, "The Oneidas tout the fact that they bring in 3 to 4 million visitors a year to central New York, and they *do*. The idea is—you come in, you spend your money, we will have nineteen restaurants or whatever it is; we will have 8 golf courses; we'll have all the things so that you can spend your money right here (at OINNY enterprises)—then you get back on the Thruway and we don't want to see you. Or we'll bus you to Syracuse to catch a plane. Our restaurants in Sherrill see very little business from the casino. In fact they are seeing competition from the casino and losing business."

These conversations occurred in October 2004. The U.S. Supreme Court had docketed the *Sherrill* case for a full hearing, Oral Argument, set for January 11, 2005.

We returned to the Bachmans in the mid-afternoon so that Kamie and I could re-organize all the luggage, cameras, books, and clutter we had loaded in and out of the car for 25 days. We would be returning the rental car at the Syracuse airport the next morning, and It was clear that we had far more than the airlines would allow us to carry home. Fred Bachman helped Kamie and I pack everything possible into boxes for separately shipping back home, while Judy got things ready for a group of guests coming to visit with us later in the evening.

Our heads were spinning. We had absorbed so much over 6,000 miles, were so very tired, and eager to get home. We were in some sort of surreal "zone" realizing that we had actually started and completed this long road trip, and we had done so without any major calamities, not withstanding some tense moments on several reservations.

Fred and Judy had invited about a dozen local folks to come by for a gathering the night before we left. They shared their personal concerns that are generally expressed in within this chapter, and they wanted to hear all about our journey. It was a very pleasant, final evening for our trip. I would have one more morning to take in the spiritual calm that seems to enwrap the Bachman lands, then we were off to the Syracuse airport.

One would think that two women having spent 26 days around the clock would have a momentous or congratulatory farewell as we headed to catch separate planes home. Some scenarios are just too powerful to contend with. We knew what we had been through, and Kamie's plane was about to board. We turned in the rental car, wheeled our luggage into the terminal, and stopped for a very brief moment.

Kamie said, "See ya, Elaine. It's been terrific." We had a quick hug and she disappeared into the crowds. It was just too emotionally heavy to even speak of, at goodbye.

The next time I would actually *see* her was April 2005. We both have very busy lives, but from October until April, we have worked on the film and the book via the Internet and phones, as we live three hours apart.

On January 11, 2005 "*David and G*oliath" were heard in Oral Argument by the U. S. Supreme Court. On the City of Sherrill's website is their Winter 2005 Newsletter, which includes a lovely photograph of City officials standing in front of the U.S. Supreme Court on January 11th. The caption states, "Traveling to Washington, D.C. and pictured are: City Manager, David Barker, Mayor Joseph Shay, City Clerk Michael Holmes, and Commissioners Jeffery Gilbert and Bill Brewer."

The Bachmans also attended the Oral Argument at the U.S. Supreme Court. Few can ever discern where the nine justices seem to be headed, based upon anything discussed in the Oral Argument, but there was serious hope that the Court had not taken the Sherrill case, simply to affirm it. No one anticipated a ruling to come down from the Court before May or June 2005. On March 29th, however, the news came. The first sentences in the first article published in Indian Country Today newspaper, owned by 4-Directions, an enterprise of the Oneida Indian Nation, stated:

> Invoking the Doctrine of Discovery, the Supreme Court said repurchased Indian land does not unilaterally revert to tribal sovereign status. In an 8-1 ruling, the court determined that the Oneida Indian Nation of New York "cannot unilaterally revive its ancient sovereignty, in whole or in part, over the parcels at issue. The Oneidas long ago relinquished the reins of government and cannot regain them through open-market purchases from current titleholders. [Indian Country Today website, March 29, 2005]

Score one for *David*, as reported by *Goliath*.

Upon hearing the news, I had two immediate thoughts. The first was a remembrance of a naturally beautiful smile that David Barker, Sherrill's City Manager occasionally flashes. I imagined that Dave would be smiling for months to come. Then I flashed on the possible reaction of our friends in Salamanca, and I just wept. No doubt the families of the Salamanca Sixteen would be delighted for their neighbors not too far away in Madison and Oneida counties—but it would be a joy mixed with deep pain. I so wished, and still do, for some measure of justice for these wonderful people.

Another true value for the City of Sherrill was the services of Attorney Ira Sacks, and the fact that the entire legal process through all levels of the judicial system, was a total expense of just $100,000 for the City of Sherrill, extremely reasonable considering the elapsed time, nature and scope of the legal process involved.

The ruling by Justice Ruth Bader Ginsburg, and supported 8-1, with a sole dissent from Justice John Paul Stevens, will take months, perhaps years before its breadth and scope is fully understood. Several important findings should be noted, as provided in the Court's ruling for *City of Sherrill v. Oneida Indian Nation*:

- "Fee title to the lands occupied by Indians when the colonists arrived became vested in the sovereign— first the discovering European nation and later the original States and the United States." *[Doctrine of Discovery]*.

- "The distance from 1805 to the present day, the Oneidas' long de-lay in seeking equitable relief against New York or its local units, and developments in Sherrill spanning several generations, evoke the doctrines of laches, acquiescence, and impossibility, and render inequitable the piecemeal shift in governance this suit seeks unilaterally to initiate... the doctrine of laches focuses on one side's inaction and the other's legitimate reliance to bar long-dormant claims for equitable relief." *[Doctrine of Laches]*.

- "The longstanding assumption of jurisdiction by the State over an area that is predominantly non-Indian in population and land use creates "justifiable expectations... a contrary conclusion would seriously disrupt the justifiable expectations of the people living in the area" *[Acquiescence, Impossibility, Justifiable Expectations]*.

- "Congress has provided, in 25 U.S.C. §465, a mechanism for the acquisition of lands for tribal communities that takes account of the interest of others with stakes in the area's governance and well being. Section 465 provides the proper avenue for OINNY to reestablish sovereign authority over territory held by the Oneidas 200 years ago." *[Trans-ferring Indian-owned lands from fee into federal "trust" status]*.

The *Sherrill* ruling is a true, much deserved, and necessary victory for New York's smallest city, if as Barker promises, "our people have expectations and we meet them." They are, for now, less at risk of being parceled into tribal sovereign "patches" within an existing local government system. The case will undoubtedly have substantial impact upon other jurisdictional conflicts arising from federal Indian policy in New York, and likely across the Country.

There's so very much more to be accomplished. For example, to preserve the civil rights of tribal members, clear enforcement language and mechanisms must be required in the Indian Civil Rights Act for so long as tribal governments continue to exist. The Shenandoah family struggle is but one of thousands of similar struggles occurring within federally recognized Indian reservations ruled by forms of government that are not compatible, nor consistent with U.S. Constitutional guarantees such as the Fourteenth Amendment, and other provisions in the Bill of Rights.

The Sherrill ruling is, to quote Neil Armstrong's famous words, "one small step." It is a step, however, that will keep the charming little "City of Integrity" from going to pieces.

They that can give up essential liberty to purchase a little temporary
safety, deserve neither liberty nor safety.

— Benjamin Franklin
American Revolutionary Philosopher and Diplomat
(1706 - 1790)

Chapter 18
Hawaii: Last Star On, First Star Off?

Native Hawaiians owe an immense debt to Senators Daniel
K. Akaka (D-HI) and Daniel K. Inouye (D-HI) who have served
for years on the Senate Committee on Indian Affairs. There are
no federally recognized Indian tribes in Hawaii, and there are
few American Indians in Hawaii, but this Committee has oversight for legislation; which the two Hawaiian Senators, and Ben
Nighthorse Campbell of Colorado (R-CO), now retired, have
sponsored. That legislation provides special preference funding
for Native Hawaiians, too. The largesse facilitated by Hawaii's
senators to ethnic-based programs has resulted in a near political
coup that carries inordinate political clout throughout elected
offices in Hawaii.

The political and economic expansions benefiting federally
recognized Indian tribes have not gone unnoticed by powerful
ethnicity-oriented political activists in Hawaii. Although our
road trip obviously did not include Hawaii, I have recently returned from a fact-finding visit to Honolulu, to hear and see firsthand, the local political climate.

Here is a sample of communication I have received from
supporters of Senate Bill 147, "The Native Hawaiian Government Reorganization Act of 2005":

"As President of the Hawaiian Women's Patriotic
League (1893-Present) [sic!] our history will show you
what we are all about. First of all, Hawai'i was never
annexed to the U.S. We are being held hostage by your
government and want to be set FREE from the illegal

U.S. military occupation. This is what we want because the U.S. could never pay us back for over 112 yrs. of occupation.

"However, the U.S. and it's military can repair what they broke, polluted and destroyed i.e. water sources, land sources and other natural resources such as Kaho'olawe and other military bases that have pollutants buried in ground, in the ocean and in the air.

"We can, [sic] through the acting Council of Regency you can read about in the website.

"Coveting according to God's Law is a sin.

"The U.S. has committed many sins and we want to help heal them through repentence [sic] and prayers."

The above was written by an intelligent U.S. citizen who appears to truly ignore Hawaii's legitimate statehood, and considers the islands to be "held hostage" by the United States. The writer is not alone. She represents an alarmingly growing voice in Hawaii.

The Senate Indian Affairs Committee under Senator John McCain (R-AZ) conducted a hearing on March 1, 2004 before the Senate Committee on Indian Affairs to seriously consider Senate Bill 147, the long-standing proposal of Senator Daniel Akaka (D-HI). The "Akaka Bill" would split the island state into two foreseeable unequal parts by creating a "sovereign and independent" Native Hawaiian state with control of all property to which such "natives" lay claim and full control of their own law enforcement and justice system while continuing to enjoy all of the benefits of what remains of the present State of Hawaii after the separation is achieved by Congressional enactment and a White House signature.

The legislation calls for all descendants of native Hawaiian islanders to be represented by a "United States Office for Native Hawaiian Relations" somewhat similar to the federal Bureau of

Indian Affairs. All applicable, current, federal programs for health, education and welfare, supported by American taxpayers, would be funneled to the "Native Hawaiian Interagency Coordinating Group."

As our youngest, and fiftieth State, Hawaii's present status is being politically and psychologically overtaken by separatists. The Akaka Bill seems almost a foregone conclusion in Honolulu, to be averted only by a Congressional rescue by Hawaii's 49 sister states. The movement to secede is real and strong by a vocal part of the ethnic Hawaiian population. The Hawaiian separatists motto is: *Last Star On, First Star Off!*

The Office of Hawaiian Affairs (OHA), a state agency no less, wields the predominant clout in the political process here, beginning with GOP Governor Linda Lingle and permeating the largely Democrat state legislature, island newspapers and educational institutions.

OHA administers programs exclusively for "native Hawaiians" (any descendant of not less than one-half part of the blood of the races inhabiting the Hawaiian Islands previous to 1778) and 'Hawaiians' (any such descendant of any blood quantum, i.e., one drop). OHA is abundantly funded by the State and most of its funds, including the approximately $350 million it now holds, are earmarked for 'native Hawaiians' of not less than one-half blood.

Another State agency--the Department of Hawaiian Home Lands (DHHL)--controls 200,000 acres (14%) of the State's public land exclusively for 'native Hawaiians.' It awards homestead leases (residential, farming and ranching) exclusively to "native Hawaiians" for a term of 99 years at $1 per year, renewable for an additional 99 years.

Kamehameha Schools, created in the mid 1890's by Bernice Pauahi Bishop, just published an annual report listing $7.2 billion (with a B) in assets. These schools are available only to ethnic Hawaiian children (although the Bishop's Will does not require that restriction). OHA, DHHL and the Kamehameha Schools are being legally challenged because they practice race discrimination, and therefore drooling for a wondrous and anticipated Plan B - a 'Native Hawaiian governing entity,' over which the will all hold sway.

A single public hearing on the first version of the Akaka bill was held by the Hawaii delegation here in Hawaii in September of 2000. One talk show host & TV commentator, Bob Rees, estimated then that opposition exceeded supporting testimony 9 to 1. Despite that overwhelming opposition, the Hawaii delegation reported broad support for the bill. Opponents of S. 147 believe that despite the taxpayer-funded multi-million dollar advertising/propaganda campaign over the last twenty years, most people do not buy it. The last time the people of Hawaii were allowed to choose their form of government was in 1959 in the Statehood plebiscite. Over 94% voted Yes for statehood. Today, that statistic is being ignored and supporters insist that ALL Hawaiians support the proposed legislation.

Dr. Kenneth R. Conklin, Ph.D., reporting on a September 2004 "Red Shirt March" of Native Hawaiians who are pursuing a separate, race-based government, makes the following observations:

This red-shirt march, like the others that preceded it during the previous 12 months, maintained the tradition of anti-Americanism found in the Hawaiian sovereignty movement. That anti-Americanism is clearly shown by the total absence of any American flags among the sea of Hawaiian flags. It is also shown by the presence of scattered signs saying "Yankee Go Home." It is also shown by the presence of anti-war and anti-Stryker marching units in the parade -- of course it would be possible for loyal Americans to oppose the war in Iraq, and to oppose the coming of a Stryker brigade to Hawai'i; but in the Hawaiian context those protest topics are anti-American because their long-range purpose is to force the U.S. military to leave Hawaii and, eventually, to force the U.S. to completely abandon Hawaii to independence.

Dr. Conklin is an independent scholar in Kaneohe, Hawaii, and has, over the past ten years, extensively researched Native

Hawaiian history, culture and politics. Dr. Conklin has a considerable website that reports on a growing anti-American movement in Hawaii. The website is:

http://www.angelfire.com/hi2/hawaiiansovereignty

One of the most prominent and vitriolic voices that leads the anti-American movement in Hawaii, is Haunani-Kay Trask, a Professor at the Center for Hawaiian Studies at the University of Hawaii at Manoa. In June 2003, *FrontPageMagazine.com* reporter, Ryan O'Donnell, wrote an illuminating article about Professor Trask. It begins with her statement: "We need to think very, very clearly about who the enemy is. The enemy is the United States of America and everyone who supports it."

McDonnell describes Trask in the following manner: " A guru of the racial separation/ethnic nationalism movement, Trask routinely abuses her position an educator (and American tax dollars) to spread racist and anti-American doctrine throughout the University of Hawaii student body, sometimes violently opposing the dissenting voices that arise on campus and elsewhere on the Island.

Professor Trask may have altruistic beliefs; however, it is not inconceivable that she would be urged by her follows to assume a leadership role in a newly formed race-based government, so altruism could be but one of the agendas contemplated.

Toward the end of February 2005, the nefarious Ward Churchill had been in Hawaii the week before I arrived. During the week I spent in Hawaii, in early March, a two-hour replay of Ward Churchill's talk and time spent at the University of Hawaii was repeated on public television In Honolulu, at least two or three times daily. I watched this charade one time, and was chilled at the reception Mr. Churchill received. His performance was preceded with a traditional Hawaiian welcome of solemn, prayerful chants, nearly a dozen Hawaiian leis, several pre-speakers heaping accolades upon their majestic guest, including complete adulation by his hosts, the primary host being Haunani-Kay Trask.

As Churchill held forth like an arrogant lion, ranting and repeatedly shaking his mane, the camera would pan around the audience to a standing-room-only crowd, with faces that looked as though they were in the presence of the Messiah himself. Very young minds are being molded in an alarming manner, at the University of Hawaii. Academia nourishes and promotes analysis, argument and independent thought; however, a clearly Anti-American message is fomenting on numerous campuses across our country.

The last 'Star' is dimmed for lack of legitimate governance by those sworn by Oath to protect Hawaii's statehood. I find this to be a completely alarming scenario among so many elected officials serving a constituency that is ignored, and constantly bowing and curtseying to all requests from the leadership of this anti-State, anti-United States of America movement.

The Akaka bill is intentionally vague as to the type of 'Hawaiian government entity' that will be designed by Native Hawaiians. The short-range goal is to be free of all state interference. The long-range goal is to restore a nation of, by and for Hawaiians, defined by race alone. The desire to be an independent monarchy or other type of Hawaiians-only governing entity, operating tax-free, regulation-free and capable of negotiating treaties with other countries, and honored by its international colleagues is the dream. This now seems regrettably imaginable, once the political machinery is in place.

An in depth analysis of S. 147 is provided in 'Killing Aloha' by Attorney Paul Sullivan which is available at the following link: http://tinyurl.com/63lu9 "

A Senate Floor vote, up or down vote on Senate Bill 147 (the "Akaka Bill") is promised no later than August 2005. I wish I were simply having a bad dream about a lovely place. The grim reality for Hawaii is that it stands to become one of the next major areas at risk of going to pieces.

*Let's put it this way: you don't hear the word usurpation in Congress
for the same reason you don't hear the word fornication in Las Vegas.
When a vice becomes popular and profitable, it loses its proper name.*

— Joseph Sobran
Contemporary Syndicated Columnist

Chapter 19
Indian Gambling

It is not gaming. It is gambling. The proper name is gambling. It lacks sportsmanship. It lacks social utility. It is more about wreckage creating than recreating. And, it is epidemic in the American fabric, likely worse than the days before and during Prohibition. It is as debilitating to individuals and entire families as crack cocaine. Gambling money has now entirely corrupted the American political process.

The Indian Gaming Regulatory Act of 1988 (IGRA) brings an undeserved shame and scorn to legitimate American Indians, and will in the long term, be viewed as a foul deed foisted upon legitimate American Indian families and culture.

Gambling, whether at a tribal casino or private sector casino create the same socio-economic consequences. The distinctions to be made here are those of regulation and taxation.

Congress finds this vile pastime to be a perfect economic tool for Indian tribes and congressionally mandated a gambling monopoly in direct defiance of the Sherman Antitrust Act and all the previous Congressional statutes that attempt to keep the American economy and marketplace fair, competitive and equitable.

I call such federally sanctioned gluttony, IGRA, by a different name: "*McDonalds for the Mob.*"

Think about it:

- How else could limited, destination gambling of Las Vegas, Atlantic City, Tahoe or Reno spread

242 — Going to Pieces

across the country, often ignoring State sovereignty or State laws respecting gambling?

- Where else better to place such a gambling monopoly than on lands unaccountable to federal and state regulations applicable to all other gambling entities?

- How fortunate is it for such a federally created monopoly to also benefit from tax-exempt revenues, unlike all other gambling entities?

- How clever was it to have the Federal Election Commission rule that tribal governments, recognized as *governments* for the federal government-to-government funding subsidies, are *not* governments, for purpose of unlimited political campaign contributions flowing in from Indian gambling revenue? (FEC Advisory Opinion No. 2000-05)

- How visionary was it to deliberately exclude *Indian tribes* as language inserted into the Campaign Finance Reform legislation has exempted Indian tribes from campaign finance regulations affecting all other major entities?

The political collaboration discussed above, gets a little too close to collusion between tribal lobbyists, elected officials, federal agencies and appointed federal commissioners when one considers the end result. Congress created a gambling monopoly that has special land status (federal trust), special tax advantages, and exemptions from political campaign contributions. Were private sector corporations to have constructed such a system, they would be hammered with the Sherman Antitrust Act of 1890 that prohibits "direct or indirect interference with freely competitive interstate production and distribution of goods." (Blacks Law Dictionary, 7th Ed.).

While we are discussing federal statutes intended to preserve a fair and equitable American marketplace, it may be worthwhile to suggest that many federal and tribal collaborations with those in the corporate gaming industry may not survive daylight examination under the Racketeering Influenced and Corrupt Organization Act of 1970. RICO frowns on syndicates, bribery, fraud, extortion and other conduct known to follow in the wake, or surf along the waves of a gambling industry, now blessed and protected by Congress.

As if IGRA today, is not sufficient to create a significant monetary stream for political parties and elected officials, consider that there is yet another proposal being floated by Congressman Richard Pombo (R-CA), under the guise of limiting tribal off-reservation casinos, to create *two* Indian Economic Opportunity Zones (IEOP) in *each* state, wherein an unspecified (read: unlimited) number of tribal casinos may be installed. This is IGRA Super-sized.

This contemplated legislation would create two "mini-Las Vegas's" and spread tribal tax-free gambling, along with tribal governing systems. Only seven of our fifty states have budgets that are operating in the black. Forty-three state budgets are operating with flaming red deficits. Not coincidentally, most of these states already host tax-exempt tribal Class III casinos. Available disposable income within many states cannot much longer carry a tax-free tribal gambling industry that erodes a tax-paying private sector economy.

There could soon be two "Mini-Las Vegas's" in each state. Las Vegas gambling enterprises at least follow all federal and state gambling regulations, including the remittance of appropriate federal and state taxes. Tribal casinos are "Kings-X"—tax-exempt. Revenue goes straight to the *Kings* of tribes and the systems funding political *Kingmakers,* and directly to elected officials and candidates willing to carry tribal government water.

The entire IGRA industry would not pass the smell test of the Clayton Act of 1914 that "prohibits price discrimination, tying arrangements, and exclusive-dealing contracts, as well as mergers and interlocking directorates, if their effect might substantially lessen competition or create a monopoly in any line of commerce." (Blacks, again). What is a State-Tribal gaming compact if not a "tying, exclusive, interlocking directorate?"

It is no surprise that folks like Stations Casino, MGM, Donald Trump, David Wilmot, Sol Kerzner, Malaysian and Saudi financiers and service providers would be all too willing to help Indian tribes finance and process federal recognition for new Wanna-be tribes. Is there any reason to wonder why such interests will go out of their way to secure funding, construction plans, management and operations training, security, transportation and hospitality systems?

According to data provided to the March 2005 Western Conference of Governor's "Executive Summit on Indian Gaming," only 40 tribes pursued requests for federal recognition between 1934 - 1978; this was an average of just about *one tribe per year* during this 44 year period.

Compare the above data with 254 tribes pursuing federal recognition during a 26-year period of 1978 - 2005. This is an average of nearly *10 new tribes per year*, seeking federal recognition. To think that IGRA is not *driving* this tribal recognition process would be sheer insanity.

Class III tribal casinos are rolling out among communities with off-reservations at a rapid clip. There are currently 22 requests for off-reservation casino sites being processed by gambling tribes. Four of these are associated with large land claim battles; two requests are related to "restored lands" requests. Nearly half, ten of these requests are coming from tribes that already have at least one Class III casino in full operation.

The bulk of Indian gambling revenue is pumping straight in to tribal leadership, tribal lobbyists, and the political process of Americans legislative systems.

Nationally, there are now over 411, Class III tribal casinos, with over 217 additional "tribes" seeking federal recognition. Many of the recent tribes have gained federal recognition and then immediately sought off-reservation locations to build a tribal casino with outside investors.

Even the proud and noble Navajo Indian Nation, that intentionally avoided gambling for over fifteen years, is now working on constructing six new casinos as soon as possible.

Two new trends—*tribe shopping* and *reservation shopping*—are spreading gambling and tribalism as a governing system to all new areas of the United States, far beyond any existing federal Indian reservations. Congressional investigations are taking place and a moratorium on all new tribes has been requested by Connecticut legislators. California is trying to enact a brief moratorium on the new Class III Indian casino epidemic in their state, but there is urgent national need to do far more.

Connecticut and Washington State are very timely and active examples of how states are dealing with IGRA.

The socio-economic impacts of the Foxwood and Mohegan Sun casinos in Connecticut have been profound upon adjacent communities and their burdened infrastructure. It only took two tribal casinos for Connecticut legislators and citizens to immediately see the writing on the wall for their small state. Led by voices such as Jeff Benedict, author of "Without Reservation," and Connecticut's Attorney General, Richard Blumenthal, a statewide citizen coalition organized and has repealed their state's "Las Vegas Night's" legislation, preventing any more Class III tribal casinos in the state, thus far. But the battle in Connecticut is ongoing. To their credit, Connecticut's federal and state elected officials are not dazzled with big money, and stand nearly alone among their colleagues in Congress and other states.

New York, Minnesota, Wisconsin, New Mexico, are different stories. On the door of these State's Gubernatorial Offices, hangs a virtual flashing, neon sign: "Welcome All Tribal Gambling." As for Washington State—it stands out as a leader in such company.

Currently, the National Indian gambling Commission (NIGC) web site lists 30 tribal casinos in Washington State alone. This places Washington State as number three in the nation, regarding proliferation of class III tribal casinos.

Former Governor, Gary Locke's legacy of tribal legislation guarantees that each of the 29 federally recognized tribes may have up to three casinos each. Washington State could see the number of 30, multiply to 90 soon. There are only seven large cities in the whole state, and there are fewer than 50,000 enrolled tribal members in the entire State. Do Washington's tribes really need *90* Class III casinos to accommodate less than the population of a medium-sized city? The answer is of course, a resounding "No!" But remember the four L's that gambling revenue buys, mentioned in an earlier chapter:

1. Land
2. Lobbyists
3. Litigators
4. Legislators

The above "L's" have been purchased in large quantity with tribal gambling revenue flowing through the political process in Washington State. Ninety casinos will be economically and politically crushing. The state has been sold by the current and previous several governors, whose duty is to protect all citizens and the state's natural resources. Washington State is rapidly being handed over to the 29 tribes for governing.

More insidious for states and citizens, is the spread of *tribalism* as a governing system that is growing proportionally to the expansion of the tribal gambling industry. Tribal gambling money is supplanting tribalism over traditional American governance in numerous zip codes.

Washington State has only one major interstate in each direction: Interstate 5 North and South, and Interstate 90, East and West. The small communities located at convenient exits of these two freeways are the targets. The local property and sales tax base of any community located near a convenient, heavily-trafficked freeway exit, will be economically overtaken, by such prototypes as Quil Ceda Village, the Tulalip Indian Tribe's alleged "municipal village," economically draining the life out of Marysville, Washington.

The recently federally recognized Cowlitz Indian Tribe has partnered with the Connecticut behemoth, Mohegan Sun, to construct "the largest casino on the West Coast," in an environmentally lush and sensitive region of the state, next to tiny La Center, Washington. There has not been a single peep, not a tiny murmur from a state elected official, concerned about an out-of-state gambling monstrosity, the size of Mohegan Sun, rumbling into Washington. Ohio, Connecticut, Illinois and many other states vehemently guard their constituents against out-of-state tribal gambling efforts. Not Washington.

Washington remains one of the few states that continues to decline to collect any type of fee or percentage of slot revenues. Financial contributions agreed to in gambling compacts signed by a tribe and the Governor, are seldom actually received, and gambling compacts are not enforced.

In 2004, Washington State temporarily placed a moratorium on free healthcare to children in need, citing lack of funds. In Connecticut, however, the state has collected over $400 million from tribal gambling revenue, and has still determined that this is not enough to cover actual costs to the state and local municipalities. Currently, Washington State legislation promotes tribal gambling without reimbursement to directly impacted areas, and without any enforcement of tribal gambling compacts negotiated with the Governor.

Former Governor Locke and the Washington State Gambling Commission (WSGC) have recently approved at least two Class III casinos, on taxable parcels, regular non-trust lands. This is expressly prohibited by state and federal law. Tribal class III casinos operating in Fife and Suquamish on land not held in federal trust, are in direct violation of federal and state law, and have resulted in lawsuits citing state discrimination against non-tribal casinos that are limited to Class II or Class I casinos.

There is no current process in place in Washington State that allows municipalities or citizens or even state elected representatives to participate in gambling compact negotiations, according to legislators. Negotiation of gambling compacts is one opportunity for local communities to gain reimbursement for substantial annual costs to counties and communities. Currently affected communities and governments, as well as citizens, however, are uninvited to the closed-door negotiations between the Governor and tribal governments.

It took the private-sector gambling industry in Las Vegas over 70 years to reach the 6 billion dollar mark in annual gambling revenues. Tribal gambling revenue in California alone has surpassed this mark, just since passage of Indian gambling Regulatory Act—less than 20 years. Nationally, tribal gambling revenue generated over 18.5 billion in a single year, 2003.

This is cited to illustrate the proliferation statistics, and why the difference between regular and tribal gambling facilities should be considered much more carefully. Counties that host these developments are reporting major property, sales and B&O tax shortfalls and higher property, sales and business taxes being imposed upon non-tribal business and residents to compensate for loss.

Counties that host Class III tribal casinos show no change in unemployment numbers even though these casinos are touted as "major employment generators". Studies show that after the construction phase, an initial boost to area economies occurs, but this is short term. Non-union jobs that typically offer lower than family wage pay, lack of regular safety and injury protections, are listed as the possible reason for the lack of employment improvements in host counties.

Non-reimbursed infrastructural costs, increased traffic constraints, and a startling number of increased fatalities or drunken driving incidents associated with 24-hour gambling operations, are often listed as some of the largest negative impacts.

Connecticut and New York public school districts located within impact areas of Indian casinos report substantial costs associated with multi-language special needs, loss of property tax, and overcrowded classrooms. The significant impacts upon area schools from tribal gambling facilities are often the second highest concern, right behind crime and law enforcement issues.

Fueled by gambling revenue, increasing tax-exempt tribal retail and alternative business ventures are further eroding the sales and property tax revenues available to host counties, unable to compete with the advantaged tribal businesses. Local, non-tribal enterprises cannot compete with the significant competitive advantage of tribal businesses that are exempt from local and state regulations, and federal and state tax requirements.

IGRA statutes and regulatory policies allow private tribal gambling monopolies and other tax-exempt tribal businesses to settle into stable communities and nibble the local economy to death. That is Marysville, Washington. That is Vernon, Sherrill and Verona, New York. That is Ledyard and North Stonington, Connecticut. That is many communities in California. With Congressman Pombo's proposal to create "Indian Economic Opportunity Zones" specific to class III tribal gambling, tribal economic vacuum cleaners are coming soon to many new states and communities.

It is up to state and counties to protect constituents from the loss of local tax bases, from increased taxes, both property and sales, while simultaneously maintaining and encouraging ongoing efforts to respect and foster preservation of American Indian culture.

Elected officials at every level of government must work diligently to understand the full implications of an unfettered gambling monopoly and its impact upon American society. It is imperative that our elected representatives uphold a sworn Oath of constitutional and fiduciary duty, and ethical responsibility to fully represent all constituents, as guaranteed by the 14th Amendment

This chapter deserves an additional quote:

Never underestimate the stupidity, greed and self-interest of the American Congress. They produce the best legislation that money can buy.

— Jim Lynch, Community Manager, Extreme Tech and PC Magazine.

Is there not some chosen curse, some hidden thunder in the stores of heaven, red with uncommon wrath, to blast the man who owes his greatness to his country's ruin.

— *Joseph Addison*
English Essayist, Politician (1672 – 1719)

Chapter 20
Treatment Similar to States - A Horrendous Fiction

Power lies in ambiguity in federal Indian policy. This concept is discussed more fully in a forthcoming chapter, but let's start with the ambiguity of the word, *similar* as used by a federal agency for purpose of granting tribal governments jurisdictional, administrative and regulatory power over citizens and properties that do not belong to Indian tribes.

Webster defines *similar* as "somewhat like, resembling, having resemblance with...". To even embrace the unconstitutional premise that Indian tribes are *similar* to states, and that they should be treated as such, one must blindly accept the newest environmental weaponry facilitated by the Environmental Protection Agency (EPA) known today as "Treatment Similar to States (TSTS)". It was initially known as "Treatment *As* States (TAS), but this acronym was formally changed by EPA, with apology to Indian tribes, for politically *reducing* Indian tribes to simply the *same* as states. The apology was, for a time, and may still be, posted on the website of the EPA's American Indian Environmental Office (AIEO).

The new tribal government regimes insist upon being treated as *nations*. States are political subdivisions of nations, so the national tribal economic strategy demanded a change to the title of this brand new EPA perks for tribal governments. For these empowering political courtesies granted by EPA, *similar* actually means *superior* to States. Where TSTS is granted to a federally recognized tribe, State environmental authority and jurisdiction is substantially reduced or removed.

"I have videotaped Yakama tribal employees spraying pesticides on tribal crops, across the street from my organic cherry orchards three times now." Chris Klebaum, a Wapato, Washington orchardist has lost thousands and thousands of dollars, and at least 6 years of his State Certification as an organic farmer, thanks to Yakama Tribe's negligent spraying of pesticides on high wind days, wafting the toxins across Klebaum's organic orchard.

"Can you imagine what would happen to me, if I sprayed pesticides on *their* organic crops?" says Chris. And yet, Chris has pleaded for three years, with the local Tribal Pesticides Program, with EPA, with the Washington State Department of Agriculture—with anyone and everyone—for relief and compensation for chronic pesticide negligence that is costing him dearly. Help is not forthcoming.

Incidents like this occur frequently between landowners across the country. The difference, however, is in the resolution of such problems. The incident above is an example of how the empowerment of tribal governments to have separate environmental programs and accountability, apart from those of the State and federal government, are causing conflict and monetary damage across the country.

Congress passed the first federal environmental legislation in the 1960s; the federal air pollution control act was enacted in 1963.

Congress, through the 1960s and 70's passed federally mandated environmental legislation giving EPA administrative and regulatory authority over air quality, water quality, safe drinking water, a range of pesticides, and toxic contamination cleanup needs, among others.

During the Clinton Administration, significant Executive Orders (E.O.) were enacted that guided federal agencies regarding matters of federal Indian policy implementation. Among them was "Executive Order No. 13175—*Consultation With Tribes.* This executive order requires "that federal agencies include early consultation and continuous involvement of federally recognized Indian tribes in all matters impacting Indian reservations and tribal governments."

E.O. 13175 affects "all federal policy and matters having a substantial direct effect on one or more Indian tribes, on the relationship between the federal government and Indian tribes, or on the distribution of power and responsibilities between the federal government and Indian tribes." No mention is made within this E.O. of its affect on the several States of the United States, nor upon its citizens.

[More recently, with the codification of 26 U.S.C. 7871 in 2002, the Internal Revenue Service now *also* offers TSTS for eligible tribal governments to claim the same tax benefits as are available to 50 states and local governments. This would be less troublesome, if there were not so many *tax-subsidized* tribal governments.]

Just for a moment, consider EPA air quality issues occurring in Washington State. The reader need only replicate the many issues mentioned by multiplying the number of existing tribes, times the range of EPA Indian Environmental Programs, to see how quickly and comprehensively tribal governments can overwhelm State environmental programs.

EPA Indian TSTS programs affecting water in Oklahoma, for example, are reaching a political boiling point. Likewise, EPA Indian water and pesticide issues are promulgating near-violence in Nebraska, and escalating issues in Minnesota, Wisconsin, and numerous other states.

What happens when a societal need for something such as clean air, grounded in hard empirical science, is to be regulated within soft boundaries of multiple political jurisdictions? How do regulators make a precise, scientific distinction between Indian and non-Indian *air*? Do we also have Hispanic and Black American *air*?

Has Congressional correction of an environmental *oversight*—failure to include Indian reservations in major environmental laws—now resulted in an *overkill* of appropriate regulatory remedies? Apparently, EPA has discovered something new—there is such a thing as *ethnic* air!

The conflict of federal, state and recently proposed tribal regulations imposed upon urban and rural communities is illustrated by EPA Region 10's Proposed Tribal Air Rule, published in the Federal Register on March 15, 2002, as it is made available to 47 tribal governments in Idaho, Oregon and Washington.

There are ten separate regional clean air authorities in Washington State that are charged with full accountability and compliance with the federal Clean Air Act (CAA) as administered by EPA. Each of these authorities have inspection, permitting, regulatory and enforcement capabilities to ensure that their assigned region and State of Washington maintain acceptable air quality attainment standards that comply with the CAA. Nowhere is the State of Washington out of compliance with the CAA, in spite of the fact that the state is host to 29 federally recognized Indian tribes.

The proposed Tribal Air Rule would authorize EPA "to protect air quality throughout Indian country, including on fee lands, until a Tribe is approved for TSTS (Treatment Similar To State) and Tribal programs are approved. Upon approval of a Tribal Implementation Plan and application for TSTS, EPA would then conduct a statutory *delegation of authority to eligible tribes over their reservations.*"

EPA boasted of working with the tribes in Idaho, Oregon and Washington *for over 12 years*, since before 1994. However, EPA made little, if any, discoverable contact with any State regional air quality agencies in Idaho, Oregon or Washington, nor did EPA request or receive input from state or local governments when developing the proposed tribal air rules during this 12-year period. The first word, and opportunity for affected states, air quality districts, local governments and citizens to comment on the proposed rule was publication in the Federal Register on March 15, 2002.

The federal "trust" relationship with Indian tribes is apparently not a public process, nor one that requires even courtesy inclusion of state and local governments, nor other affected citizens.

Upon a concerted effort by the Yakima Regional Clean Air Authority, and a local community group, one single public hearing was coerced from EPA, held in Toppenish, Washington on September 10, 2002. This public hearing would be the only public hearing EPA would allow, for all three states. This was the only collected public input, after 12 years of ongoing and full discourse with the 49 tribes in Idaho, Oregon and Washington.

The proposed EPA Region 10 Tribal Air Rule would authorize regulatory authority of Indian tribes over all lands within exterior boundaries of Indian reservations. It would also provide tribal governments with "weighted comment" on all projects occurring within a 60-mile distance of any Indian reservation boundary. However, most inhabited land of Indian reservations in the states of Idaho, Oregon and Washington are owned in fee-simple and occupied by Washington citizens who are *not* enrolled tribal members, who are guaranteed a republic, participatory form of government under the federal and state constitutions, and who have no access to tribal government or voice in tribal government legislative or judicial processes.

Here is how EPA's new Cat And Mouse tool for Indian tribes (TSTS) would work. Tribal governments have no authority to enforce federal law upon non-members. EPA has no authority to enforce *tribal* law against non-members. So TSTS crafts a ploy wherein tribal governments provided with Treatment Similar to States for air quality (or other environmental programs) may initiate *investigations* against any citizens or their properties.

Tribal employees may access and investigate private properties to discover any air quality (and other environmental programs, too) problems. Tribes then report their findings to EPA. EPA has congressionally provided regulatory (enforcement) authority. The unfortunate business or landowner caught in this web will likely incur "investigational" harassment from tribal members at his/her place of business, harassment from EPA officials, and significant legal fees, trying to defend against this insane "ethnic" air program proposed by EPA Region 10.

Neither EPA nor Indian tribal governments can avoid the United States Supreme Court case of *Oliphant v. Suquamish* [435 U.S. 191], which ruled in 1978, "that Indian tribal courts do not have inherent criminal jurisdiction to try and to punish non-Indians, and hence may not assume such jurisdiction unless specifically authorized to do so by Congress." A later judicial ruling in 2001, to be discussed shortly, also provides EPA with regulatory, but no *jurisdictional* authority over lands.

Indian reservations in the Northwest are predominantly populated [60% - 95%] by other Washington residents, who are not enrolled tribal members, and many of the Indian reservations include high-density urban areas, whose air quality is currently regulated by one of the 10 State air quality authorities.

Treating tribes *similar* to States to encourage attainment of air quality within tribally controlled lands located within state boundaries, creates a plethora of very serious conflicts, some, but not all of which include:

1. Jurisdictional conflicts between state and tribal air quality agencies as to which government has jurisdiction within significantly "checker boarded" reservations. Using the Yakama Indian Reservation as an example of checker boarding, there are currently over 9,760 private, fee-simple parcels, most of which are owned by Washington citizens who are not enrolled tribal members. The Reservation is over 90% non-Indian. Private properties located within an Indian reservation boundary are not considered "Indian Country," subject to tribal government authority, nor are Washington citizens subject to tribal governance, unless by mutual consent or by tribal enrollment.

2. Exposure of state air quality agencies and management plans to non-attainment risks and penalties emanating from tribal lands.

3. Constitutional and civil rights of citizens located within exterior boundaries of Indian reservations.

4. Economic disincentive to job creation needs of existing and new businesses forced to comply with State and one or multiple tribal air quality permitting agencies, simultaneously.

5. Foreseeable scenarios within Indian reservation boundaries such as vehicle owners being forced to obtain dual air emission inspections and permits, or major community events (parades, rodeos) cancelled by tribal governments if air quality is perceived as even potentially harmful to sacred or cultural neighboring (within 60 miles) tribal lands.

6. Proposed authority of tribal governments in Washington State alone is disproportionate to the population of enrolled tribal members in the State. Washington State has nearly 6 million residents, of whom only 2.7%, or about 160,000 people, are identified as American Indians; but less 50,000 enrolled tribal members (.008%) live in the State. 29 tribal ("nations") governments are quickly overwhelming the sovereignty and integrity of Washington State—on behalf of less than 1% of the State's population.

7. Taxpayers currently subsidizing a statewide clean air regulatory program, will be asked to subsidize a duplicative program for 29 Indian tribes, while simultaneously incurring the regulatory burden of dual or multiple agency air quality programs.

In a 2001 D.C. Appellate Court ruling, _State of Michigan v. EPA_ (No. 99-1151), EPA was admonished that where Congress has delegated EPA with authority to implement major environmental legislation, Congress has not, in fact, delegated EPA any _jurisdictional_ authority. Respecting any specific parcel(s) of land having questionable jurisdiction, EPA either "stands in the shoes of a state or the shoes of a tribe," but has no jurisdictional 'shoes' of its own. Further, that when a jurisdictional question arises about a specific property or area, the jurisdictional question must be determined first, in order to guide EPA as to whether the property is subject to state or tribal governance.

258 — Going to Pieces

EPA did not appeal the *Michigan* case, and actually filed an Order of Compliance with the Court in early 2002. The Michigan case was a consolidated case that included a case arising from the Navajo Nation as well. EPA has, since filing its Order of Compliance with the court, seemingly ignored the Appellate Court's guidance, when implementing Indian Environmental Programs and TSTS. When confronted with frequent reminders of judicial rulings, EPA Region 10 continues its memory lapse.

Those who control America's air and water, control America's industries, private sector market places, farming, energy and natural resources. This statement bears repeating: *Those who control America's air and water, control America's economy.*

TSTS is the stealth bomb that has been launched and is heading for the target. Highly urbanized areas such as Portland, Seattle and the entire West Coast could soon become beholding to multiple environmental permitting processes and approvals required by Indian tribes in order to open a business or conduct any activity within their jurisdictions, or in areas even 60 miles away.

Soon, entire farming regions in Nebraska, and other Mid-Western States will find themselves answering to a tribal government for permission to use needed pesticides. The irony is that tribes such as the Omaha and Winnebago in Nebraska have almost no farmers.

Fast-tracking policy implementations and unlawful delegations of authority transferred from EPA to private tribal governments are oozing out across one state after another, for control of air, water, and pesticides—life-giving and life-taking resources of America's food supply and grazing lands.

So, if the conduct of BIA tribal police in dragging Nebraska farmers off their tractors, and beating elderly farmers down into gravel roads isn't incentive enough to drive farmers off the land, EPA is rolling out other tools to bully farmers and businesses within the historical and actual boundaries of federally recognized Indian reservations.

The simple math problem of only 50 states and some 562 tribal governments thus far, poses enormous consequences arising from EPA's Indian Environmental Programs and TSTS, in particular. Again, as an example, 29 *nations* within the State of Washington alone, have escalated significant tribal government authority overreaching control of natural resources and the environment that are quite adequately addressed by State programs. Imagine this power seeping into every other state in the United States where tribes are a factor. It is already happening.

When a government takes over a people's economic life it becomes absolute, and when it has become absolute It destroys the arts, the minds, the liberties and the meaning of the people it governs.

— *Maxwell Anderson*
American Historical Playwright
(1888-1959)

Chapter 21
The Ruse of Tribal Sovereignty

Some words have an unlimited life; sometimes words die or disappear from current usage. Often words become so associated with one particular subject that they seem abandoned, stolen from other subjects. The word "sovereignty" falls into this latter category, with respect to the frequent use of "tribal sovereignty" and the diminishing use of federal, state and citizen sovereignty.

It is important to encourage awareness about what the word, "sovereignty" really means to all American citizens, including enrolled tribal members, and federally recognized Indian tribes. There are only three specified sovereignties identified within the United States Constitution:

> **1. Federal Sovereignty**. The unimpeachable sovereignty of the United States of America as a nation and federal government, through the enumerated powers of the federal government as defined in the U.S. Constitution;
> **2. State Sovereignty.** The clearly defined sovereignty of each state of the United States as set forth in Article IV of the U.S. Constitution, inclusive of the preservation of a republican form of government within each state, and the protection of each state from invasion (Article IV, Section 4).
> **3. Citizen Sovereignty**. The sovereignty of each citizen (The "Body Politic") is whole and controlling in a government "of the people, by the people and for the people," as expressed in the Declaration of Independ-

ence, and as further described in Article V, Section 2 of the U.S. Constitution. No government entity that is not republican in form, or consistent with the U.S. Constitution, may be imposed upon a U.S. citizen unless through consensual agreement, as effected through enrollment in a federally recognized Indian tribe.

Congress and judicial federal Indian policy have acknowledged two additional types of sovereignty:

1. Federally Recognized Indian Tribal Sovereignty. Granted by Congress to federally recognized tribes, this sovereignty is a *dependent, quasi-sovereignty granted expressly to Indian Tribes* to shield such tribes from intrusion by external governments and citizen interference. Dependent, quasi-sovereignty of Indian tribes arising from Congressional acts is a lesser, more limited (quasi-) sovereignty than the perpetual sovereignties identified in the United States Constitution. Tribal dependent, quasi-sovereignty is a grant that is subject to the pleasure of Congress; tribes can be de-recognized and tribes that are not "federally recognized" have no legally recognized sovereignty.. Tribal sovereignty is limited to tribal jurisdictional, regulatory and adjudicatory authority over its members and properties. Dependent quasi-sovereignty of federally recognized Indian tribes *should* have no legal force and effect upon:

- U.S. citizens who are not enrolled members of a federally recognized Indian tribe;

- Public lands under the ownership and control of federal or state governments;

- Private properties under the ownership and control of U.S. citizens;

- Natural resources adjacent or exterior to any federally recognized Indian reservation boundary;

2. Inherent Tribal Sovereignty. The term, *"inherent,"* pertaining to Indian tribal sovereignty is a culturally recognized acknowledgement and respect for the existence of Indian tribes on the North American continent, predating the formation of the United States of America. Inherent tribal sovereignty acknowledges a cultural continuity of an Indian tribe, commonly referred to "since time immemorial," and has no legal force and effect upon non-members.

The National Congress of American Indians (NCAI) and the Indian lobbyist industry fueled and funded by casino revenue, has successfully erased the use of the legal term, *"dependent, quasi-sovereignty"* of Indian tribes, and has, at least politically and psychologically, imposed the concept of inherent tribal sovereignty as having legal authority over all persons within reservation boundaries. It does not. Inherent tribal sovereignty is specific to cultural tribal governance only. Unfortunately, too many Americans, including many elected officials, have embraced the larger view of tribal governance over non-tribal persons and properties. It is incorrect to expand *inherent* (internal, tribal members) to governing others (external, non-tribal citizens).

Inherent tribal sovereignty does not, and was never contemplated even within Indian Treaties, to allow tribal chiefs or tribal council members to govern persons (settlers, homesteaders) who are not members of the tribe. *Internal* inherent tribal sovereignty may well have existed *since time immemorial,* and as such deserves respect by all other cultures. However, inherent tribal sovereignty has, and should have, no *external* au-

Going to Pieces

thority by which to allow tribal governments to govern U.S. citizens or their properties protected by the U.S. Constitution.

And, by the way, is time truly *immemorial*? This phrase is overworked in Indian communication, much like the phrase, "as long as the grass grows," for future timelines, and "from time immemorial," referring to past timelines. First recorded manifestations of actual time-telling clocks did not appear until the mid-14th century, in Italy and England. Early Babylonians, Greeks and Egyptians were the cultural origins of calendars. Less civilized, earlier cultures had a ritual sense of a succession of sunrises and sunsets, and called them dawns or suns or moons. The bottom line, however, is that time is not immemorial; its discovery or construct was born of man's evolving ability to utilize logic, reason, scientific inquiry and other mental processes that led to such sciences as astronomy and mathematics. There is a specific point in time—in man's evolvement—when time, or the ability to define and quantify *time*, was discovered. Time was only *immemorial* to cultures less evolved in earlier centuries.

Ambiguity is imaginative and useful in Indian legends and oral history, and has actually been canonized in legal principles applied in court rulings that interpret ambiguous phrases in the best interest of Indian tribes. Ambiguity has been masterfully applied regarding Indian tribal sovereignty.

Imprecision, ambiguity and lack of written record has been both a cultural and permissible legal strength for Indian tribes; seldom is it a weakness. The legal principle requiring absolute evidence or a clear burden of proof, seems to apply to all other cultures in the United States. These legal standards should also be made equitable across all venues and cultures.

For example, I could not walk into a court room with a legal claim that many acres of ground in the Spokane Valley once belonged to my grandfather since time immemorial because my ancestors told me so, so I want my grandfather's land back. My ancestor's words and my memory carry no weight in American courts, lacking factual evidence. This is exactly what Indian tribes are doing. The difference in a courtroom is that minimal hard evidence is required of tribal land claimants. The power of oral history and tribal memory, and the ambiguity factor will sway decisions to their benefit. Neither State and local governments, nor corporations or citizens are provided such latitude in a courtroom.

Rather than laying precise claim to ancestral grounds in mathematical increments of metes and bounds, tribal land claims are often discussed in terms of rivers, walking days, as far as the eye can see, or where ancestors once walked, hunted or roamed. No other citizen could get away with such imprecision regarding property rights in an assessors office or a courtroom.

Sovereignty is at the top of the list of nebulous words that have empowered Indian tribes to reach out to acquire almost anything requested. To say no or to decline a request is viewed as unapologetic for a sad yesterday continually foisted upon today, or worse, to be called racist.

"You stole our lands. We were here first. Our oral history is gospel. You are a racist." Tribal governments win—again, and again, and again. Multiply this strategy by 562 federally recognized tribes thus far, with 217 tribes pursuing federal recognition, and the warm mother's milk of American taxpayers in 50 United States is unable to even contemplate a weaning.

The actual word, sovereignty, has a simple definition in Black's Law Dictionary, 7th, Edition:

Sovereignty: **1**. Supreme dominion, authority, or rule.
2. The supreme political authority of an independent state.

Neither of these definitions fits for federally recognized Indian tribes. The federal *recognition* process is a Congressional authorization that allows tribal governments to exist within the United States. Congress funds them as *dependencies—dependent wards of our sovereign USA.* How can tribal governments be dependent wards and sovereign simultaneously?

Congress acknowledges a tribe's inherent sovereignty to govern itself. Congress does not acknowledge tribal governments as separate nations, freestanding from the United States. Indian tribes exist at the plenary power and pleasure of Congress. *Nations* is another inappropriate term; however, it is certainly true that tribes are all about nation building.

Americans and their elected officials have a genuine desire to respect, acknowledge, assist and empower Indian tribes to thrive and prosper. Frankie Sue Del Pappa, former Attorney General of Nevada, put the principle of tribal sovereignty very clearly in her analysis defending the decision in a U.S. Supreme Court ruling, *Nevada v. Hicks* (2001). *Hicks* ruled that "a state's jurisdiction does not end at an Indian reservation boundary."

The *Hicks* ruling co-mingles federal, state and tribal sovereignty. Ms. Del Pappa wrote that federally recognized tribal sovereignty was always intended as a shield by which to protect Indian tribes from intrusion or interference from others. Tribal sovereignty was never intended as sword by which to "wield its sovereignty offensively."

Today, many of the 562 recognized tribes have the sovereignty sword unsheathed and are wielding that tribal sovereignty in an offensive manner to reclaim state and privately owned lands, capture and control vast natural resources, energy systems, and to create severe competitive advantages in gambling and other forms of manufacturing, contracting or retail industries. It is as though other neighboring citizens and governments not only do not matter, they simply do not exist in negotiations between Indian tribes and federal agencies. This is the dilemma of the North and Central Idaho people, as well as folks along the entire 6,000-mile trip we have taken.

Unless the fifty United States respectively assert their Constitutional sovereignty, and individual citizens assert their Constitutional sovereignty, the pattern of events over the past thirty years will allow tribes to expand *their* sovereignty—erasing all other. The political attitude expressed continuously by national and tribal government leadership emphasizes that no one else's best interest is a concern to them. It is not about the well being of the United States or its citizens. It is about expanding tribal government. This is certainly not the attitude of individual American Indians that I know and love. Nor is it mine as a Cherokee descendant. But it *is* the national and tribal mantra of Indian leadership today.

Federal Senators, Congressmen, State Governors and legislators, heavily funded by Indian gambling contributions, have no incentive whatsoever, to whisper an occasional "No" to a tribal whim, unless and until you and I, as voters, demand it.

I now pay very close attention to the campaign contributions of elected officials, and if they have been purchased by tribal government entities or organizations, they do not receive my vote.

Since 1924, every American Indian is a U.S. citizen on equal footing with all other Americans. The ability to honor one's ancestry and culture does not require a government. It requires a personal decision, a desire to do so because it is the right thing to do.

There has been no legitimate purpose served by continuing Indian treaties or tribal governments since 1924. But Congress and tribes insist upon playing *Let's Pretend*, because it is so very lucrative for them to do so.

It is time to remove tribalism as a governing system in this country. The expansion of hundreds of tribal "sovereigns" is beyond our countries economic or political carrying capacity.

Let's Pretend—needs to be *Game Over*.

Clearly, a civilization that feels guilty for everything it is and does will lack the energy and conviction to defend itself.

— Jean Francois Revel
French Philosopher (1924 -)

Chapter 22
Appeasement and Apology

In his recent bestseller, *Off With Their Heads,* author Dick Morris provides an insightful discussion of the principle of Appeasement, related to historical political philosophies in France. As I read Morris' illuminating discussion of appeasement, I was struck with how Congress has historically practiced appeasement in continuous escalation of special preferences, tax exemptions and endless funding resources that abound in federal Indian policy. Morris states, "Appeasement is a philosophy, founded in fear and uncertainty, in which contradictions abound and live alongside one another." I will paraphrase and redirect the focus of Mr. Morris's brilliant insight to make an important point.

Appeasement in federal Indian policy begins with an unmentioned wish by Congress and the White House that tribal government demands would go away like a bad dream. It then leads to Washington's refusal to believe anything critical about tribalism as a form of government for its American citizens, and a fear of what tribal leaders and lobbyists might do if riled.

Morris defines appeasement as "the tendency to give an aggressor what he wants, in the hope that he will go away and leave you alone." Using this definition regarding federal Indian policy, it is understandable that Congress has an ingrained will to seek the easy way out. This reluctance to confront an industry promoting tribalism in America stems from political cowardice and a deep fear of reprisal.

Congressional appeasement legislation is running amuck. Each Congressional act essentially replaces the Constitutional rights of enrolled tribal members and often, other citizens, with a grant of more tribal power and authority. Appeasement legislation allows tribal government authority to trump the rights of individual citizens.

The Indian Child Welfare Act (ICWA) usurps rights of enrolled tribal members, transferring their parental rights to a tribal government. The Indian Gaming Regulatory Act (IGRA) creates a gambling monopoly for tribal governments with no enforceable requirement that gambling revenue be directly distributed to upgrade the quality of life for impoverished enrolled tribal members.

More recently, a failed Senate Bill 578 would have provided tribal government with full criminal, civil and adjudicatory authority over *all* persons within boundaries of Indian Reservations, for the purpose of defending "tribal homelands," whether or not there is a direct relationship to the safety of America's national homeland.

Rather than risk the wrath of aggressive, wealthy, tribal lobbyists, too many elected officials devote attention to battling those who would seek equality for all American citizens. This confusion of allies and adversaries is a hallmark of appeasement. It resembles a political variant of the famed Stockholm Syndrome, which leads hostages to see their captors as friends and their rescuers as enemies. Far too many of our 535 senators and congressmen have been seduced and co-opted by exorbitant political campaign contributions, and can now be viewed as monetary and political hostages to radical tribal influence.

We currently have elected representatives at every level of American government that fit the Stockholm Syndrome definition to a tee. Governors, state legislators, Congressmen, and specifically the Senate Committee on Indian Affairs, refuse to acknowledge a greater population of other American citizens than Indians, residing within exterior boundaries of Indian reservations. They blindly cosign all whims and desires of tribal lobbyists, refusing to acknowledge any public input or comment from other affected Americans, to the absolute and direct harm of these citizens. To do otherwise could send them on the pathway of the former Senator Slade Gorton.

Senator Gorton simply suggested "means testing" so that federal funding would be proportionally reduced for wealthier tribes and redistributed to poorer tribes. That was his undoing. That reasonable, logical suggestion, cost him the loss of a highly respected and productive career as a Senator for Washington State. The loss cost Washington State severely, when he was replaced by Senator Maria Cantwell, who headed directly for her chair on the Senate Committee on Indian Affairs.

In his book, Morris's quotes the Reverend Fr. Charles T. Brusca:

> Initially, hostages come to identify with their captors as a defensive mechanism: The victim, "in an almost childlike way," tries to win the favor of the captor so he will not be harmed. He comes to fear the efforts to release him may expose the hostage to a renewed risk of violence, from the authorities or from the captor... The captive seeks to distance himself emotionally from the situation by denial that it is actually taking place. He fancies that "it is all a dream," or loses himself in excessive periods of sleep, or in delusion of being magically rescued." Hostages in such situations may even reverse the moral dynamic in their minds, becoming convinced that the criminals are in the right and the would-be rescuers are the problem.

Nothing could better describe the appeasing net effect of Congressional reactions and tendencies to escalate Federal Indian policy than:

- Trying to win the approval of a few aggressive tribal leaders and lobbyists so as to minimize chances of political uncertainty or harm;

- Ignoring the voice of other constituents because of fear of political or financial reprisal from tribal governments and lobbyists;

- Engaging in busy work (avoidance) to keep their minds off the real crisis;

- Denying that the situation is really taking place.

The most egregious example of federal Indian policy appeasement that now expands into international venues is reported in an unsigned, and thus cowardly, "*Indian Country Today*" editorial article published July 31, 2003 with an accompanying cartoon. In the cartoon, an Indian whispers in the ear of an Iraqi worker, while pointing back at an Uncle Sam caricature, "....And whatever you do, don't sign a treaty with *that* guy!" The editorial then states: "Never underestimate the ability of American Indians to be ambassadors of the best of America and its varied peoples."

The editorial also boasts that "as many as ten high-tech Indian-owned companies are being awarded non-competitive, multi-million-dollar contracts to take on various reconstruction duties in Iraq." With absolute seriousness, the *Indian Country Today* editorial states: "The often-expressed value in Indian cultures, of respect as a governing attitude in guiding relations between nations and peoples is very important. For American Indian entities entering that troubled region this is the best common motto: Let respect among peoples prevail." The very next sentence in this "thumb-in-America's-eye" editorial calls attention to the cartoon noted above. Now, those same megabuck, non-competitive contracts given to Indian-owned contractors are currently under serious federal investigation.

The similarity of political thought, action and behavior between the principles of appeasement and the typical Congressional response to the radical tribal government industry is striking. Federal Indian policy reeks of appeasement and cowardice. It is distressing to note that no less than 562 federally recognized Indian tribes with such adversarial attitudes toward other cultures, now constitute a monetary and political force that is created, fueled and funded by Congress to balkanize and spread tribalism as an acceptable form of governance in the United States. The fifty separate States cannot long withstand such political and economic implosion.

The legislative practice of appeasement has created an insatiable, ungrateful governing system called *tribalism* spreading across America. This we do, while spending billions and spilling American blood to free Middle Eastern cultures of the tyranny of the very same oppressive tribalism. Something is terribly wrong here.

Apparently, tribal government representatives now have a free pass to spread anti-American venom to foreign shores, such as Iraq. The irony should not escape us.

On April 6, 2004, Kansas Republican Senator, Sam Brownback submitted a Senate Joint Resolution, S. J. 37, "a bill to acknowledge a long history of official depredations and ill-conceived policies by the United States Government regarding Indian tribes and offer an apology to all Native Peoples on behalf of the United States." Within the text of this Apology is the following statement:

> Whereas the foundational English settlements in Jamestown, Virginia, and Plymouth, Massachusetts, owed their survival in large measure to the compassion and aid of the Native Peoples in their vicinities....

At about the same time this "American Indian Apology" was moving through Congress, I was immersed in a marvelous new historical book, "*Love and Hate in Jamestown*," by David A. Price. An example found in Price's book, of the alleged *compassion and aid* extended to Jamestown colonists by Indians, is in Chapter 14, *Skyfall*, describing an event on March 22, 1622:

> The sky was about to fall. For the colonists, Friday, March 22, 1622, started as a day like any other. Morning found native men visiting the plantations in their usual manner, bringing deer, turkeys, fish, and fur to trade in return for beads, glass, and metal. Some of the men joined the English at their tables for breakfast. Others mingled among the English in their workplaces—in the fields, at their brick-firing kilns and their forges, at their building sites and workbenches. The visitors carried no weapons.

At those sites, the colonists and the natives interacted in their everyday manner until the natives abruptly began their assault. They slaughtered men, women, and children with the colonists' own swords and work tools—axes, knives, saws, and hammers. In an instant, hundreds of English were lying lifeless. 'Not being content with taking away life alone,' noted a report after the attack, 'they fell after againe upon the dead, making as well as they could, a fresh murder, defacing, dragging, and mangling the dead carkasses into so many pieces, and carrying some parts away in derision, with base and brutish triumph. . . .'

At the morning's end, at least 347 English were dead, and possibly as many as 400. The colony's population before hand had been roughly 1,240, so the mortality amounted to somewhere between a quarter and a third of the colonists. Of equal significance, the membrane of normality that had recently surrounded the English in Virginia—or which they had assumed to be surrounding them—was now punctured. "I thinke the last massacre killed our countrie," wrote colonists William Capps in a letter to a friend. "Beside them they killed, they burst the heart of all the rest.'

Where *is* that *compassion and aid* in dire need of an apology? Now, in 2005 in Virginia, Jamestown is about to celebrate its 400th anniversary. However, once again, Jamestown is being threatened by the Indians. Six tribes in Virginia, currently seeking federal recognition, are saber rattling about plans to boycott and interfere with this celebration if they fail to receive federal recognition prior to the upcoming historical commemoration.

I find it a sorrowful irony that today, Jamestown, the very community that barely survived the often cruel and hostile Indian *compassion and aid*, 400 years ago, is being threatened yet again. So, no, I am not inclined to support any apology to American Indians.

Harm and brutality occurred on all sides from all ethnicities. Tribes took slaves from each other, kidnapped children (Sacajawea) - fought each other unmercifully, and fought the white settlers (Whitman Massacre). No part of our society was without accountability for uncivilized behavior. But one race in this society has for decades been receiving ongoing reparation in the form of land, huge federal dollars, separate governance authority, special privileges to the direct harm to others—with seldom a word heard, of appreciation or mutual respect for other cultures that share the great country that is now unraveling in its dysfunctional quest for over 400 years, to get tribal governments to accept us all.

To formally apologize to Native People requires a troublesome premise. We must first admit that all those who ever came to North America, or participated in the Revolutionary War, or helped forge the United States, or homesteaded and settled The West —were bad people, doing wrong things.

Then, too, we must denounce the limitless opportunities now available for citizens of all cultural persuasion, including American Indians—as equally bad things, wrong things—conditions for which guilt must reign for *time immemorial*. This is sheer insanity, and this is the root principle for which federal Indian policy continues to exist. All humans residing on this continent who are not aboriginal, or blood-quantum descendants of aboriginals are forever bad and wrong, and must forever pay.

Would tribal governments prefer that the United States—this bell of liberty—have never rung? Unfortunately, for some tribal leaders, the answer to this question is a resounding "Yes!"

There is simply incessant mantra: "We were here first! You stole our land! You owe us!" These chants lack historical truth on all three counts. The only true resolution to this continuous assault upon the soft, decent underbelly of the American spirit, would be for all persons not of Indian bloodlines to depart the continent, as descendants of unworthy, ashamed, guilty and mean-spirited ancestors.

Do Indians really want their old life ways? I see no tribal governments doing without electricity for a day or two, or foregoing automobiles, cell phones, indoor plumbing or precious slot machines. I see Indian tribal governments enjoying the best of America's inventions while continually bashing their source. It is tiresome and it needs to stop. It is unbecoming, if Indians claim that theirs is a "noble culture."

If an apology to American Indians were necessary, it would be more appropriate to apologize for the unintended consequences of our government's failed federal Indian policies that now fuel an apartheid mentality and conditions of continuous shortcoming upon tribal lands under non-democratic, unaccountable, and often oppressive, tribal governance. Contributing billions of tax dollars annually has not remedied the failures. Providing a unique government monopoly for unlimited more billions, annually, through Indian gambling has not remedied the lack of quality of life among Indian reservation families.

The Constitution places a higher value upon individual rights of American citizens than group rights, a principle not well regarded by tribal governments. Tribal governments are systems built on collectivism and socialism, with needs of individual members placed far behind the needs of a tribal government.

We might apologize only to the extent that our elected officials thought that more money could make life better for American Indians on reservations. Our elected officials have overlooked the obvious: that in this land of opportunity, individual attitude and effort creates its own best result.

There is only one race...the human race. There are hundreds of wonderful cultures, but only one race.

— *Edward James Olmos*
Actor, Director, Producer
(1947 -)

Chapter 23
Racism

It may be naive, but I choose to believe that at the fundamental core of most us is a basic sense of decency and worth. I think we simply want to live the best life we can, and wish no harm or ill upon others. This is our vulnerable, psychological underbelly. This soft space in American hearts is the prime target of those who would continuously slather on demands of guilt and apology for all things occurring yesterday.

A child will experience guilt when his parents are not getting along. It is a false guilt but it feels very real to the child. Fomenting guilt for historical events of yesterday can produce the same effect —a false guilt.

We are the children of yesterday's parents. The soft side of the American mindset quickly absorbs even false guilt. An American's deep sense of responsibility is married to an instant absorption of false guilt when things are not perfect. We are indomitable spirits determined to strive for perfection for everyone. We are not there yet, nor will we arrive through a pathway of perfection. Americans will never achieve perfection but we will never cease the effort.

In the two and a quarter centuries since the American Revolution, and the ultimate establishment of the United States, blood has been shed, land ownership has been exchanged, and literally thousands of cultures now call the United States home. Heroes and villains can be found among all cultures. We stand, however, as the one free society on the globe that welcomes and holds promise for everyone. Our governing documents foster "equality for all."

We stand and salute the American Indian and say, "You stand with us as American citizens. The promise of this country is yours equally."

This salute, however, is seldom returned by tribal governments. they are still trying to "get even" for real and perceived grievances of 150 or more years ago.

In Union Springs New York, Upstate Citizens for Equality (UCE) Chapter President, Dick Tallcot puts it this way: "It is openly obvious racism that is being set up and promoted in this country. With the 14th Amendment alone, we are all U.S. citizens, we should be one nation, on equal footing and with equal standing— and we are not."

Within tribal governments, mutual respect for other cultures that call America home is minimal. American Indian culture, as with all cultures in our country, are socially, technologically and intellectually advanced far beyond conditions 500 years ago. Lifestyles, and quality of life today depend upon these advancements. Enjoying the very best of today while honoring the very best of yesterday are not mutually exclusive. Forever mourning or haranguing the worst of yesterday is debilitating, futile, and potentially self-destructive.

In Wisconsin, Scott Seaborne makes a reasoned observation when he says, "We have competing governments. Here, we have a state and county/town system for non-Indian people, and for Indian tribal members we have the reservation, tribal government. So we have competing governments. That's the political part of it. They have their jurisdiction for their lands and we have jurisdiction for our lands, so in that regard, that is legal. However, when we try to talk about ways to resolve these problems, the tribe always introduces the fact that because we have a different opinion; we are, therefore, racist."

"The racist issue is used to divide," Seaborne continues. "The racist issue is a red herring that tries to discredit and eliminate debate. These are issues that are not discussed openly and fairly. The race card is played consistently in order to discredit an opposing view. We have been called racist and bigots. I have continually asked our opponents who raise this argument to please show me one thing that I have said, one thing that I have written, one policy that we take (referring to local and national groups addressing federal Indian policy), that is anything other than political or legal. And I have *never once* had anyone come forward and say, 'here is your racist comment.' or 'here is your racist writing.' "

All of our ancestors struggled and suffered from the 1600's to the current time. None of our ancestors were perfect, nor is a single American citizen perfect now. But our country is closer to freedom and opportunity than any other space in the world. It still seeks the perfection of the vision of the Founders who dreamed of the freedoms we now live.

Minnesota State Representative, Sondra Erickson, puts it this way: "In the area of human rights I think it is a travesty that across this nation, those of us who are just regular working people, regardless of race, gender, ethnicity, or whatever, are getting a bad rap. There is a special group with special rights—Indian tribes, that are seeming to become all powerful and seeming to point the finger at *us*, as being racist or being unfair or discriminatory, and Congress just turns the other way and disregards that, and lets the human rights attacks against us go on."

David Price says, "The idea that it is racist to talk about equal rights or something like that is, first of all, absurd, but this is not an argument between White people and Indians. You know, tribes will push their agenda to a certain point—with a strategy that says 'we have a "tribe-utopian" agenda where we are going to get everything we want,' and when enough people notice it or cry foul, then Voila! The strategy immediately shifts to 'We are all in this *together*. We just want to be a *part* of you guys. We just want to be *friends*. And there is nothing we are trying to take over. We are not trying to exploit you. It's just a crazy idea—it's just those *racists* groups that are coming up with that." Price continues, "So tribal strategists keep going back and forth. But they are willing to wait hundreds of years to get this done. They are educating kids in kindergarten curriculum in Minnesota, that starts with 6-year olds being taught that Indian tribes are sovereign nations and can do whatever they want."

Price is in progress with another manuscript, and says, "In my new book, one of the things I'm writing about is a new Native

American hereditary aristocracy because you have people who are tax exempt, who believe that they should get free medical care and education forever. Senator Inouye has said that, based on what he interprets from things he believes were granted in Indian treaties. I've read all the treaties; I haven't seen that yet. I don't believe it's in there. There is an idea that for enrolled Indians only, there are some entitlements that go on forever.

If you look at aristocracies in Europe," Price continues, "that is typically what they do. Aristocracies have some kind of monopoly, and Indians have a monopoly over here, a casino monopoly. Well, European aristocracies might have had a monopoly on a road in France somewhere, or so forth. And I know that's going to fly in the face of people who think that every Indian is poor, but when you have Indians making a million dollars a year, and the tribal casino only pays voluntary taxes, this hereditary aristocracy is something that they aspire to. That is part of the tribe-utopia idea."

Price concludes: "Well, keep *giving* all these benefits, prerogatives and special preferences, and tribal governments will certainly *take* them."

David Price's observations illustrate that federal Indian policy is absolutely not about our federal government's duty to protect the rights and well being of individual American Indians. The federal "trust" relationship is to protect the poor, "dependent ward" *tribal governments*, getting rich on the backs of all American taxpayers, and more egregiously, on the backs of poor American Indian families kept in squalor on Indian reservations. The 20% of enrolled tribal members remaining on reservations are needed for head-count to increase federal subsidies, and to qualify tribes for casinos—not much more.

Absolutely no one that I know is racially disparaging 80% of American Indians who have voted with their feet and left Indian reservations, for freedom from the yoke of enrollment, and a chance to pursue the American dream. The culture of any American Indian is as worthy of respect as any enrolled tribal Indian, or a member of any other culture in America.

We might apologize because appeasement has never made life better for American Indians or anyone else. Now that it is glaringly clear that money cannot reach Indian families when it is processed through tribal governments, perhaps we should apologize for the continued funding of tribal governments that usurp the Constitutional and civil rights of their enrolled tribal members.

The only way that tribal families will be able to fully embrace the same freedom and opportunity available to all other Americans, is to be freed of the shackles of tribal government, while preserving their cultural traditions held dear. This could be congressionally accomplished by transitioning the status of federally recognized tribal *governments*, to non-profit tribal *corporations*, and by allotting all lands currently held in federal trust back to fee, deeded status to Individual enrolled tribal members, or to the non-profit tribal corporation.

All other cultures in America honor their ancestors and cultural traditions without a government appropriation or program to do so. American Indians will too, if and as they desire. But first, they must be free of corrupt tribal masters and tribal governance, and the limitations of a repressed reservation lifestyle.

One day soon, that soft space within the American spirit will fully realize that: 1) it has taken every single action to the current date, to create and preserve this America of opportunity for all cultures; 2) there is no assignable or real guilt associated with growing this wondrous land; and 3) apartheid and reservations have been largely destructive to wonderful tribal families.

The only hope is that one day soon, appeasements, apartheid and apologies will be duly retired. For purpose legitimate domestic tranquility, that day cannot come soon enough. The absence of federally sanctioned race-based policies and programs would restore the Constitutional and civil rights for all persons of all cultures who reside within or near Indian reservations.

One day soon, we must acknowledge the guidance written ten years ago by Justice Antonin Scalia:

> Individuals who have been wronged by unlawful racial discrimination should be made whole; but under our Constitution there can be no such thing as either a creditor or a debtor race. That concept is alien to the Constitution's fo-

cus upon the individual, nor shall any State deny to any person the equal protection of the laws and its rejection of dispositions based on race, or based on blood. To pursue the concept of racial entitlement—even for the most admirable and benign of purposes—is to reinforce and preserve for future mischief the way of thinking that produced race slavery, race privilege and race hatred. In the eyes of government, we are just one race here. It is American.

— *Justice Antonin Scalia, (<u>Adarand v. Pena</u>, 1995)*

Rather less prudently, the British refused to pacify the Indians with either an overwhelming show of force or a systematic program of bribes, both of which the French had long found necessary to (achieve) comfortable and profitable relations with the red men.

— *Encyclopaedia Britannica, 15ᵗʰ ed., Vol. 29*

Chapter 24
Dual and Dueling:
The U.S. and Separate National Indian Economies

It is easy to imagine thousands of Sears and K-Mart stores sprinkled across the country. It took each of these corporations over one hundred years, including many national economic downturns and corporate bankruptcy periods to reach a point that in November 2004 resulted in K-Mart acquiring Sears for a venture encompassing assets worth 12.3 billion dollars and an estimated annual revenue of 55 billion. At all times, Sears and K-Mart had to comply with all federal, state and local laws, and had to contend with substantial competition of other big-box retailers.

In just one year—2003—tribal casinos produced $*18.5 billion* in revenue alone. That's just *one* year of revenue, not the accumulation reached after a century of enterprise. Tribal gambling revenue is at 35% of the combined revenue of Sears and K-Mart, and they're just getting started. Tribal gambling customers do not receive product and merchandise like Sears or K-Mart customers do. Casino customers receive perhaps a good time for a few hours, while pouring disposable money straight into tax-exempt slots or worshiping at green felt card tables. Since 1988—in less than two decades—tribal casinos are now bringing in annual revenue greater than one-third of the annual revenue of all the Sears and K-Mart assets combined.

When Sears, K-Mart or Wal-Mart comes to town, they have to compete with other retailers, play by all the rules, follow all federal and state wage requirements, and turn in tons of tax revenue to states and local governments. Their presence in town frequently increases traffic and generates substantial environmental impacts, for which they are held accountable through land use and zoning, and other local government requirements. They do, however, provide a needed resource and contribute to the local economic base. Not so, with tribal casinos.

When a tribal casino comes to town it also generates substantial traffic, creates significant environmental impacts, but it often skates free of this accountability, or taxes, and wage requirements. A tribal casino-resort complex contributes almost nothing to the local economy while it sucks up the disposable income from other businesses in the community. A tribal casino has no competitors, and adds to the legal, economic and social burdens of communities. Tribal gambling revenues do not flow back into the community money stream. Casinos simply pull out the local money, putting nearly zero back.

Indian casinos are protected by Congress and are *guaranteed* a federal-state monopoly, unlike say, Wal-Mart, Sears or even other non-tribal gambling facilities that must compete with each other and follow all laws.

There was national outrage over even the possibility that Microsoft was behaving as a monopoly. The American marketplace just wasn't about to stand for unfair business practices so Congress and the federal Department of Justice quickly weighed in to slap Microsoft's hands severely. One must play fair in America. Competition is the American way—except Indian casinos. The government creates, protects and facilitates a tax-exempt and tax-erasing monopoly to slither into any marketplace and start the local money erosion. Where's the Sherman Anti-Trust Act when needed? It apparently does not apply to the Class III Indian casino monopoly.

Many citizens and head-in-the-sand, coin-operated elected officials have been stunned to learn of the breadth and depth of the tentacles of federal Indian policy. What is this machine? How did we get here? Why is the momentum of federal Indian policy just now building with such explosive, exponential force?

First, the Game: The Indian gambling Regulatory Act of 1988 (IGRA), is the Bad Seed that is spreading faster than dandelions to erode the American economy. It has accelerated the federal tribal recognition process causing non-tribal gambling corporations to actively *recruit* new tribes from thin air and miniscule genetics. IGRA is the engine behind significant conversion of fee land (taxpaying) into Indian "trust" land (non-taxpaying), fast-tracking vast lands back to tribes and prime interstate-exit lands for new tribal casinos. Originally intended for lands only within actual reservations, the new game is called "cherry picking" or "reservation shopping" for prime sites in urban areas for *off-reservation* Indian casinos. Large urban areas are the new targets. With IGRA, Congress set in motion the opening of over 411 mega-million-dollar Indian casinos, with 100 more looking for startup in California alone. There are currently 217 additional, loosely defined, "tribes" including as few as 3, 5 or 7 members, that have received or are awaiting *their* federal recognition approval from the Department of Interior so they can get *their* casinos rolled out to *your* neighborhood.

IGRA set tribes on a path intended for economic self-sufficiency, but as so-called easy money ventures always do, epidemic greed has ensued. Now *self*-determination isn't enough. Power and determination over the lands and lives of *others* is rapidly enlarging tribalism as a form of governance that is shredding the fabric of American communities, democracy and government.

Second, the Money Machines: Indian gambling revenue, endless federal appropriations and subsidies, and gullible, naive or otherwise misled philanthropist nonprofits throw tons of money at the *poor Indians* because some of your ancestors *stole their land*. The problem is that the tons of federal, gambling and nonprofit dollars seldom reach a single tribal member's family to actually improve quality of life.

Billions of federal funding dollars and billions of Indian gambling revenue have does little to improve the continued poverty and squalor on reservations. The disconnect between all the money and actual tribal families, is in the redirected funds going into land grabs, or to corrupt gambling operators and tribal leaders, and tribes that buy political largesse.

On the Yakama Reservation, as example, the Yakama Legends casino celebrated its seventh year of operation in May 2004, but tribal members still cry out to see an actual annual revenue report. Except for a few very low-wage jobs, tribal families derive almost no benefit from casino revenue. It is impossible to discover if Yakama gambling revenue has built a single home for a tribal family, or provided health or education resources for tribal families. There is no discernible improvement in the quality of life for tribal members.

But Legends Casino boasts of million-dollar days. This is far too typical of Indian casinos on reservations across the country. Tribal members are clueless about their tribe's gambling revenue and only inquire at great risk of censure or retaliation. Their quality of life remains stagnant or gets worse. Across the country, under current tribal gambling policies on most reservations, tribal members will be in poverty fifty years from now. Tribal leaders, gambling developers, the legal and partisan political industry are, however, the fat cats feasting in new opulence.

Third, The Pathway: President William Jefferson Clinton's 1998 Executive Order 13084 requires an Indian Policy desk in twenty-five Federal agencies, ready and waiting to fast-track paperwork and quickly accommodate any tribal request. Campaign finance reformers and their ardent promoters and manipulators, such as several major liberal foundations, have recently confessed that they made it possible for the Federal Elections Commission to create an additional piece of the pathway in May 2000, just in time for the Gore/Bush presidential election funding needs. Where tribes demand and enjoy a "government-to-government' relationship with the federal government, the Federal Election Commission, in its Advisory Opinion 2000-05, determined that tribes are *not* governments for purpose of campaign finance and election activities. Indian tribes are not subject to the prohibitions that all other governments have respecting political activity or contributions.

American towns, cities, counties and states may not contribute a single penny to political activities, but tribal governments may do so with abandon. So tribes are governments in order to *receive* federal subsidies, but they are *not* governments for the purpose of unlimited, unregulated, and unmonitored campaign contributions from checks issued directly from tribal general treasury funds or from Indian gambling revenue - two sets of huge bottomless-money pots, over 1,000 of them and growing monthly. The bottom line: taxpayer dollars that go into tribal general funds can be redirected back to elected officials to do the bidding of tribes. Republicans and Democrats alike, profit from this scheme. Federal Indian policy is forcing taxpayers to fuel the demise of their own traditional democratic, accountable government.

Fourth, Special Preferences and Exemptions: Where early federal election codes such as the Tillman Act of 1907, and the Taft-Hartley Act of 1947 had never before specifically included *Indian tribes* as subject to election rules, "Indian tribes" was *intentionally* omitted in the McCain-Feingold Campaign Finance Reform. If these specific words are not expressly included in legislation, Indian tribes are not subject to the legislation. After significant grassroots efforts calling attention to this egregious Indian *loophole* in the McCain-Feingold legislation, both the Senate and House offered amendments to include *Indian tribes* in the McCain-Feingold bill, but the amendments were defeated. Leaving Indian tribes out of Campaign Finance Reform significantly increased the financial clout of Indians in elections across the country. Indian campaign and lobbying funds are now wide open, at a time when contributions of all other citizens and entities are substantially restrained.

Recently tribes have cried foul over the payment of 86 million dollars paid over a three-year period to two Washington D.C. lobbyists who may have bilked them. Questions: Isn't a loose 86 million dollars from Indian tribes a small clue as to the abundance of casino dollars flowing into American politics? And, how much annual federal funding dollars do these wealthy tribes still receive?

Federal Indian policy has created two classes of persons in the United States, taxpayers and free ride, non-taxpayers, based entirely upon race. Just for fun, browse the IRS website online, keywording "Indian" to see hundreds, perhaps thousands of special IRS tax waivers, exemptions and benefits enjoyed by tribal governments and members, and unavailable to any other Americans. Did you know that two military personnel of equal rank and duty, perhaps sharing the same foxhole or sand dune in Afghanistan or Iraq, get different paychecks? Enrolled Indians in the military do not pay state taxes, but the guy or gal fighting shoulder-to-shoulder with them do. Indian money, exempt from most taxes, goes farther of non-Indians that is held strictly accountable to the IRS.

Fifth, The Players: The players are Indian lobbyists, the entire national gambling industry, tribal leaders, a burgeoning Indian legal industry, and elected officials. Mainstream media, particularly major newspapers that benefit from substantial casino advertising dollars, also slant their "news" in a manner that meets the approval of their Indian gambling advertisers. The bleeding-heart academics—the university professors who are on permanent retainers for tribes across the country—all gather around the Indian money-pots. Harvard heads the list here. The Oneida Nation recently endowed the Harvard Law School with 3 million dollars, and Harvard does specialized gambling research "promoting recreational and educational benefits of gambling as sound economic development," especially if Indian-owned.

An especially unholy alliance is the conspiratorial triumvirate of environmentalists, tribes *and* the federal government, joining *together* to aim a cannon called the Endangered Species Act, destroying everything human in its path. That is exactly what happened to the Klamath Farmers in Oregon, Methow Valley farmers in Washington State, and numerous other areas that remain at high risk. Just one tribe, for example, the Agua Caliente Band in California, now retains 14 fulltime Washington D.C. lobbyists to ensure that federal legislation and funding increases benefit their tribe. Imagine the cumulative hordes of lawyers and lobbyists representing 562 other tribes, with 217 wannabe tribes swarming the halls in Senate and House buildings in Washington, D.C. How much pressure can only one hundred senators and

435 congressmen representing 50 states endure without caving to either the money or the menacing?

Last, the Losers: Very, very little of this great money adventure trickles down to uplift the quality of life among enrolled tribal members and their families. Tribal lifestyle continues to be a welfare state run by monarchial, and often malevolent chieftains. Poorer tribes that don't cough up monies into the political process do not get to play in this game. That happened recently when the Chinook and Duwamish tribes in Washington were de-recognized, and it happens in small ways among federal funding agencies and grant competitions. The bigger the political contribution, the greater in frequency are federal waivers, exemptions and maneuvers to give politically strong tribes political booty and sledgehammers. The National Congress of American Indians appears to be the choir director here, influencing who's in and who's out among tribes.

Too many Indian casinos do not pay minimum wage, have no health and food inspections, nor decent labor programs, and customers are at their own risk in the event of illness or injury, because tribes incessantly file lawsuits. Yet the tribes cannot be sued.

The other losers in this sorry mess are you and me. We were just polite kids, growing up, trying to be good neighbors, doing our best to get along with all cultures, raising our families, being respectful to each other as fellow Americans of all ethnic origins, and largely unaware of this morass that is *now* forcing so many out of their businesses, out of their homes and off of their farms, ranches, forests and lands.

Most of us learned early on that a deal is a deal, regardless of the circumstance of the parties—but not so with federal Indian policy. Every deal can come undone with federal Indian policy, and America is coming undone. It is coming undone with more tribes awaiting recognition, and they'll need new reservations (more lands leaving the property tax base) and casinos too. This process is dramatically overwhelming for fifty states when you add in the financial clout and economic drainage caused by over 411 megabuck-Indian casinos hastening the undoing.

Since when did slot machines and casinos become traditional Indian culture? The answer to that is: Since the gambling industry, legal and otherwise, saw an unlimited gold mine. The most evil of marriages is between the *You-Owe-Me* people and the *I'm Gonna Make An Offer You Can't Refuse* gambling guys. It is actually a menáge-a-trois that includes the federal government as one of the key players. The Indian gambling Industry, including foreign investors and legions of lawyers, now essentially funds, entices, overwhelms or intimidates Congressional and state elected leaders.

The fact that millions of Americans now fear the economic, jurisdictional and quite possibly judicial takeover by tribal governments, of their communities and government, is testimony to the escalating power of Indian gambling money and how quickly political pressure works.

An aggressively marketed *Tribal Wealth Management* conference was held In November 2004 at the Seminole Indian's Hard Rock Hotel-Casino-Resort in Tampa, Florida. The pre-conference hype included competitive advantages of Indian tribes such as being:

1. Exempt from taxation
2. Exempt from most federal, state and local regulations
3. Protected by "Sovereign immunity."

Indian tribes are being encouraged to diversify casino profits into a range of new business enterprises. Never mind that tribal families for the most part are still living in poverty, squalor, oppression and fear. Most tribal families have no wealth to manage; but obviously someone does - tribal leaders and the Indian lobbyist industry.

Considering that the *wealth* of these tribes is grounded upon annual federal (taxpayer) dollars and a congressional economic monopoly, some very serious questions need to be asked.

1. Is it appropriate for American taxpayers to subsidize Indian tribes to a point where they may use additional profits for making foreign direct investments?

2. In the current time period of homeland security difficulties and questionable conduct of many foreign countries, will somebody be watching as to *which* foreign countries tribes choose to invest in, and for *what* purposes?

The National Congress of American Indians (NCAI), and other national tribal-related entities are pushing to create a *National Indian Economy*. This is apparently the new national goal. Are we now segmenting out America's economy by race and tax-status? The tribal wealth management conference was a brazen thumb in the eye to a very generous America.

To promote and grow a *dual* economy creates a situation where one very prosperous (tribal, non-taxpaying) economy is being fueled and subsidized by American taxpayers to the direct loss and erosion of the primary, (taxpaying) economy. This is a huge economic crisis emerging that is rapidly bleeding out far beyond just unfair competitive advantages in gambling. The first victims are small rural, tourist-oriented communities. Now tribal enterprises, able to rely upon federal subsidies for all basic needs, can move forward with profits to erode the American marketplace in a range of new areas - hotels, golf courses, marinas, shopping centers, gas stations, cigarette and fireworks shops - a list limited only by imagination.

Tribes poised for expansion into foreign direct investment should first be tribes that no longer require annual federal subsidies, shouldered on the back of American taxpayers. This is a particularly troublesome area when prominent writers in the Indian Country Today newspaper and other Indian media refer to the rest of America as "the enemy."

American Indians have been full citizens since 1924. It is one thing to balkanize the country with separate Indian reservations and private, tribal governments. It is quite another thing to pro-

292 — Going to Pieces

mote separate economies, untaxed, and taxed; the former dependent upon the latter.

As President George W. Bush frequently states when he considers our international relations in the war on terrorism: "You
are either with us, or against us." The same must now be the case
when dealing with Indian tribes and their ardent promoters.
There should be one fair marketplace, one level playing field for
all American businesses, and equal taxation of all citizens in One
America.

Just because you do not take an interest in politics does not mean politics will not take an interest in you.

— Pericles
Ancient Greek Statesman
(495? - 429 B.C.)

Chapter 25
Whose Land is it, Anyway?

We are not a country that turns on a dime. Nor should we be. We change with deep thought and dialogue; "of...by...and *for*...the people." Historically, the closest we have come to instant action is Pearl Harbor on December 7, 1941, and sixty years later, the attack of September 11, 2001. Major intentional shifts and upheavals that have forged and shaped this country have not come easily, or quickly.

Nearly century passed between the colonists of Jamestown and the American Revolutionary War. Thirteen years would pass before the birth of our country and the ratification of the U.S. Constitution.

It would be another sixty-three years before the wrenching call to action for the end of unconscionable slavery, *"Uncle Tom's Cabin,"* was penned by Harriet Beecher Stowe in 1852, and even then, eleven more years would be required before the Emancipation Proclamation of 1863 emerged during a bloody Civil War. Nearly another century would pass before the U.S. Supreme Court, in <u>*Brown vs. Board of Education*</u> technically ended "separate but equal" in public education in 1954, and another dozen years before enactment of full civil rights, 1967-1968.

The tentacles of tribalism as a governing system in the current century are permeating much of this country as significantly as was the British rule in the 1700-1800s, and slavery through the 1800s. All three systems—monarchy, slavery and tribalism—are birthright, class and race-based.

294 — Going to Pieces

Monarchies, slavery and tribalism have a common denominator: They require the absence of equality.

Either a ruling family, or a ruling or preferred race are fundamental to these three political systems. What could be more defeating to a federal, republican form of government and society that is "of the people, by the people, for the people," if *all* of the people are not afforded an equal relationship with each other?

Federal Indian policy has created a spreading system that is separate and unequal. Congress allows tribal governments to benefit from two separate conditions strapped down until *time immemorial* upon the United States and its citizens:

1. Tribal governments insist that the federal government maintain a "trust" responsibility for their "dependent, ward" status, and demand that the U.S. subsidize all tribal needs through taxes paid by all citizens.

2. Tribal governments insist that they are separate, "sovereign nations" apart from the United States, and superior in their status to the individual States of the U.S.A.

Tribal governments positioned themselves to secure perpetual funding when they chose to play the dependent, ward role. Conversely, they secured jurisdictional overreaching and continuous efforts to govern other citizens when they chose to wield the "sovereign nation," role. It is not a matter that tribal governments are either one (dependent) or the other (sovereign). They should be neither.

Tribal governments are comprised of and managed by American Indians who also enjoy full U.S. citizenship, equal to all other Americans. There should be no tribal governments and all American Indians should be equal—not superior, not inferior—equal.

Whose land is it, anyway? It is my country, and yours. A piece of the soul and spirit of America belongs to the newest immigrant who became a legal citizen today, to the oldest living citizen alive today, to the infant of any ethnicity born in this country five minutes ago, and to all of the descendants born here, of former and current immigrants, settlers, American Indians - *equally*. Period.

Tribalism as a governing system does not, and never will, fit within a governing system founded on freedom and equality for all people. Cultural, religious, or ethnic-based business corporations are fine, so long as all are held equally accountable to the laws of one land—one country—the United States.

It does not matter how much catsup, horseradish or mayonnaise you smother on a piece of rotting hamburger, - it remains rotting hamburger. Tribal governance is a spreading, contamination of democracy in America's governing system.

Casino cash flows from the pockets of millions of happy seniors from church groups, women's clubs and fraternal organizations who go on busses to Atlantic City, or Foxwoods, or go with their family to Las Vegas or Turning Stone, or who go to the country store for a lottery ticket, etc. etc. Gambling is a national attraction, a vice to some, and a sport to others.

Casino cash, and most especially tribal-government controlled casino cash, pouring from the pockets of gamblers, dumps directly into the pockets of a few wealthy and corrupt tribal leaders, then straight into the pockets of political power. From there, tribal casino revenue is the power exchange that transfers control of lands, waters, communities, energy systems, national parks, natural resources and every whim desired by "the dependent wards"—Indian tribal governments.

We were here first - You stole our land. My answer to this mantra has always been, "You are *so* very lucky that some morally driven pilgrims and colonists were among the *second* ones to arrive. Had it been any other culture on the planet in the 1600's, American Indians would be studied today as we do extinct dinosaurs.

All of us rightfully choose to self-identify our political, religious, cultural and social preferences. These values are personal choices, a direct gift to Americans from their country. Race has no place in the taxation system administered by the Internal Revenue Service.

The root cause of special preference, separatism and apartheid systems begins with benign little boxes to check on U.S. Census Bureau forms. Are you an American Indian? Are you Black American? Are you Caucasian? Are you Hispanic or Non-Hispanic? Are you different, meaning not equal? Are you different, meaning that your needs are more special than, or less special than another American's, based upon some genetic distinction?

As Americans we can be any or all these categories, or none of the above. That is what the word "American" represents—the only national name embracing all of humanity.

The most respected cultures, religions or social systems are those that voluntarily exert the necessary effort to cherish, promote and preserve themselves. The Sons of Norway and other ethnic fraternal entities remain as cohesive as they wish. Hispanic cultural traditions are a respected part of daily life. Groups such as the Amish, Jewish, Catholic, Islamist and Protestant religions are clearly definable within their cherished beliefs and practices. None of these require or demand federal government assistance or forced subsidizing by others.

Tribal cultures can, if so desired, remain culturally in tact, without a tribal government, by reorganizing as non-profit corporate entities or some other non-governmental system.

A groundbreaking shift in the matter in which this country collects its demographic data and distributes funds to those in need would be to set one foundational criteria for the distribution of funds to meet the needs of American families: *Annual household income.* Nothing more. If race, age, gender, marital status, even sexual lifestyle—if nothing matters but annual household income for the census, we could easily reallocate resources so that children of low-income households and families have equal opportunity. How simple and how fair.

An irony is that actual household needs and government agencies to meet them would remain fairly constant. A shift in agency missions and purposes would be required. Employees of the Bureau of Indian Affairs and other ethnic-based federal programs would simply be reassigned to other pertinent and long established federal departments and agencies to accommodate special needs of all Americans, absent the race criterion.

The separatist argument that one genetic DNA should take preference over another has politically escalated into an apartheid system with tentacles reaching into the public education systems, access and control of some of our nation's vast natural resources, and the extortion of the America system of government.

Therefore, based upon an illuminating journey that Kamie and I took across seventeen Indian reservations, after thirteen years of actually living within the boundaries of an Indian reservation, and six years of intensive doctoral and political study and dialogue, specific to federal Indian policy, I submit that a reasonable path to restore a cohesive and culturally diverse United States of America is possible, when each citizen is provided equal accountability and access to and for the duties and resources of this amazing country.

The process of ending tribal governments may cause some readers to experience emotions ranging from apprehension, shock, or outrage, to stark terror. What? No tribal governments? Will they attack? No. Will tribes survive as a culture? Yes, if and as they so desire. Will America ever be the same? No, any more than we were the same after freedom from Great Britain, or the same after slavery. Will we be *One Nation Under God, Indivisible*, as was intended and spelled out by our Founders who developed, debated and enacted the Constitution and our Bill of Rights? Yes.

Every culture that desires to protect and preserve its history for all posterity, will do so, or maybe not. But race must never again be a basis for federal, state or local government policy. Our states, counties and towns, which are presently being adversely impacted by the chaos caused by the Indian reservation system and federal Indian policy, will be fully restored. We will have a seamless Homeland Security system. Regional economies and local businesses, now unfairly put at a disadvantage by special tribal tax exemptions and regulatory exceptions, must be returned to a level playing field.

Equal treatment of all citizens will allow the final achievement of the fraternity of all in a national melting pot where all men and women are brothers and sisters of one country. We must seize the time and opportunity to make this happen.

Providing equal treatment for all of our citizens really shouldn't be so terribly difficult. We have faced more difficult challenges. For example, after the Civil War, three amendments to the Constitution helped former slaves enter American society. The Thirteenth Amendment abolished slavery. The Fourteenth provided citizenship, due process and the equal protection of the law, and the Fifteenth guaranteed the right to vote to all races. Applying these constitutional amendments to everyone currently affected by federal Indian policy would go a long way towards correcting the problems now so prevalent in "Indian country."

Ten years after the Fourteenth Amendment was ratified, Chief Joseph, the famous Nez Perce warrior chief, gave a speech to President Rutherford B. Hayes at a large gathering of cabinet members, congressmen, diplomats, generals and others in Washington, DC. In his speech Chief Joseph gave this eloquent plea:

> If the white man wants to live in peace with the Indian he can live in peace. There need be no trouble. Treat all men alike. Give them the same law. Give them all an even chance to live and grow. . . . all people should have equal rights. . . . I have asked some of the great white chiefs where they get their authority. . . . They can not tell me.
>
> I only ask of the government to be treated as all other men are treated. . . .We ask that the same law shall work alike on all men. . . .with one sky above us and one country around us, and one government for all. . . .that all people may be one people.

Over one-hundred and twenty-five years ago, Chief Joseph pleaded for equal rights. The Fourteenth Amendment of our Constitution requires "the equal protection of the laws," and our American traditions and culture demand nothing less.

For over 60 years, since 1934, the governing system of tribalism has removed democracy from large land spaces within the states of the United States. Since 1988, however, with the Indian Gambling Regulatory Act, tribal governments are rapidly accomplishing the financial capture of Congress, governors' offices, state legislatures, and even significant portions of America's marketplace.

As citizens of Constitutionally provided individual sovereignty—the Body Politic—we will either fix this, or we will suffer increasing erosion of America's political processes, our democracy and our economy.

"The preservation of the sacred fire of liberty, and the destiny of the republican model of government, are justly considered as deeply, perhaps as finally, staked on the experiment entrusted to the hands of the American People."

— *George Washington*
American General and First U.S. President
(1732 - 1799)